WHERE HAVE YOU BEEN?

FARRAR, STRAUS AND GIROUX   NEW YORK

WHERE HAVE YOU BEEN?

SELECTED ESSAYS

MICHAEL HOFMANN

Farrar, Straus and Giroux
18 West 18th Street, New York 10011

Printed in the United States of America
First edition, 2014

Grateful acknowledgment is made for permission to reprint "Remembering Teheran,"
by Ted Hughes, from *Collected Poems*, copyright © 2003 by Ted Hughes.
Reprinted by permission of Faber and Faber Ltd.

Library of Congress Cataloging-in-Publication Data
Hofmann, Michael, 1957 August 25–
    [Essays. Selections]
    Where have you been? : selected essays / Michael
Hofmann. — First edition.
        pages   cm
    ISBN 978-0-374-25996-9 (hardback) —
    ISBN 978-0-374-70916-7 (ebook)
    1. Poetry—History and criticism.   2. Poetry—Translations into
English—History and criticism.   3. Poetics.   I. Title.

PN1136 .H64 2014
824'.914—dc23

                                              2014020501

Designed by Abby Kagan

Farrar, Straus and Giroux books may be purchased for educational, business, or
promotional use. For information on bulk purchases, please contact the Macmillan
Corporate and Premium Sales Department at 1-800-221-7945, extension 5442,
or write to specialmarkets@macmillan.com.

www.fsgbooks.com
www.twitter.com/fsgbooks • www.facebook.com/fsgbooks

1   3   5   7   9   10   8   6   4   2

FOR BARBARA H., LIGHT OF MY LIFE

CONTENTS

PART TWO

I have translated novels (a lot of novels) and written poems (not so many poems), but probably what the Germans call the "red thread" of my life is here: in what I have written about novels and poems and, more occasionally, paintings and films. Here, safely between covers, you will find my most regular and responsible writing, the hand on the shoulder, the earnest or incredulous voice in your ear, the animated gestures of deprecation or delight or indifference or bafflement. Here you will find a history of my spontaneity, a requiem to my intransigence, calipers for my taste. Here you will see—if you are disposed to at all—my version of what to read, why to think, how to like.

In 2001, a first book of my "pieces on writing and pictures" came out—fifty-six of them, called *Behind the Lines*. That was taken from twenty years of work—if you call literary reviewing work—and was adventurously assembled from an array of carbons, photocopies, and newsprint, three things that probably need footnotes nowadays. Even then, it felt like a late book of its kind. And now here we are again, the same but different, with thirty more pieces from the dozen years since, turned out at the rate of two or three a year (given the time it takes me to prepare and write them, an almost unbroken chain). Is there—aside from the sourcing of everything on computer files, where "documents" are so effortlessly preserved and traced, though less well by your maladapted writer—a difference?

The pieces seem to have become longer and more rounded. Their blending of service to the reader (information, summaries, background, quotations, dates, titles) and self-delighting freedom of expression is more pronounced. Their occasions—Lowell, Seidel, Hamilton, Antonioni, Zweig—mean more to me, and I have had more time to rise to them; many I have spent years, sometimes even decades, waiting for. Just as the publications—the *Collected Poems* of Ted Hughes or the *Selected* of Adam Zagajewski, the life of Weldon Kees—are events, so it was my hope that my consideration would be something of an event too: Schnitzler in 2003, Herbert in 2007, the Bishop/Lowell letters in 2010. As I was taught, by my father and others, I wanted my words and noticings to be of a piece with my subjects'; I aimed to write an homage (for the most part) to literature in something that itself approached the condition of literature. If there is something monumental about most of my subjects, something marble or granite or bronze, then maybe (I thought) I can investigate and animate them, make them resonate, play with and in and over them, like the water in a fountain.

Just as it was my hope and part of my brief in the original writing to pique and amuse everyone from the author (if alive) and the devotee to the skeptic and the happily or unhappily oblivious, so now I hope this book can be read with profit and enjoyment by anyone from *littérateur* to layperson. I like to think the reader of Schuyler might (in spite of all) make his way back to Lowell, or the reader of Bishop to Solie, or of Seidel to Bernhard (I don't believe in a language island or a poetry island or even a literature island, though that would come closest!). I don't see why books have to be written on purpose, or by design, and from scratch. Wouldn't there be as much intensity, originality, adventure, and revelation here as in, say, a single-author study or a book with a thesis to fail to prove? So, yes, as the TV chefs say, here's one I made earlier. These are pieces that were written, most of them, to commission, and that have appeared here or there. I wrote them, even at the time, so that they might be reread years later, and why not a gaggle of them, "scratching each other's backs," as Lowell says, "like cans in a sack"? Why not in fact a book already tested by its separate occasions, by the discipline of print, and the challenge of propinquity?

Last thing. My title, *Where Have You Been?* As is often the way, it *was* the last thing. I imagined it leveled—personally or impersonally, kindly or accusingly—at me, and this my answer. And then, I thought, isn't it also the constant clamor or refrain, bandied from book to reader, reader to critic, critic to book, in an endless farce of ill timing? And vice versa, too, of course. Where increasingly everything is global and blogal and instant and on demand, where the things we think we want talk to us (or at least the things that have been told to want us), isn't it odd and lovely and even a little reassuring that there's so much itinerant lostness about? This book is a sort of baroque convenience, a vade mecum, a few more connections, a few more lines, a further wrinkle of mapping.

PART ONE

BISHOP/LOWELL CORRESPONDENCE

Words in Air is such a formidably and dramatically and lingeringly wonderful book, it is hard to know where to begin. Well, begin in the manner of the physical geographer and the embarrassed statistician and the value-for-money merchant, with quantity, though that's absolutely the wrong place. Here then are 459 letters, 300 of them not previously published, exchanged over thirty years, between 1947 when the two great poets of late twentieth-century America first met—Robert Lowell just thirty, Elizabeth Bishop thirty-six, both with one trade book and one round of prizes under their belts—and 1977 when Lowell predeceased his friend by two years; covering all told some nine hundred pages from Bishop endpapers—one hand-scrawled, one typed—to Lowell endpapers—one in his laborious, also not greatly legible child-print ("I know I'm myself beyond self-help, and at least you can spell"), one typed. The apparatus of footnotes, chronology, and compendious glossary of names—take a bow, Saskia Hamilton—is modest, helpful, and accurate. At this point in our postepistolary (no joke), postliterary, almost postalphabetical decline, we would probably receive any collection of letters with a feeling of stupefied wistfulness and a sigh of valediction, but *Words in Air* is way beyond generic. It feels like a necessary and a culminating book, especially for Bishop. To read, it is completely engrossing, to the extent that I feel I have been trekking through it on foot for months, and I don't know where else I've been. "Why, page 351," I would say. "Letter #229; March 1, 1961. Lowell's forty-fourth birthday. Where did you think?"

But what is it like? How in fact do you read it? "I am underlining like Queen Victoria," Bishop remarks at one stage. How do you filter, assimilate, crunch it down to the space of a review? Its eight hundred pages of letters—every one of them bearing my ambiguous slashes of delight, interest, demurral, startlement—still left me with eight sheets full of page numbers of my own. It's like starting with a city and ending up with a phone book—hardly useful as a redaction. Really, I might as well have held a pencil to the margin and kept it there, for bulk reread.

It's an epistolary novel, if not a full-blown romance, then at least at moments an *amitié amoureuse*. It's a variation on García Márquez's *Love in the Time of Cholera*. Or it's an *Entwicklungsroman* in later life, both parties already poets but perhaps more importantly still on the way to becoming poets, as perhaps one only ever and always *is becoming* a poet. It's an ideally balanced, ideally complex account of a friendship, a race, a decades-long conspiracy, a dance (say, a tango?). It's a cocktail of infernal modesty and angelic pride. It's a further episode in Bishop's increasingly sweeping posthumous triumph over her more obvious, more ambitious, more square-toed friend. It's a rat-a-tat-tat Ping-Pong rally, an artillery exchange, a story told in fireworks, a trapeze show. One can read it for gifts sent up and down the Atlantic, from Lowell's traditional northeast seaboard to Bishop's serendipitously arrived-at Brazil, where she mostly lived from 1951, having disembarked from a freighter for a short visit; for projects completed, adapted, revised, abandoned, published, and responded to; for blurbs solicited, struggled with, and delivered to greater or lesser satisfaction; for houses bought and done up and left; for other partners encountered and set down; for visits and time together passionately contrived, put off, and subsequently held up to memory or guiltily swept under the carpet; for gossip and the perennial trade in reputations; for a startlingly unabashed revelation of mutual career aid ("we may be a terrible pair of log-rollers, I don't know," writes Bishop in 1965, having asked Lowell for a blurb for *Questions of Travel* after he had asked her for one for *Life Studies*); for loyalty and scruple, independent thinking and prudent silence, insistent generosity and occasional self-seeking; a longing to submit to the other's perceived discipline and a desire to offer unconditional admiration; for personal, professional, and public events. One can read it for movements of place, gaps in time, and discrepancies and disharmonies in feeling or balance; for the dismayed Bishop's agonized criticism of aspects of two of Lowell's books, the rather coarse free translations in *Imitations* of 1961, and the use of private letters from his second wife, Elizabeth Hardwick, in *The Dolphin* of 1973; for various other crises and cruxes: their heady, teasy-flirty mutual discovery of 1947, Bishop's difficult visit to a near-manic Lowell in Maine in 1957, Lowell's visit to Brazil and another manic episode in 1962, the death by suicide of Bishop's companion, Lota de Macedo Soares, in 1967, Bishop's uneasy return to Boston (to fill in for Lowell's absence, if you please), and Lowell's ultimate shuttling between wives and countries of the late 1970s. It's social history, comedy of manners, American dissidence, the search for a style. It's not least a gender myth more astute about men and women than that of Atalanta and Hippolytus (in any case, I always think Atalanta, like Bishop, should have won—*she* should have been provided with the apples, and Hippolytus, the ambitious, distractable male, goofed off in their pursuit, rather than the other way round). He is her anchor, she his kite.

The haunting issue in these letters is how much the vast difference between their authors brings them together and how much it pulls them apart. Because that Lowell and Bishop are unmistakably and unignorably and quite intractably dissimilar, of that there can be no doubt. The letters might as well have been printed in different type or different colors, so little is there ever any question of who is writing. (Which, if you think about it, is rather striking over some eight hundred pages of often close personal communication.) Even when, in the manner of friends, Lowell mimics Bishop, or Bishop teases Lowell, there is no real blurring of identities. The attraction of opposites is a simplification in this context, but the Lowell-Bishop association does bring to mind the school construction of a molecule: the proton (Lowell) massive, positively charged, hugging the center, and the electron (Bishop) almost weightless, negatively charged, speedy and peripheral and orbiting.

All this is exacerbated, of course, by the way one reads, which is to question, to cross-refer and compare, to doubt, to go behind the back of words, to tap for hollowness and cracks and deadness. One reads not with a vise or glue, but with a hammer and chisel, or an awl. It's not—or at least not by intention, or not immediately—a consolidating or fortifying activity, but more like looking for safe passage across a frozen river. Hence, the very form of this book—not one voice, but two voices, and then such different voices and such completely different temperaments—inclines one to further doubt. It's as though two incompatibles had rebased themselves and in some Nietzschean way sworn undying loyalty. The loyalty, whether un-spoken or occasionally voiced along the lines of "I don't know what I'd do without you," one tends to disregard—it makes, as it were, the hard covers for this book—while the reader is again and again made aware of the incompatibility, which is everything in between.

The thought came to me early on that this is a dialogue of the deaf, or to put it in the way I first conceived: it's like an arm writing to a leg. It's all a matter of what you want to do: tickle or walk. Bishop is acute, Lowell obtuse; Bishop sensitive, solicitous, moody; Lowell dull, sometimes careless, rather relentlessly productive; she is anx-ious, he, when not shockingly and I think genuinely self-critical, in-souciant; she is open to the world, whereas with him—and this is an understatement—"sometimes nothing is so solid to me as writing"; her poems in her account of them are fickle, small scale, barely worth pursuing—and how many of them seem to get lost in the making—whereas his are industrial-scale drudgery and then quite suddenly completed. It seems symptomatic that as these letters begin, Lowell is working on his long poem, "The Mills of the Kavanaughs," "12 hours a day—it's now 24 sections of almost 400 lines, and I think it may go to about 50 sections," only for that to be followed by his prose memoir in the '50s, various translations and dramatic adaptations in the '60s and '70s—*Imitations, The Old Glory, Oresteia, Phaedra*—and the several versions of another "section" poem, *Notebook*, followed by another long poem, *The Dolphin*. He writes like a man consumed— and not at all made happy—by his own industry, a sort of tin Midas: "I have a four hundred line sequence poem which might make a book, twenty pages on a New England essay, and my obituary on Randall. Thank God, we two still breathe the air of the living." If Lowell proceeds like a bricklayer—you see the string and the plumb line, everything is so and so many courses of bricks—Bishop is like a butterfly hunter, now one, now another, in pretty pursuit, a little forlorn, and likely to come home at night with nothing to show for a day's gallivanting. (Strange to think that they were both fisherfolk, and on occasions fished together.) She is much more protective of her poems too, either not mentioning them at all, or else habitually dep- recating them: "I have two new ones I'll send you when I get back, but not very serious ones I'm afraid." Even length—and the term is relative—is not comforting to her, but rather the opposite: "However I have just about finished a long & complicated one about Key West." The poem in question is "The Bight," which is all of thirty-six lines.

The catalog of differences goes on. Not only is Lowell a sort of monad of literature, with little interest outside its bounds—his oc- casional comments on painters seem dull and contrived, and in music as well he lags way behind Bishop, a one-time music major, who is capable of recommending jazz clubs in Boston, Gesualdo, Purcell, Webern, and Brazilian sambas, all with deep knowledge and un- derstanding—even within it he is drawn with laddish—or loutish— insistence to the monumental, the papier-mâché, the *Ben-Hur*. The contrast in their reading is illuminating: he comes to her, at various times, with Faulkner, Pope, *Middlemarch*, Chaucer, Dryden, Tasso, Shakespeare, Carlyle, Macaulay, *Dr. Zhivago*, "all of Thucydides. Isn't Molière swell!"; she counters with *Marius the Epicurean*, Frank O'Hara, Captain Slocum, Mme. de Sévigné ("so much better than most things written on purpose"—which might be an epigraph for the present volume), Sergey Aksakov. It's not that her writers are impressively obscure or recherché—though they are that, too!—they bespeak a taste as his, frankly, don't. They are the product of longer and more grown-up searching. This emerges beautifully in one of the most lovely and softly assertive passages of hers in the book, where she is talking initially about an Anton Webern record, then makes this into nothing less than an *ars poetica*:

> I am crazy about some of the short instrumental pieces. They seem exactly like what I'd always wanted, vaguely, to hear and never had, and really "contemporary." That strange kind of modesty that I think one feels in almost everything contemporary one really likes—Kafka, say, or Marianne, or even Eliot, and Klee and Kokoschka and Schwitters . . . Modesty, care, *space*, a sort of helplessness but determination at the same time.

This brave and smart piece of improvisation, on an aesthetic that is not even wholly *her own*, and fighting contrary tendencies in Kokoschka and Eliot, at least, is surely quite beyond Lowell, whose programmatic remarks in books and interviews are few, lazy, and approximate—which might not seem to matter very much, except that the regrettable "confessional" label has gone by default.

Literary style is another constant source of difference. Bishop has humor—the lovely air of amusement and being amused that plays over almost everything she writes—Lowell has the more deliberate, more solitary quality of wit. I don't think Oscar Wilde ever wrote or said anything wittier than Lowell's observation—itself a witty variation on Juvenal—on his friend (and regular bone of contention in this correspondence: he likes him, she doesn't) Randall Jarrell: "Then Randall thinks nothing adult is human." Bishop seeks balance and harmony, even in her most far-flung sentences, so that one's impression is of a chord: "The man wore a very strange buttoned bow-tie, and as a youth he had carried gold, around his waist, for Wells Fargo." (Who else would have thought to make one sentence out of that?) Lowell is drawn to energy, imbalance, exaggeration, caricature; here he is on his son, aged just one: "We'll be at Bill Alfred's sometime after the 15th, though I dread the effect of Sheridan on Bill's fragile furniture. Unfortunately he has made great strides in the last month and now walks, and I think takes strength exercises. A little girl visited him and he looked in contrast like a golden gorilla." To such a distanced, perhaps word-bound, way of looking (remember, please, those "great strides" are literal), everything is apt to seem monstrous;

and did anyone ever use the little word "girl" with that undertow of sexual speculation with which Lowell always endows it? Bishop noticed it too: in "North Haven," her marvelous elegy for him, she has, "Years ago, you told me it was here / (in 1932?) you first 'discovered girls.'" There seem to be almost two competing notions of literature at work here: to Bishop it is seeing everything clearly and fairly and in complicated harmony, through to the horizon; to Lowell it is something compacted and impacted, often a single quality driven in and in on itself, somehow caricatured even when kind. He *does* have some wonderful passages, but they seem—compared to hers—so utterly planned and worked: the account of a literary conference in New York, the description of a weekend's sailing in Maine with the Eberharts and others, a piece of passionate recollection of Delmore Schwartz (on July 16, 1966), which reaches the level of his brilliant published memoirs of Randall Jarrell and Allen Tate:

> Delmore in an unpressed mustard gabardine, a little winded, husky voiced, unhealthy, but with a carton of varied vitamin bottles, the color of oil, quickening with Jewish humor, and in-the-knowness, and his own genius, every person, every book—motives for everything, Freud in his blood, great webs of causation, then suspicion, then rushes of rage. He was more reasonable than us, but obsessed, a much better mind, but one already chasing the dust—it was like living with a sluggish, sometimes angry spider—no hurry, no motion, Delmore's voice, almost inaudible, dead, intuitive, pointing somewhere, then the strings tightening, the roar of rage—too much, too much for us!

This is hammer work, a hammer on the piano or a hammer on the drums; Bishop makes writing seem like breathing.

If one leaves the sheltered hunting grounds of literature—as to an extent we have already—then the differences grow still more apparent. Bishop likes strong Brazilian coffee, Lowell drinks American dishwater coffee (or tea, sometimes he's not sure). Bishop is the one who brings in words—*desmarcar*, "when you want to get out of an engagement," or "found a lovely word at Jane Dewey's—you probably know it—ALLELOMIMETIC. (Don't DARE use it!)," and she is the one, too, whose work requires a dictionary: "Dearest Elizabeth: It was fun looking up echolalia (again), chromograph, gesso, and roadstead—they all mean pretty much what I thought. Oh and tab-oret, an object I've known all my life, but not the name." It's as though these correspondents have separate vocabularies! And of course separate lives, or rather—to put it a little too brusquely—one life as well: hers. She is the one who travels on freighters, who likes bullfighting, whose "favorite eye-shadow—for years—suddenly comes in 3 cakes in a row and one has to work much harder at it and use all one's skill to avoid *iridescence . . .*" (I belatedly realize what a strangely Hemingwayesque collocation this is). It's not just that Lowell didn't do these things, but that even if he had done them, it seems probable that they would have been wasted on him. He after all was at different times in three European cities—Florence, Amsterdam, and London—and was reminded in all three of them of Boston. Meantime, from Boston, *his* Boston, she wrote him in 1971: "It is nice autumn weather—the ivy turns bright colors but the trees just an unpleasant yellow. On the library steps I realized the whole place smelt exactly like a cold, opened, and slightly rotten watermelon—." It is hard not to contrast this gift to him of his own place with his hard, raptorlike, plaid-golfing-slacks announcement: "We would like to come and see you and then rapidly a little more of South America."

A great majority of the arresting and beautiful observations in this book are Bishop's, and one's sense of the book as a whole is largely conditioned by her part of it. From tiny sparkling details like the salutation "Dear Lowellzinhos" or the signing off "recessively yours," to a charming haikulike sentence on a postcard from Italy, "Lovely weather—green wheat, wild-flowers, swallows, a ruin with a big fox," that is like a fast-forward of the creation, it seems she is always good for a vivid and pell-mell and noticing transcription—if not, to use I think it was Derek Mahon's Joycean neologism, "danscription"—of the natural world that is a match for anything in her poetry:

All the flowering trees are in blossom, delicate patches of color all up the mountains, and nearer to they glisten with little floating webs of mist, gold spider-webs, iridescent butterflies—this is the season for the big pale blue-silver floppy ones, hopelessly impractical, frequently frayed, in vague couples. They hover over our little pool, and pink blossoms fall into it, and there are so many dragon-flies—some invisible except as dots of white or ruby red or bright blue plush or velvet—then they catch the light and you see the body and wings are really there, steely blue wire-work. We sat out in the evenings and the lightning *twitched* around us and the bigger vari-ety of fireflies came floating along like people walking with very weak flashlights, on the hill—well, you missed this dazzlingness—and the summer storms. Lots of rainbows—a double one over the sea just now with three freighters going off under it in three differ-ent directions.

The Lowells had paid a more or less calamitous visit the previous year ("hopelessly impractical, frequently frayed"), and this magnifi-cent paragraph is nothing less than a remaking of paradise ("steely blue wire-work") and a sign of forgiveness ("a double one") for them all. Even an occasional striking a pose of brisk, tweedy, maiden-auntish refusal is delightful in her: "A very cursory look at the Munch Museum—it was too beautiful a day and I was feeling too cheerful to be bothered with all that nordic nonsense." For much of this book, Lowell makes really remarkably little showing compared to Bishop's ironically proffered "superbly underdeveloped country and this back-ward friend!"

Why this matters I suppose is that—other things being equal—one likes a poet to have (ugly Tory word!) some hinterland—some hinterland basically of prose: to have experiences, to hold opinions, to store memories, to lead a rich and varied life of the senses. (The other type of poet is a unicorn who lives in an ivory tower: he's fright-ening and different and real, and we don't get him. When Lowell spends an evening reading poems aloud with I. A. Richards, that feels like unicorn behavior to me.) It's the famous Louis MacNeice pre-scription: "I would have a poet . . ." and so forth. This, Elizabeth Bishop embodies triumphantly, to the extent that over the course of her life her poems—four short books—have a hard time emerging. She gets involved in the turbulent Brazilian politics of the '50s and '60s (and the characteristically ham-fisted American responses to them); Lowell writes: "Let's not argue politics. I feel a fraud on the subject," but that sort of retrenchment applies everywhere, and to some extent the feeling of fraudulence too. Bishop is so prodigal with sympathy, attention, interest; Lowell, by contrast, seems to endow even people quite close to him (even Elizabeth Bishop, as we will see) with very little reality. It comes down to something like focal length—his is about a foot. See him in his heavy, black-rimmed spectacles, recumbent on a leather sofa in the Fay Godwin photograph ("my tenth muse, Sloth"), in a study described (in the poem "The Restoration") as "unopened letters, the thousand dead cigarettes, open books, yogurt cups in the unmade bed," and writing things like:

> Dear Heart's-Ease,
> we rest from all discussion, drinking, smoking,
> pills for high blood, three pairs of glasses—soaking
> in the sweat of our hard-earned supremacy,
> offering a child our leathery love. We're fifty,
> and free! Young, tottering on the dizzying brink
> of discretion once, you wanted nothing
> but to be old, do nothing, type and think.

This is the poet as houseplant, as aspirin-munching studio beast, as day-for-night velvet hairband. Lowell is the linebacker-turned-pasha as poet, Bishop is the lifelong dervish.

Small wonder that Lowell (maybe) felt fraudulent. He knew the value of Bishop's letters—when he sold his papers to Harvard, he made sure she was paid a decent sum for hers, but that's not what I mean—even as he apologized ("your letters always fill me with shame for the meager illegible chaff that I send you back") for the thinness of his own. "You & Peter Taylor both make me feel something of a fake—so I love you both dearly," he remarks in 1949. It sounds flip, but of course it was deadly earnest. Lowell understood that there was an agility and a naturalness in Bishop that he would never have; he and most of the rest of his generation were manufactured. To my possibly anachronistic modern ear, he sentimentalizes and patronizes her all the time. His letters keep her in place, and almost invariably the wrong place; telling an audience that with her he "felt like a mastodon competing with tanks" is typically inept, but maybe no more than telling her, "Honor bright, I'm not a rowdy." For decades he championed her prose, the story "In the Village" in particular ad nauseam—an obviously ambiguous accolade to any poet—and praises her poems—it's a heretical thought, but it did cross my mind—without much sign of having read them. One succeeds the other in his "billfold," but maybe they didn't do him much good there: "It's like going on the pilgrimage of your Fish, or the poem ending awful and wonderful, yet the journey is as utterly new and surprising as a first discovery of what life is all about. And so it is. If I can't stop what I've already done, I must stop. Maybe, if I carry your '[Under the] Window' around long enough, I'll learn. It's a kind of patience and freshness." The enthusiasm is vitiated by the confusion around the "what" and by the stale terms at the end. I've developed a thoroughgoing aversion to the (now routine) cult of Bishop as a perfectionist slow coach (Lowell was an early high priest): she was a fast and sure and instinctive writer, but when a vein or a jag broke off, it was much harder to patch or extend than with less sensitive matter. Beyond that, it's mystifying how anyone could misremember "awful but cheerful." But then, in a letter near the end, he manages to misremember the whole of her: "I see us still when we first met, both at Randall's and then for a couple of years later. I see you as rather tall, long brown-haired, shy but full of des[cription] and anecdote as now. I was brown haired and thirty I guess and I don't know what." This elicits a characteristically accurate harrumph of friendly fire from her:

> However, Cal dear, maybe your memory *is* failing!— Never, never was I "tall"—as you wrote remembering me. I was always 5 ft 4 and ¼ inches—now shrunk to 5 ft 4 inches— The only time I've ever felt tall was in Brazil. And I never had "long brown hair" either!— It started turning gray when I was 23 or 24—and probably was already somewhat grizzled when I first met you. I tried putting it up for a very brief period, because I like long hair—but it never got even to my shoulders and is always so intractable that I gave that up within a month or so. I think you must be seeing someone else!*

The asterisk is to her footnote: "so *please* don't put me in a beautiful poem tall with long brown hair!" which of course, as she very well knew, is just what he would have done.

He knew she had everything he didn't; she—in terms of his persistence, his confidence, his diligence—will have known the same. A kind of justice and a kind of vicariousness prompted each of them in hopes for the other, though in the end I don't believe that either helped the other's *writing* very much. (The title, "words in air"—the words are Lowell's, incidentally—tells its own story.) She is afraid to read him while writing; it influences her too much. While her praise and minute criticism, droppered out over years ("'ganging' is just right"), would have made him think she was responding on an insignificant, immedicable scale, and beyond anything he could do. "I'm mailing you a copy and wish you'd point [out] any correctable flaws. *Correctable*—the big ones alas I'm stuck with," Lowell wrote to accompany a typescript of *Life Studies*. But of course he was stuck with the little ones too, in the end not so little. With his swaggering inexactitude Lowell was absolutely wrong—a red rag for Bishop. In one dangerous letter, she wonders: "If I read it ["The Old Flame"] in *Encounter* under someone else's name I wonder what I'd think?" He, too, had cause to wonder from time to time: "I see in a blurb you've written you object to confession and irony"—it doesn't leave much of him, and he sounds accordingly bemused and hurt. They were contraries. Each enshrined the other. Short of enmity, it was all they could do.

ROBERT FROST AND EDWARD THOMAS

I thought all the mails had gone down in the Laconic, *but evidently not.*
—*Helen Thomas to Robert Frost*

Parnassian friendships—in particular friendships between poets—
are rarer than one might imagine. A friendship late in life is unlikely,
poets are so botanically specialized and overdetermined, each one
stuck at the extremity of his or her personal development, craning
and twisting apotropaically toward his or her personal light. Early
friendships are subject to volatility, the vicissitudes of life, competi-
tiveness, and the torque—or torc—of the Muse. When one has further taken away such things as alliances (Pound and Eliot), dalliances
(Lowell and Bishop), rivalries (Goethe and Schiller), dependencies
(Spender and Auden), romantic entanglements (Verlaine and Rimbaud), and mentor-pupil relationships (Akhmatova and Brodsky),
one is left with really not very many.

Montaigne's marvelously, irreducibly simple formulation for
friendship, "*Parce que c'était lui, parce que c'était moi*"—because it was
him, because it was me—can have few juster claimants among poets
than Robert Frost (1874–1963) and Edward Thomas (1878–1917).
Friendship is such a mystery (and therefore such a provocation, a
diaphanous rag to a bull) that it's no surprise scholars have queued up

to explain this instance of it, but it doesn't come down to such things as more or less one-sided influencings, or the critic Linda Hart's impressively foolish list of congruencies. For Frost, who outlived by the best part of half a century the friend he saw for one year, and wrote to for another two, the relationship was unrepeatable and irreplaceable. For Thomas, it was both an enabling agency—but for it, we might never have read him, or even heard of him—and an object of intensest focus. One could do worse, as one reads through the letters, poems, and reviews assembled in *Elected Friends* than murmur Montaigne's words to oneself from time to time.

A starting point better than the second-guessing and computer-matchmaking of some of the critics, is to understand that the friendship between Frost and Thomas came about, in a strange way, out of time and out of place. This creates the space for some of its electiveness. Frost, evidently, was not in his own country but in the England he had bravely and arbitrarily plumped for a year earlier; nor did Thomas have home advantage either. Often, he was guesting in his hated London, touting for work ("I hate meeting people I want to get something out of, perhaps"), or else, in the Edwardian fashion, passing himself around like the port among various addresses (Eleanor Farjeon he met in the course of a "cricket week"). In fact, if one imagines, in one of P. G. Wodehouse's "Psmith" novels, a meeting in a London chophouse or a country pile—say, Blandings in Shropshire—and a fast friendship being formed between Psmith's likable friend Mike Jackson and—not Psmith but instead Ralston McTodd, "the powerful young singer of Saskatoon"—I don't think the story of Frost and Thomas is altogether unlike a serious version of that. Even when they were living in adjacent cottages, in Ledington and Ryton, Thomas didn't know that particular bit of country (not far from the imaginary Blandings); there was a local hill from which he could see Wales, but basically he was no more "at home" there than the American visitor.

Nor could either man draw on the authority of years, family, accomplishments. True, they both had families—Frost with his four children, Thomas his three—but to some extent, both were on the run from them. They were in settled, or serious years, mid- to late thirties—Frost the older by four years, and seeming older than that,

I would guess, by virtue of being American and having traveled, of having grown up half-orphaned, of having come into money from his grandfather—but basically neither had very much to show for his time on earth, and both were well aware of the fact. If anything, Thomas, who was a hugely prolific and hardworking literary journalist with a string of books to his name, should have had the upper hand on an erstwhile farmer and occasional teacher, an idle and irascible man who had published hardly anything—only he saw in his own extensive production chiefly grounds for shame. (In fact, he was a wonderful writer of prose: the original texts have long since disappeared from sale, and even selections like Roland Gant's *Edward Thomas on the Countryside* and Edna Longley's *A Language Not to Be Betrayed* are not easy to find, but they are all worth the trouble: marvelously alert and rapturous prose.) Both Frost and Thomas had the discontents and aspirations of much younger men, though both, evidently, had seen and experienced far more of life. This strange mixing of ages characterized them, separately and together. On the one hand, the immoderateness and capacity and ebullience of youth, and youth's faith in friendship's great exchange, and on the other, the urgency and narrowing purpose of midlife, what the Germans call *Torschlusspanik* (fear of the gate closing). It was one of the conditions of their friendship, the inability of either man to "be his age." They were unfinished, unappreciated, adrift, and thrown together.

Their time, their era, too, left them alone. The whole beginning of the twentieth century was in a somewhat similar muddle to themselves, a sort of soft interregnum. It was old and young, and it didn't have long to go. Historians don't know quite what to do with it; often, they simply add those fourteen years to the nineteenth century, as if that was where they really belonged. The great reputations—James, Hardy, Yeats—had all been founded in the Victorian age. When Frost's favorite living poet died in 1909, it was George Meredith. The reputations of the 1900s and 1910s, of the Edwardians and Georgians (those characters listed in the "Biographical Table" at the back—I would almost call it a glossary!) have disappeared more thoroughly than those of any other decade. No one now reads those poets Edward Thomas spent a great part of his lifetime sifting in the *Daily Chronicle*. And against that, the Modern had pushed its foot in the door. "On or about December 1910," as Virginia Woolf would have us believe, "human character changed." Lawrence is a dangerous presence, Pound is at home in London—"sometimes," as he wrote on his visiting card to a predictably nettled and crestfallen Frost—and the soon-to-be Imagists Flint and Hulme are there to be met, and always our knowledge of the impending war. It is a confused and unimpressive waiting, the situation of Saul Bellow's first book, *Dangling Man*, George Orwell's *Coming Up for Air*, or Julian Maclaren-Ross's *Of Love and Hunger*.

In this brief abeyance, the friendship took hold and grew. They met twice in 1913; 1914 was "their year"; in February 1915, the Frosts sailed (taking with them—as a kind of wonderful pledge or earnest—Thomas's oldest child, Mervyn or Merfyn); Thomas started to write poems and enlisted, Elinor Frost suffered ill health and a miscarriage, Frost embarked on his prodigious career as a professional bard and performer ("Dear Edward: First I want to give you an accounting"). Everything is changed, changed utterly. This was, for all involved (even, one suspects, the onlookers), a transformative relationship. The plot has the bold X shape of a perfect short story (say, Chekhov's "Lady with Lapdog") and, indeed, the friendship has absolutely the intensity of an affair.

This "story"—a kind of natural, unprocessed narration, with beginning, middle, and end—is most exquisitely set off, or inverted, by the epistolary form. Because there can be no doubt that its deepest moments were when the two men were together at Ledington, improvising walks and conversations. It was not in its essence a written (or even primarily a *literary*, except inasmuch as both men were literary) relationship at all—not *Fernliebe*, heady and disinhibited—but one founded on time eagerly and intensely spent together, and it is of precisely this that we are necessarily ignorant. First names—the *tu* or *Du* form that registers electrically upon a European ear—are only used once the Atlantic has come between the writers. Intimacy, perhaps, to redress distance. Strikingly, and sadly, there seems not to be a single photograph—what one might jokingly call prima facie evidence—of the two men together. A handful of poems (one by the awful Gibson), a few paragraphs of recollection from the principals, and by Helen Thomas and Eleanor Farjeon. What is proposed to us is the form of an arch, but all we see of it are the beginnings or foundations. We see the men building toward each other. The middle, their meeting, eludes our inquisitiveness. Letters are predicated upon absence; in an extreme instance of this, one single letter from Frost to Thomas seems to have survived from the time before his departure. They have a natural, aleatory tact, very much in keeping with the characters of both men. In her wonderful memoir, *As It Was*, Helen Thomas wrote of Edward: "for though he needed and loved my impulsive and demonstrative nature, these qualities were foreign to him." Frost, meanwhile, wrote to Edward Thomas: "I have passionately regretted exposing myself"—though not to Thomas.

Precisely because of what one might call its refusal of distance, though, the collection displays a characteristic and very appealing exaggeration, blandishment, almost flirtatiousness. Again, this is supplied almost as much by what isn't there—the "silence" from Frost, which of course isn't a real silence—as by what is: Thomas's tireless charm, solicitude, address, seductiveness. There is just no way for him *to be* without his friend, and Frost's absence or unavailability leads him—almost from the beginning, "Dear Frost (if you don't mind)"—to the brink of excess, impropriety, fantasy, whatever one wants to call it. The early notes from Thomas seem to live always toward their next meeting, to sigh, almost romantically, for more favorable conditions, where cake can be had and eaten: "There must be a world where that is done. I hope you & I will meet in it." He is like a man pressing his suit upon some chilly fair, or even—such is the force of so much charm, desire, wistfulness—a woman. In 1910, Thomas had published a book called *Feminine Influence on the Poets*; "till I got to his signature," he writes of Richard Burton, "I thought he was a she"; his concluding presentations of himself are regularly "feminine": "but you know already how much I waver & on what wavering things I depend," the odalisquelike "It is purely disinclination to sprawl about before your eyes as I feel I should do, more than usual, just now," or the frankly eye rolling "If you were there I might even break away from the Duke for 3 days, but it would be hard." (I'm sure I overstate Thomas's femininity. It's just my somewhat coarse approximation for the combination of youth, pliancy, respect, teasing that he offers Frost. And of course, with his "strength and silence," Frost plays his male part.)

All this, of course, is not to suggest there was any homoerotic component in the relationship, but rather to propose that something of what one thinks of as merely or exclusively sexual—the gallantry or flirtatiousness of seduction—inheres in many, if not most great friendships. (The magnificent thing about Montaigne's sentence is that it is as applicable, or rather more obviously applicable, to love as to friendship.) In fact, I would say there is something a little strange where it's not there. There is something, in Robert Lowell's words, "too little nonsensical" even in the twinkle of Brecht's invitation to Walter Benjamin to share his Danish exile with him: "How's your health? How about a trip to the northland? The chess board lies orphaned; every half hour a tremor of remembrance runs through it; that was when you made your moves." There is something deliberate and deflected and third-person neuter about this; too much depends on the cartoon-animated chessboard; it is not torrid but cool, witty-whimsical rather than charming, and seems already to accept the possibility of defeat. Thomas, by contrast, like the heroine of a bodice ripper, seems always ready to hurl himself quixotically against any let or hindrance: to walk anywhere, cycle any distance, use any pretext, accept any lodging. It's as though he always has their coordinates plotted on a map, and has in his pocket a compass with Frost his true North. And in this he is even occasionally—happily!—outdone by a still more exorbitant Frost, who makes the amazing suggestion that he take a little three-week leave of absence from the army so that Thomas can cross the Atlantic to talk to him. After all, he says, reasonably (because reason also is part of the process), "They ought to consider that you were literary before you were military." The assertion of primacy, like the—naked or exaggerated or (to the writer) surely irresistible—expression of need, seems to me a term from love's lexicon.

The romance of friendship is to me a beguiling trait in these letters. And while Thomas, who wrote most of the letters that have come down to us—and most of the longer letters at that—seems to make most of the running, this is an accidental impression (although it is one of the minor pleasures of reading this collection deliberately to entertain it). Frost's letters may be less engagingly volatile—less *frisky*, almost, than Thomas's—but rarely can he have come over as so attractively involved as he does here: one cannot say with any degree of confidence that "the more loving one"—Auden—is Thomas. Rather, dangling before his friend such heavenly and Kafka-ishly impossible notions as the "lecture-camp" in New Hampshire, Frost entered fully into the solicitous optimism of the relationship.

At the same time, most movingly, Thomas quit it. It's as though the torch of hope and ambition (and illusion) had passed from him to Frost. In his last two years of soldiering and poetry, he seems to move, consciously, into an unreachable final solitude. At the end of a tightening spiral—shorter, more "mannish" sentences, less self-reflection and self-censure, renunciation (of his Gloucestershire village of Steep, of reading, of friendship, of the idea of a future), the affirmation of more and more negatively couched perspectives—there is only death. "All the anchors are up," he writes. He sees himself in a sort of continual masquerade, in strange, tight clothes, an artilleryman's mustache, rising through spectral ranks, a dirty somnambulist, and yet—absurdly—a schoolmasterly figure among much younger men, quite unrecognized ("I wonder would you recognise me with hair cropped close & carrying a thin little swagger cane"; "Nobody recognises me now"; "my disguises increase, what with spurs on my heels & hair on my upper lip") to the point where he simultaneously becomes himself and doesn't know himself ("*Niemand, der mich kennt*"—no one knows who I am—are Rilke's dying words). Thomas seems to rebalance himself in negation. Frost, meanwhile, is a tender irrelevance, not quite knowing whether to cheer from the sidelines of American neutrality—very much as at a sports event—to praise the personality of Lloyd George, to recall old memories of their times together, to envy Thomas's uncomfortable mastery of "black talk," or to give him an anxious shaking: "Don't be run away with by your nonsense." Many of these pages are at the extremity of friendship.

I haven't talked much about poetry. Poetry seems to come naturally and variously out of the relationship. It is Frost telling his friend that of course he can imagine him "taking to verse." It is in both Thomas's sublimely candid and intelligent reviews of *North of*

Boston—and his bantering references to "North of Bostonism" in his own work. ("Influence" seems to me such a ridiculously, barbarously heavy notion here: I don't think Thomas set himself to write Frost poems any more than Frost set himself to write Thomas poems. Thomas may be vastly less known than Frost—especially in the United States—but I don't think he has anything to fear from the comparison. Rather, I should say that their poems, as I should take it their wives and their children, were on friendly terms with one another.) It is Frost sending Thomas "The Road Not Taken"—and I don't suppose anyone who reads it in such a context will ever view Frost or the poem in the same way again. It is Thomas taking exception to the closing line of a poem, and his discreetest reservations about plays, about plainness, and—less discreetly—about things being "made up" or "thought out" or "done too much on purpose." It is in innumerable felicities of expression one finds on the wayside, as it were, in these letters, such as Thomas's feeling "thinned out by all this reading & smoking"; or his writing about "little trees & some great pears," and wishing Frost, in an utterly Keatsish way, "I hope you have some as good, so that you eat them till your teeth are sad with them"; his comparing "a foxhunting major" to "a mandrill" (though what else is an officer, if not someone who drills men?); it is Frost's astonishing, unpunctuated, inverted, unquestioning question: "For what has a man locomotion if it isnt to take him into things he is between barely and not quite understanding." It is Thomas saying, "I could read Frost, I think," and later, in his last letter, revising this— you see, these really aren't bookish letters—assuring his friend: "yet you are no more like an American in a book than you were 2½ years ago."

WELDON KEES

There is a short story by Weldon Kees called "Farewell to Frognall," one of the last he wrote before giving up prose at the age of thirty, where there is the following memorable little exchange:

> "What have you been doing?" said Frognall. He was a tall man, no longer so very young, with bushy carrot-colored hair and bad teeth. He did not look straight at one when speaking.
>
> St. Clair said, "Translating the poems of Gröbman-Pauli."
>
> "Never heard of him."
>
> "Few have. He is quite unknown here. His poems are virtually untranslatable and depend for their effectiveness on an almost unbearably tedious repetition of guttural sounds. It is very difficult to reproduce their flavor in a translation. He wrote exclusively in septenaries. Little is known of his life. He abandoned poetry in his twenty-fourth year and seems to have allowed himself to be supported by women of a low sort from that point on until his death, a peculiarly revolting one at the age of forty."

The humor of the description is a strange and uncomfortable blend of the drolly academic—the silly poet no one has ever heard of, for very good reasons—and the savagely self-mocking: because surely, whether it was by accident, intention, or merely prophecy, Gröbman-Pauli has a lot of Kees in him.

Weldon Kees (1914–1955?) is the nearly man of twentieth-century American poetry, and not just poetry but—as above—fiction; art, music, and poetry criticism; Abstract Expressionist painting; traditional jazz (both pianism and composition); avant-garde theatricals; and documentary filmmaking. Until I read James Reidel's biography, I hadn't realized how "nearly" Kees was, and how far he came, in how many fields of artistic endeavor. Here was someone who ate hamburgers with Mary McCarthy, dined with William Carlos Williams, took over as *Time* magazine's cinema editor from James Agee, and as the *Nation*'s art reviewer from Clement Greenberg; who wrote a splendid piece for *Time* on Fats Waller, and had poems in *The New Yorker*, on one occasion two in three weeks; who helped edit Paramount's historic newsreel footage of *To the Shores of Iwo Jima*; was friends with John Cheever, Malcolm Cowley, Conrad Aiken, Theodore Roethke, Mark Rothko; had his paintings hung next to those of Jackson Pollock, and had several one-man shows in New York; talked about films on the radio with the youthful Pauline Kael; who published his first story as an undergraduate aged twenty, and as late as 1955, his (so far as we know) last year, was awarding a poetry prize to Robert Fitzgerald. Nor would it be right to think that these luminaries condescended to Kees, or that he was in any way, in any of these fields, an also-ran, a water carrier, someone to help fill the room: he was met, always, as an equal.

As impressive, in all his many fields, is Kees's discrimination. He was an intuitive cosmopolitan—born in a small town in Nebraska, never once went abroad—of a kind that I wonder whether the universities and the "fly-over states" of America can still produce. At twenty-one, he was lugging the two-volume translation of Alfred Döblin's *Berlin Alexanderplatz* with him to read on the train. He adored the Modernists—Joyce, Eliot, Pound, Crane, Wolfe. "Back to the Twenties!" was a battle-cry of Kees's, "Or even further!" Of Denver, where he spent some time as a librarian, he wrote: "The intellectual life here is very saddening." He proposed an edition of the extremely little-read Victorian poet Thomas Lovell Beddoes to James Laughlin at New Directions. He admired Arthur Waley, Rilke, Cavafy decades before everyone else did. He read and reread Malcolm Lowry's masterpiece *Under the Volcano*, which appeared from the same publisher, in the same season, and with the same editor, Albert Erskine, as Kees's own one and only trade book of poems, *The Fall of the Magicians*. He tried to invite Robert Lowell to a series of events he put on in Provincetown in the late 1940s. He championed the cause of the Abstract Expressionist painters and was one of their best early spokesmen. He wrote about Jelly Roll Morton's *Kansas City Stomp*: "made in the summer of 1928, with"—wonderful phrase!— "an exceptionally knowing group of men." In San Francisco, he ran into and recorded with Jesse "Lone Cat" Fuller, who, many years later, opened for, as James Reidel says, "his fans the Rolling Stones." Where, you wonder, as you read all this, given always that Kees's own accomplishments are of a piece with these others—as indeed they are—is the wrong in any of it? Where did the magician fall down?

There are probably four answers. He was, first, in a way the ancient Greeks would have understood, too gifted. He spread himself over his different fields, serially and simultaneously, too thin. To do anything else would have bored him; but to others it made him seem uncommitted and even a little implausible. Not only is it not really "done" for American poets to paint and play the piano and make films; most of them don't even write prose. Even Frank O'Hara, ten years after Kees, as bubbly and as diversely interested, didn't paint his own pictures.

Second—it seems banal to say so—he was quite genuinely unlucky. If a lot of things had fallen out even a little differently, it would have made a huge difference: if the United States hadn't joined the war, then his Midwest campus novel, *Fall Quarter*, might have been published at the time, rather than posthumously, in 1990, and he might have had a career in fiction; as it was, it was rejected two days after Pearl Harbor. If his poetry publisher, Reynal and Hitchcock, hadn't been bought up by Harcourt, Brace, and World (whose editor, Robert Giroux, published Lowell and twice rejected Kees), then he might have had more of a showing in the poetry world. If Clement Greenberg had written the piece it seemed he was going to write on Kees's paintings, that might have been the making of him as a painter. If the San Francisco theater building where he was working hadn't been shut down by the fire department as unsafe, he might have stayed longer in the area of performance and "happening." And so on, and so on, and so on. Much more than with other artists and writers one might think of.

Third, there is an important element in Kees that much preferred, in John Ashbery's phrase, "the mooring of starting out." It is easy to sentimentalize his failure and probable suicide (on July 18, 1955, his car was found abandoned on the approach to the Golden Gate Bridge); to some extent Robert Knoll is guilty of this in his otherwise excellent book *Weldon Kees and the Midcentury Generation* with his formulation "ten minutes too soon." The fact is that, probably, Kees's career was going nowhere, probably he didn't want it to go "anywhere," and the idea of a "career" as anything other than a plunge into a combination of death and deathless obscurity didn't have much appeal to him. Reidel has a nice phrase about "the *subtlety* with which he operated his own career." It is interesting to note, in this context, the description of Kees's longtime friend, Norris Getty, of Kees's "unearthly cleanliness," and of his much-remarked upon "aloofness." At any rate, the repeated pattern with Kees is that of a sudden, spectacular beginning and a failure to grub and grind it out thereafter. A revealing instance of this is when, newly arrived in San Francisco from New York (another sideways, if not backward move), Kees started circulating ideas for cartoons to *New Yorker* cartoonists like Charles Addams, with whom he had, in some cases, acquaintance, the sort of humble and speculative behavior one would hardly expect from—after all—a *New Yorker* poet and multidisciplinarian at the height of his prowess. Not the sort of thing Elizabeth Bishop would have done.

Fourth, and last, there is throughout Kees's *writing*, at any rate, an element of the macabre and the fastidious. He is a blackly funny writer, in prose and verse, who compounds satire and dread. In a representative line of his, say, "The tambourine did not function with its usual zest," one hears the pert disengagement of Eliot and Oscar

Wilde. He is a wonderful poet of rooms and atmospheres. Social and external details are produced with a bracing and inexhaustible dysphoria. Here is his short poem, "For H. V. (1901–1927)":

I remember the clumsy surgery: the face
Scarred out of recognition, ruined and not his own.
Wax hands fattened among pink silk and pinker roses.
The minister was in fine form that afternoon.

I remember the ferns, the organ faintly out of tune,
The gray light, the two extended prayers,
Rain falling on stained glass; the pallbearers,
Selected by the family, and none of them his friends.

("The pure products of America go crazy," William Carlos Williams wrote once; a puzzling remark, it would seem, to many.) Perhaps one has not to be an American to relish this comprehensively ruined account for its dry, almost scurrilous wit, and not merely to find it "depressing." Most poetry written nowadays is again as sanctimonious and as imperially overblown as in the 1940s and 1950s. What a tonic a wider appreciation of Kees would be! He still seems, as his editor, Donald Justice, remarked back in 1960, the sort of poet readers discover for themselves, and by accident. Now, thanks to this really good, well-written, and thoughtful biography, by James Reidel, himself a Keesian of twenty years' standing, he will be just a little harder to ignore than before.

JOHN BERRYMAN

I don't write these damned things willingly, you know.
—J.B. to Allen Tate, June 26, 1963

"I look less weird / without my beard," he tells us, but I'm not sure I agree. It's strange to think of him for so long as buttoned-up and repressed and preppy and clean-shaven and starchy; blue jaws like Nixon's, and small, rather shifty eyes. Like a middle manager and tweed fancier, with a secret penchant for golf: "They set their clocks by Henry House, / the steadiest man on the block." A strange, doomed effort to pass. "He knocked himself out to be like everybody else," Saul Bellow confirms in his gorgeous memoir of his friend. And then with the beard—the badge of his emancipation and loss of control—in Terence Spencer's magnificent *Life* photographs of him in 1967 in Ireland, hunched over, possessed, in spate, the beard gesticulating and waving like a third hand. The one pursed-lipped and Anglo-Saxon and mute; the other an uncontrollably gabby sage. From an unhealthy tightness to an unhealthy looseness.

John Berryman did not get to publish his first full-length book, *The Dispossessed*, until 1948, and it was only in 1953 that he graduated from the realms of the "promising" with his long poem *Homage to*

Mistress Bradstreet; and then it was not until the appearance of *77 Dream Songs* in 1964, when he was fifty, that he established a poetic identity and achieved enduring renown. The following year, he won the Pulitzer Prize. In 1967, he brought out *Berryman's Sonnets* (an account of an adulterous love affair written twenty years previously and never published before) and a retrospective *Short Poems*. In 1968, he published *His Toy, His Dream, His Rest*, a selection of a further 308 Dream Songs (four times the number of the original volume, and for the most part rather more straightforward). For this he was given the National Book Award in 1969. *The Dream Songs* were then published in one volume—385, count 'em—and they were followed by a couple of chatty, rather prosy, sporadically highly attractive books, with earthy and heavenly sections, *Love and Fame* (1970) and *Delusions, etc.* (1972). By the time *Delusions* appeared, it was posthumous, for on January 7, 1972, Berryman had killed himself by leaping from Washington Bridge in Minneapolis (where he lived and taught) onto the frozen banks of the Mississippi. One further posthumous selection was put together by John Haffenden, called *Henry's Fate and Other Poems* (1977); disappointingly but not altogether surprisingly, it contained many pieces in the Dream Song mode (which he was supposed to have forsworn)—"I will not come again / or not come with this style"— and a lot of naked distress. In the decade or so after his death, there was a little spate of critical attention—much of it again from John Haffenden, who also wrote the best biography of the poet (*The Life of John Berryman*, 1982)—but recently things have been rather quiet around Berryman. Perhaps his example seems too extreme. Yet young readers have always been drawn to him, especially to *The Dream Songs*: no one writes like that, no one dares, no one would have the wild imagination or the obsession. Who knew English could encompass that flux; that whinny; those initially baffling, then canny and eventually unforgettable rearrangements of words; that irresistible flow of thoughts and nonthoughts of that degree of informed privateness?

I first read Berryman in 1977, in what still felt like his Cambridge, when I was twenty and he was five years into his posterity. It wasn't therefore possible, but if it had been, I might well have written him a letter of the kind he writes about: "A lone letter from a young

man: that is fame." Not least because I thought he was right: and it
didn't sound as though he had it in the bag, more like an invitation,
as the needing in the Dream Songs generally has it over the bragging.
For a time I thought I might become sufficiently conversant with
the Dream Songs that I could play them as a parlor game: if someone
gave me a first line, I would oblige with the number. Or even vice
versa. To this day, #4, #14, #40, #69 (such naughtiness in the num-
bering!), #75, #78–91, #145, #146–158, #171, #219, #283, and #379
(among others) are in play. Others I could do to within maybe ten or
twenty. No cigar. Ballpark. And of course I affected the ampersand
as well.

If you possess something for a long time, you tend to wear it
down. The edges come off it, whatever garishness bleeds out of the
colors; the creak goes out of the materials; and something emerges
fluffy and tender and dusty and contourless. Blue lint. Kurt Schwitters. A childhood toy, an old book, maybe a teddy bear (as in #291 or
#302?). The Dream Songs are what taught me to lie on my back
when I can't sleep ("& my thoughts are different & more straightforward / than on my side"); nostalgia for a plethora of morning mail
deliveries in the 1920s; the meaning of *"Do, ut des"* (shorter and pith-
ier than any Latin I could construe); vivid trembling through black-
and-white films; the discreet charm of the broken-armed invalid,
where "three limbs . . . take / the other for a cruise, like an elderly
lover / not expecting much" (and Berryman sounds so unexpectedly
like Zbigniew Herbert in *his* "Mr. Cogito" persona poems); little
fragrant glimmerings of Japan and India from 1957, hefty big boisterous slabs of Dublin from 1966 to 1967.

Berryman was of the first generation of American "professional
poets"—the prizes, the residencies, the summer schools, the readings
(the first creative writing department established at the University of
Iowa by Paul Engle in 1947)—but never entirely in it. He thought
about it a lot, the biz, the poe-business, sometimes drily, often in a
sour or jaundiced way: about publication and publications, success,
fame, tribulations, colleagues, and rivals. (There cannot be another
poet who mentions *The Times Literary Supplement* in his poems as
often as Berryman does, or who is so preoccupied with "honours"—

the British spelling he retained from his two graduate years in Cambridge, in the 1930s.) He was an eager participant, all right, and painfully, vauntingly ambitious, but he seems on the whole to have been what in German is called *ein Zaungast*, a fence guest, semi-excluded by a mixture of luck, tardiness, unsuitability, and being stuck out in the Midwest (his stint at Minneapolis is coeval with the Dream Songs: both date back to 1955). He always had the feeling that he had ground to make up, that success came more easily to others, that universities and serious scholarship (his book on Stephen Crane; a long-mooted edition of Shakespeare, the wreckage of which John Haffenden assembled into the posthumous *Berryman's Shakespeare*) had taken years from him that he would not get back. Now life reasserts itself, now literature, now teaching. Existence was a perpetual round of rock, paper, scissors, and mostly he had the sense he was losing. Some of his most attractively heroic poems are about the virtue and necessity of teaching: "Sick at 6 & sick again at 9." He has a poem about *exams*. He looks forward to himself as an object of scholarship and to his (infant) daughter making her way at Vassar or Smith. The newly institutional life of the American poet is nowhere better or more fully written about than in these poems and in Bellow's 1975 novel *Humboldt's Gift*, about their mutual friend Delmore Schwartz. Bellow would visit Berryman in hospital ("He was not there because he had broken his leg"), and be treated to new Dream Songs. Berryman made the connection himself: "A hospital is where it all has a use, / so is a makar." It may not have been the institution one had in mind, originally, but hey, who cares! "Open the main!"

Berryman pines for literature. He really can't wait. He is pushing things through, like a panicky spy into a shredder. His poems—his poem, as he persists in thinking of it—are coming along/is coming along, but oh the agony! "I feel my application   failing." "My framework is broken, I am coming to an end, / God send it soon." Was ever an enterprise handled with such pathos, with round-the-world yachtsmen and Gordon of Khartoum supplying epigraphs? "Lucid his project lay, beyond. Can he?" he cries pantomimically into the void. (It's as though we should all shout out together: "It's behind you!") Then repeat, this time with fresh anxiety, that of surfeit: "with a new book in my briefcase / four times too large." He doesn't know whether to stick or twist, "whether to sing / further or seal his lonely   throat." He is on the point of applying to the president personally for help: "Mr Johnson has never written one / but he seems a generous & able man." The Dream Songs are so laced with quotations and authorities and allusions, it's as though they are preemptively literary; something with so much water in it, surely it can float. There's even a song—the example that proves the rule—celebrating a book (the only book?) that Henry hasn't read: *Ubu Roi*. It's as though Berryman is set on amplifying the famous opening line of Mallarmé's *Brise Marine*, "*La chair est triste, hélas! et j'ai lu tous les livres.*" Hence the Kafka, the Housman, the Yeats, the Wordsworth, the Rilke, and dozens more besides: companions, allies, antagonists, farther along by virtue of being dead and being their books. In this frantic vision, life is a race to posterity, and, once there, perhaps, a struggle for ascendancy. "While he begins to have it out with Horace," Henry replies, contumaciously, of the barely cold Robert Frost.

The Dream Songs show the antic dance of the poet, scholar, teacher, and all-round "human American man" at its best. Berryman's style—Lowell after his death admitted, "I'm afraid I mistook it for forcing, when he came into his own"—breaks other components into an astounding new whole. It encompasses all his literariness, his versedness, I would like to call it, and all his creativity and demotic flair as well. There are astonishing things, priceless things, things that no one else could have done, not even—and he maybe comes closest—Ezra Pound: "whenas we sought, among the beloved faces, / eminence and were dissatisfied with that / and needed more," "O Adlai mine," "the weather fleured," "Go, ill-sped book," "Honey dusk do sprawl," "she leaned an ear / in my direction, here," "I will not come again / or not come with this style." Lowell in his long initial bafflement referred deprecatingly to "babytalk," Michael Schmidt compares it to Cummings, "but a cummings carrying a huge library on his back," but the best is probably Adrienne Rich, noting that "Shakespeare's English and some minstrelly refrain meet, salute and inform each other," before going on to wonder: "The English

(American) language. Who knows entirely what it is? Maybe two men in this decade: Bob Dylan, John Berryman."*

This knowledge is there already in the *Sonnets* and the *Bradstreet*, but chiefly it illuminates the Dream Songs, which seem to me to be written with as much freedom and—before a manner, a tic, could establish itself—as much necessity as anything I can think of. I love the extremes of courtliness and creatureliness in the Dream Songs, on the one hand such things as "Come away, Mr. Bones" (the occasion for Adrienne Rich's first rapture), or "There is a kind of undetermined hair, / half-tan, to which he was entirely unable to fail to respond / in woman"; and on the other hand "Gentle friendly Henry Pussy-cat," or "Henry / tasting all the secret bits of life"; or again, when the two categories are run together, as when Berryman remembers an adolescent amour: "while he was so beastly with love for Charlotte Coquet / he skated up & down in front of her house / wishing he could, sir, die," or, perhaps most succinctly: "What wonders is / she sitting on, over there?"

The best of the Dream Songs have a sort of radical delicacy. Here is one never, so far as I know, much regarded or anthologized, #19:

> Here, whence
> all have departed or will do, here airless, where
> that witchy ball
> wanted, fought toward, dreamed of, all a green living
> drops limply into one's hands
> without pleasure or interest
>
> Figurez-vous, a time swarms when the word
> "happy" sheds its whole meaning, like to come and
> like for memory too
> That morning arrived to Henry as well a great cheque
> eaten out already by the Government & State &
> other strange matters

---

*Predictably, Henry—Berryman—isn't a fan. "Yes, if only he'd learn to sing!" he is quoted as saying to students, in John Haffenden's *Life of John Berryman*.

Gentle friendly Henry Pussy-cat
smiled into his mirror, a murderer's
(at Stillwater), at himself alone
and said across a plink to that desolate fellow
said a little hail & buck-you-up
upon his triumph

The poem is about dejection and money. It is unrhymed and almost unpunctuated, but rhetorically organized ("Here . . . here . . . that morning . . . smiled . . . and said") into one strikingly cogent sentence. From the very first line—itself an extraordinary getaway or liftoff—the poem is a bristling and dazzling display of grammar: almost one's first thoughts on seeing it are to do with agreements and ("here airless") appositives! The first "here," which Henry (or Berryman) is in such a hurry to quit, is the world, a world, further, in which the world (or something very similar—an apple, or a green apple, or perhaps Snow White's poisoned—"witchy"—apple) falls into your lap, but without making you any the happier for it. The poem revisits the theme of Arthur Hugh Clough's "So pleasant it is to have money, heigh-ho!" or Brecht's "Song of the Vivifying Effect of Money," but in an agnostic or unsatisfied mode, the mode, if you like, of Midas or, worse, a Midas with a paper touch. It is a poem of accursedness or ill fortune, set up as in a parallel world (the world of depression, or perhaps a mirror world, which would help account for the role of the mirror at the end of the poem in breaking the spell?) similar, say, to the "vast landscape of Lament" in Rilke's Tenth Elegy ("*Einst waren wir reich*"—We used to be rich). From "whence," from "departed," from "airless," from "that witchy ball" and from "green living," I have a sense that the earliest Russian and American space missions—Gagarin and Shepard, both in 1961—may have played into the poem, and the very earliest satellite photographs of ourselves—mirrorings—from space. If one strand of the poem's thought is cosmic, the other is monetary; it is there in the play on "interest," "living," and "green"—with its echo of "greenback"—in "buck-you-up" and the spectacular "Figurez-vous." Berryman learned this sort of image cluster from Shakespeare, who is a constant pressure on his style. Typically, such literariness and ambition are balanced by an early use of the illiterate particle "like." The verbs are conspicuously loose fitting and vitalist: "drops," "swarms," "sheds," and "eaten." It is out of the vegetable nature of these that the animal character of "Gentle friendly Henry Pussy-cat" is compounded. "Stillwater" in the third stanza is a penitentiary in Minnesota (Berryman, as one would have suspected, actually owned such a mirror); and "plink" is a bit of family slang. There is no one else in the poem but Henry: it is he who smiles, who is "alone," then "desolate," and finally triumphant. Still, the very clever introduction of the murderer, as it were, flavors the poem (Berryman identified his particular area of expertise as a poet as the personal pronoun!). The murderer brings in society, depth, risk, an alter ego ("in feelings not ever accorded to oneself," it says with stern magnificence). The poem is an authentic Dream Song, diffusely coercive, unconventional, complex, bleak, tender in adversity, rallying.

The Dream Songs vary through every degree of lucidity and opacity: some of them, beautifully, add up; many others are at least consistent in their gestures; a few leave unanswered difficulties; but almost all make their own distinct mark on silence and the page. They are dramatic poems—few more so. Cliff-hanging or stalling episodes in a long-running series. Vainglorious or Pyrrhic, addled or plain: "His wife has been away / with genuine difficulty he fought madness / whose breast came close to breaking." Often, they end up in rhetorical reaches most poems don't go near: threat, prayer, promise, action, resolve. Berryman always insisted on their unity—"The Care & Feeding of Long Poems" was his special study—but that no longer seems a plausible or even an important claim, if it ever did. (Nor, analogously, does the siting or defining of Henry: he may not *be* Berryman, but he shares too many of the trials and tribulations of the twentieth-century American poet.) Reading through all the Dream Songs is like remaining in your seat while the lights go up and down on three hundred and eighty-five phantasmagorical-existential sketches. "He led with his typewriter. He made it fly."

IAN HAMILTON

Though Ian Hamilton died in 2001 of cancer, I still see him sometimes in party rooms, at literary gatherings, burly, almost square,
with the low center of gravity of a Scottish ex-middleweight or
-wing-half, encased in his black Crombie overcoat (indoors, radiat-
ing simultaneously cold and impermeability), invariably smoking—oh,
how we used to smoke—and making what the Trinidadian novelist,
Sam Selvon, calls "oldtalk." There was something of Lino Ventura
about him; Ian McEwan described him as having "the face of a capo
di capi, and a useful, understated cool." A conspiratorial element of
backroom, exile, spit, and sawdust clung to him. He put one in mind
of a boxing manager or a soccer coach. His father's middle name was
Tough. The habitual set of his face was a sort of tender scowl. He
had the secret sorrow one might look for in a Spurs fan and serial
founder and editor of little magazines. The cowboyishly skewed
mouth—the word "hard-bitten" might have been invented for it—
passing sotto voce ten-ton judgments was much more familiar to me
from Craig Raine's gifted and unexpectedly devoted imitations of
him than from the real thing. In fact, parties aside, I saw him very

few times, though these, oddly, seem as though they could furnish a biography. An ill-advised lunch at my instigation in the early '80s, just after his life of Robert Lowell appeared, at which Ian drank more than he spoke, and I hadn't yet learned to drink ("those played-with-but-uneaten lunches for which he was famous" in the words of his friend, the novelist Dan Jacobson; "You never ate / Just pushed things round and round your plate / Till you could decently light up again" in those of Alan Jenkins's poem "Rotisserie [The Wait]"—but how was I to know that?). Then there was the time he popped up in a playground in Queens Park, which was the wrong suburb, with a daughter I had no idea he had—he was supposed to be away in Wimbledon, and with sons—growling something about Catherine (innocently pulling at a bottle of water) having inherited her father's thirst. I saw him another time going into the publisher's to fetch some boxes of things, wearing a camouflage jacket, and with a station wagon idling outside, in the throes of moving house and changing lives. Later, there was a group reading in Manchester, even as an unbuttoned United having won the European Cup were paraded through the city on an open-topped municipal bus; we made our way through thousands of onlookers to read to a disappointed bookstore manager and a dozen nutcases—sorry, poetry lovers. I saw Ian the next morning, already ensconced in the London train, and felt far too shy to join him, but when I opened my newspaper, his name leaped out to greet me. It was his contribution to a series—this speaks volumes about a certain positively idealistic streak in English cultural philistinism—on "overrated books." Ian's chosen target was *The Waste Land*.

He was possessed of more authority—more literary authority, I suppose I should specify—than anyone I've ever met, and it was, in the terms of the social anthropologist Mary Douglas, personal not positional authority. In other words, it didn't matter that he no longer sat at the head of the table; no longer fronted book programs on the BBC; no longer had commissions to dole out, approval to bestow or deny in the columns of *The Observer* or the *TLS*; that his magazines *The Review* and *The New Review* edited (partly to avoid creditors) from a pub across the road called the Pillars of Hercules had long since been wound up—you still wouldn't want to cross him, or even disagree with him. Not because he was a—literary—gangster but, rather, the opposite, because of the virtue and delicacy of his poems. In the long and fascinating interview that Dan Jacobson conducted with Hamilton shortly before his death (Between the Lines, 2002), it is striking how often he uses a phantom or gangland first-person plural; it's always "we weren't supposed to be telling people about fads" or "so we thought yes." And yet I can't help thinking that the co-opted parties, left to themselves, would have stuck, more truthfully, to the third-person singular: "Ian this" or "Ian that." Hence the persistent take-offs (flattery) and the unparalleled loyalty to his memory and example. He ran his magazines, the one from 1962 to 1970, the other from 1974 to 1979, without really making any discoveries or launching any notable careers. Perhaps they could even be described as gloriously exclusionary enterprises, ideally diminishing to a single angel (who?) on a pin. Most of the major reputations of the 1960s—Larkin, Gunn, Hughes, Plath—were already firmly defined, and the editorial "we" was fairly agnostic on their successors; "I never had any time for Geoffrey Hill and still don't"; entertained more or less crippling reservations about Lowell and Heaney and Berryman ("I was never a great Berryman fan"); never saw the point of the Black Mountain school ("that neo-Poundian stuff"); and fought an unremitting war against the poppy, crowd-pleasing Mersey Poets ("You can imagine what [Matthew] Arnold would have said if he had read Roger McGough"). At the same time, it seems to me that the poets who passed through his magazines, like Douglas Dunn, David Harsent, Hugo Williams, Craig Raine, did some of their best work then, in an endeavor to please Ian. The fiction writers, too, Julian Barnes, Ian McEwan, Jim Crace, Martin Amis, Edna O'Brien, Kazuo Ishiguro surely bore some trace of having been through his editorial *cura*. It strikes me that Ian was perhaps the last poet routinely read by novelists (at least, if there have been others since, I am not aware of them). It was the last time there was any sort of citadel or center in English letters, even though it may have ended, in brilliantly English fashion, with the writers being called upon to pay the printers' bills. (Doesn't it all sound like something from Cavafy?) Or is that just a story?

Ian Hamilton published his book of poems called *The Visit* in 1970. It contained thirty-three poems, all of them short (more on this matter of brevity later). In 1988, the year he turned fifty, he had bulked this up to a production called *Fifty Poems*. Ten years later, that was replaced by *Sixty Poems*, always with the original thirty-three leading off. Alan Jenkins—poet and reviewer, a friend and successor of Ian Hamilton's at the *TLS*—has managed to turn up two more poems and another seventeen unpublished or uncollected pieces. Grand total: seventy-nine. You think prime number, or else of the perceived shame and difficulty of writing at such a slow rate. Ian, of course, was aware of the problem: *Fifty Poems* came with a moody though unapologetic preface ("Fifty poems in twenty-five years: not much to show for half a lifetime, you might think" included, with much other valuable material, in Alan Jenkins's edition). And when he read aloud to launch it, the difficulty was still more acute, as he threatened to gallop through the entire book in half an hour or so, because not only were the poems short, but they didn't elicit from Ian very much in the way of commentary or explanation. These problems, though real and un-get-round-able—is there any substitute for quantity in poetry!?—are ancillary, because in the end Hamilton's slender oeuvre is worth others ten times as bulky. As the man's life was a perhaps involuntary education in the difficulties of being a poet (or "man of letters"), so Ian's poems are an education in poetry. Reading them trains and civilizes one's nerves. Just as in his tastes he whittled and whittled away, "allowing" finally maybe only Hardy and Arnold and Frost and Larkin and some early Pound and Keith Douglas and half a dozen pieces from *Life Studies*, so the poems do away with luxuriance, the inessential. No filler, only killer. If you take them to your heart, you will understand how much poetry is to do with the mastery of hot and cold, of precisely heart and heartlessness: the control of side effects—semicolons, line breaks, syllables, changes of register, hurdles, internal rhymes—within its own silent and impossible speech. As his poem "Nature" has it, "counting syllables / In perfect scenery, now that you're gone."

All of Hamilton's poems are moments of equilibrium in dramatic or even fraught contexts. Sometimes the contexts can be made out, or they are revealed in the notes (though neither notes nor poems are indiscreet): they are a father's death, or a wife's derangement. Sometimes they remain mysterious, though just as urgent. Their tragedy is expressed in the absolute separation of the pronouns in these "I-you" poems: the helpless "I," the afflicted "you," the fictive "we." "The usual curse" it says in "Ties": "His, yours, theirs, everyone's. And hers." The poems stop and turn; there is something pivotal and sculptural about them, but also something instantaneous—almost the best comparison is with Bill Brandt's statuesquely tubular black-and-white sixties nude photographs (with the addition, in Hamilton, of occasional little spots of color) ("Trucks"):

> Aching, you turn back
> From the wall and your hands reach out
> Over me. They are caught
> In the last beam and, pale,
> They fly there now. You're taking off, you say,
> And won't be back.

It is so vivid, it is almost theatrically or mythologically present, this shaped snapshot. Each scene has something of beacon or semaphor: built up from the short words and artful repetitions of Frost, the contracted verbs (often, as in Larkin, couched in the negative), and the teetering piles of adjectives (the triads borrowed from Lowell) or else Hamilton's personal trademark adverb-plus-adjective pairing: "monotonously warm," "this shocked and slightly aromatic fall of leaves," "one hand in yours, the other / Murderously cold," "the delicately shrouded heart / Of this white rose," "semi-swamps / Of glitteringly drenched green," "The river weeds / [. . .] A shade more featherishly purple," for buddleia or rosebay willowherb. (These extraordinarily effective, really rather glamorous adverbs aside, Hamilton's poems have a modest and restricted vocabulary: it's hard to imagine him doing anything as officious and showy as naming plants.)

The opening poem—not so in *The Visit* but from *Fifty Poems* on—is "Memorial":

Four weathered gravestones tilt against the wall
Of your Victorian asylum.
Out of bounds, you kneel in the long grass
Deciphering obliterated names:
Old lunatics who died here.

That's the whole thing, a miracle of balance and implication. The "you" is addressed, I take it, to Gisela Dietzel, Hamilton's first wife, who became schizophrenic. There are two word groups, one subtly expressing (Pound's word!) long standing—"weathered," "Victorian," "long," "obliterated," "old," even, at a pinch, "tilt"—and the other, dementia—"asylum," "lunatics," and, arguably, "tilt" again, and "out of bounds." The stones are characterful from the beginning, like British teeth, pitched between the two interesting, almost flavorful words "weathered" and "tilt," one governing surface, the other angle. (I'm reminded of an astonishing Egon Schiele painting *Four Trees*, each one a distinct, spindly personality.) It's no surprise to have them brought out at the end in the personal, matey, borderline slang of "old lunatics" (a tone, by the way, of which Hamilton had an absolute mastery, as witness his essayistic prose, or a couple of broader poems, "Larkinesque" and the lit. crit. skit called "An Alternative Agenda"). The impersonal Pevsnerish handling of time in "weathered" has morphed into the simple personal of "old." ("We are all old-timers," says Lowell in "Waking in the Blue," a poem Hamilton will have known and, I believe, liked.) That tone—distinctly warmer, more spoken, more intimately joshing than anything else in the poem— prepares us for its last word, "here." There is a conflict, as there often is in Hamilton (and I struggled with it before, with my likenesses of photographs and sculptures), between movement and stasis: this is one shot, one frame, but with a zoom. It is the zoom that gives the poem its fear (oddly coincident with its warmth): the fear that the "you" will never leave "here"—that "here" that was once "out of bounds"; that the tenderness of a chance, meaningless occupation ("kneel" of course has something erotic about it) will turn out to have been ill omened or predictive; that the interest evinced will have become excessive and fateful; that ultimately we are attending at something symptomatic and morbid, for which there are hurtful colloquial designations, like "old lunatics." The poem is graced by all sorts of other details and symmetries: its two dynamic verbs, "tilt" and "kneel"; the way the sound of "tilt" seeds "obliterated" and that of "Victorian" "lunatics"; the play of "Deciphering"—to do with revealing figures—and "obliterated," which is destroying letters; the sinister implication of having five lines about four stones. Then "Memorial" starts to recede. It becomes what the art critics call a "*mise en abime*" dramatizing the theme of attention ("the natural prayer of the soul," as Paul Celan liked to say): it is Hamilton kneeling at what has become his wife's grave; and then it is ourselves, as it were on our knees before this "memorial." It is, after all, a poem about reading.

The other chief or recurring Hamilton subject is the death of his father, when he was thirteen. Here, again in its entirety, is "Birthday Poem":

> Tight in your hands,
> Your Empire Exhibition shaving mug.
> You keep it now
> As a spittoon, its bloated doves,
> Its 1938
> Stained by the droppings of your blood.
> Tonight,
> Half-suffocated, cancerous,
> Deceived,
> You bite against its gilded china mouth
> And wait for an attack.

This poem is strung up on one rhyme, on the letter *t* and a long preceding vowel: "tight . . . bloated . . . eight . . . tonight . . . suffocated . . . bite . . . wait." A second series, this time of short-*t* syllables, makes itself felt alongside: "spittoon . . . its . . . its . . . its . . . attack." There is something queasy and labored about the long syllables— especially "bloated"—and then the short, pedantic cymbal stroke of the *t*: it demands the careful British dental *t*, not the drawled American half *d*. The *t* is the frontier, it enacts the spit, between one "mouth" and the other, one "mug" and the other. The poem is in iambs throughout, but with striking and dramatic trochaic inversions at the beginning ("Tight in") and halfway ("Stained by"), though that hardly does justice to its supple variety. The last line, for instance, "And wait for an attack," is three iambs, but each of a completely different quality, the first, if you like, normal strength, the second almost Pyrrhic (those two unimportant words, gulped down), the third almost a spondee. I don't know why the poem is called "Birthday Poem"; either it happens to be the birthday of the father (or the son); or, a little more obscurely but sensibly, it's a reference to the year of the poet's birth, 1938, the same year as the Empire Exhibition, held in Glasgow, the city of his father and mother, which they had recently left. The year 1938, the year of the Munich agreement, of "I hold in my hand a piece of paper" and "peace in our time" and Sudetenland, and the last year of a more general "waiting for an attack," is of course far from innocent (therefore no "doves," or only bloodstained ones, "deceived" ones, if you like). But then so is Empire (shouldn't it really be "Expire" and "Expiry Inhibition," the effort to hold in one's death?), which was also awaiting its end, while still recalling those—bloated?—"distensions of Empire" that Pound's Sextus Propertius refuses (natch) to "expound." The poem moves from defense—that "tight" appears all the time in such soccer locutions like "keep it tight" or "playing it tight"—to the helpless "wait for an attack." Its climax, its knot, where one repeatedly looks to, is the triad of adjectives, brutally sectioned off by the line break, "Half-suffocated, cancerous, / Deceived": how the "you" feels, how he is, and how he reconciles the two conditions in his mind. With its undependable *c*'s, now soft, now hard, and the soft puffing ff's replaced by a long screaming *e* vowel and a slicing *v*, the combination of sounds is of a deadly masterful suggestiveness.

The poems in *The Visit* are wonderful and unequaled by any of those that so painfully slowly came later. "Memorial" and "Birthday Poem," plus "Pretending Not to Sleep," "Father, Dying," "Last Respects," "Epitaph," "Admission," "Last Waltz," "The Visit," and "Now and Then" all come from the first thirty-three, along with others almost as good, as intensely pitched, as eerily balanced and mysteriously stocked with quiddity. Hamilton—of course, of course—knew this: "In fact, I'd now say," he writes in the 1988 preface to *Fifty Poems*, "that these later poems are bruised rewrites of what I'd done before." To say there is anything like a falling-off would be like saying there was a falling-off in the work of T. E. Hulme. The poems still partake of and contribute to the same harrowed atmospheres, the same persistently denatured nature ("I sit beneath this gleaming wall of rock / And let the breeze lap over me"—in the poem called "Nature"), and harshly lit studio rooms, with curtains, neighbors, and cars outside only momentarily distracting the archaically helpless antagonists within from their drama. While almost completely neglecting the sixties—one song title, one mention of Vietnam—and with no topical nouns, no consumer language, nothing street or *veriste*, it is uncanny how much these poems are able to evoke the textures and comforts of their time. But perhaps that's one vestige of the perverse way in which, to begin with, I tried to read him, almost as a war poet, for drama and substance; whereas now I see him as the Mallarmé-like technician of stresses and syllables that in fact I think he did become, a little mannered, a little hallowed and sacerdotal, a little too self-aware, a little too good at doing without, a little too coolly canny ("Vigil"):

> These ancient lamps, diminishing each day,
> Will never taste the dark worlds they whimper for.
> These wounds,
> Though we have nourished them for years,
> Will be the freshest of sweet tears
> Tomorrow. And the lost will not be found.

The enzyme that converted pain to poetry went away or gave up. The thing is, there was something not just poetry-minded, but also simply and truly high-minded about Ian, which meant that he had a horror of exploiting those around him: Lowell, whose life he wrote, and of whom he will have seen a fair bit in London in the late '60s and early '70s, appalled him with his personal fusses and pitiless production. The cards he was left with—seventy-nine poems, not so many more than a deck—were paucity and brevity. I realize I am paraphrasing the sentence with which Alan Jenkins opens his introduction, quoting Dan Jacobson: "So far as they can be said to be famous at all, Ian Hamilton's poems are famous for being small in size and few in number." Accordingly, he wrote hundreds of reviews and essays, and eventually a subtle and simply written and enchanting group of prose books that discreetly revolved around the question that so preoccupied Hamilton of what writers did when they stopped, in any vital sense, writing. First, there was the autogyro Lowell. Then the opposite case, J. D. Salinger, the greatly loved author who "had elected to silence himself. He had freedom of speech but what he had ended up wanting more than anything else, it seemed, was the freedom to be silent." There were books on writers in Hollywood (a sort of posthumous condition), and on writers' estates (those really had put down their pens). There was Paul Gascoigne, the most gifted footballer of his generation (and a Tottenham player!), who burned out on silly drink and bad food and personal excesses, and Matthew Arnold, a Victorian slave to duty and social good. I don't think Ian chose—though of course he didn't actually choose, there wasn't a choice—any worse than any of these. Last of all there was a book called *Against Oblivion*, a set of lives of twentieth-century poets, a pendant to Dr. Johnson, agnostic, cool, sometimes drily wounding. All that I think is nacre; the pearls are the poems.

JAMES SCHUYLER

Not first sight, often enough, but a second look—it is a mysterious thing with poetry that it finds its own moment. The poets that have meant most to me—Lowell, Bishop, Schuyler—all, as it were, were rudely kept waiting by me. I had their books, or I already knew some poems of theirs, but there was no spark of transference. Then it happened, and our tepid prehistory was, quite literally, forgotten—beyond a lingering embarrassment at my own callow unresponsiveness. It was as though they had always been with me, and I found it difficult, conversely, to remember our first encounter. It is a slight relief to me that James Schuyler, who writes about reading almost as much as he writes about seeing, confesses to a similar sluggishness of feeling ("Horse-Chestnut Trees and Roses"):

> Twenty-some years ago, I read Graham Stuart Thomas's
> "Colour in the Winter Garden." I didn't plant
> a winter garden, but the book led on to his
> rose books: "The Old Shrub Roses," "Shrub Roses
> of Today," and the one about climbers and ramblers.

It is this dilatory or sidelong compliance I am talking about. There follows my own belated winter garden to the American poet James Marcus Schuyler, pronounced Sky-ler, (1923–1991).

The first time I was aware of James Schuyler was in one of those shrill American "Best of" annuals. At the back of the book, the poets comment on their own poems, in every shade of vainglory and modesty, pretentiousness and aw, shucks! The only comment I can remember from a decade's worth of these books is Schuyler's, to the effect that while his poems were usually the product of a single occasion looking out a window (his version of the unities!), the poem in question (I think it was "Haze") departed from this, by using more than one window and more than one occasion. "I do not normally permit myself such licence," the poet sternly ends. This stood out: for its idiosyncrasy and scrupulousness, for its thoughtful rebellion against unthinking unassumingness, for its (I am somehow convinced) borrowed plumminess. There's something enjoyably performed and bewigged about it. That was in 1994. From then I date my public espousal of the "poem out of the window"—though that's an old cause with me—and a little later, I finally began to read Schuyler.

It was on a morning in Manhattan, the book was *The Morning of the Poem* (typically, I don't know how it came to be in my possession), and the poems that convinced me (it's unusual to remember even this much) were a little sequence of eleven short pieces called "The Payne Whitney Poems." Payne Whitney, I knew from reading about Robert Lowell, was a New York mental hospital—in the same way I knew from reading Malcolm Lowry's little book *Lunar Caustic* that Bellevue was a New York mental hospital—and here was a clutch of texts fit to set beside that, or Lowell's "Waking in the Blue" or his sequence "Hospital." Intact records of damage, frail hints at a central neural mystery, words newly out of bandages:

> Arches
> of buildings, this building,
> frame a stream of windows
> framed in white brick. This
> building is fireproof; or else
> it isn't: the furnishings first

to go: no, the patients. Patients
on Sundays walk in a small garden.
Today some go out on a group
pass. To stroll the streets and shop.
So what else is new? The sky
slowly/swiftly went blue to gray.
A gray in which some smoke stands.

Typical of Schuyler are the adjustments and corrections—like Bishop's, only more sweeping (and yet somehow just as mildly carried out, "no, the patients," "slowly/swiftly"). Also the small thoughts and whimsical half-experimental notations, before they are countermanded: "This / building is fireproof," "Today some go out on a group / pass"—this last reminding me unfortunately of someone's altogether more robust sneer (is it Berryman?), "nuts in groups about the room." There is a clear and real external scene, a view or "subject," and yet always stronger is one's sense of the poem as being made, like a painting: the quick, nervous applications of paint, and the quick taking of it back. Schuyler is at once a painterly poet, descriptive and objective, and at the same time he uses all the subliminal, microbial quirks of language.

The poem attempts perhaps to find something to affirm, but everywhere there is either fear or envy (of the patients on their exeat) or a crippling feeling of fatuity. Something as "normal" and ordinary as "To stroll the streets and shop" can rarely have sounded as hesitant and borrowed and speculative as it does here. The infinite wistfulness of the infinitive. To know her is to love her. To walk and chew gum. To pass through the eye of a needle and enter heaven. No wonder it takes them straight out of the poem—leaving the speaker with the self-interrogation which, one senses, he has been avoiding as hard as he could. One infers that the speaker, from shame, from weakness, from "shakiness"—a condition referred to in one of the other poems—or perhaps from lifelong aesthetic preference, would prefer to stick to external, middle-distance things. His speech feels like remedial speech, the words sound odd and insecure. Having asked his question—doesn't it sound like a visitor's, easy to ask, hell to reply to, that he's unhappily parroting to himself?—he heroically interposes "The sky," perhaps so as not to have to offer information about himself. Unluckily, "The sky" sounds like a play on the poet's name, and the predicate may perhaps offer clues about his condition (and I have seen both the following ascribed to Schuyler): the schizophrenic "slowly/swiftly," or else the bipolar "went blue to gray," a past verb— more, painful, relearning of language—suggesting the change— which of course the speaker has no hope of quantifying—from depressed, "blue," to medicated, "gray." "A gray," the information carries on, in a rather unlooked-for way, "in which some smoke stands." The last word, wholly unexpected, makes the poem. Not that one had any doubts about the poem being made—it makes itself throughout—but such an ending, dutiful, dominant, at no stage in the poem seems remotely within its reach. Here is the unlooked-for affirmation, a new physics in which smoke "stands" while windows "stream" and brick is "white" and "fireproof; or else / it isn't." And of course, platitudinously, "no smoke without fire" and the patients are the first "to go," and where this one, humorously, has "gone." "Some."

What looked like a static scene—a view out the window!—is instead a little drama. The interest of the poem—fully held by the minutely controlled to-and-fro, paint-and-scrape of the sentences, its terrible, casual sensitivity—is in its naked tact and its secret optics. The form of the arch (it is hard to know where to say this) had [the suicide] Kleist's admiration for being kept up by the desire of every individual part of it to fall. "Arches" is the poem of someone with his glasses off, or his brain decoupled, of the infinitely delicate return of matter, manner, humor, humanity. What we call way, Kafka said, is wavering or dithering. The Payne Whitney poems (*pace* Heaney) waver into sense. They take very small steps tremendously irresolutely. At the beginning of "Arches," the speaker recognizes or discerns nothing (by the end, he sounds wise). Not just that, he seems to be under very low pressure. There is painfully little forward momentum. Most rhetoric is based on repetition; Schuyler uses repetition that is only repetition, that is without rhetoric. The title—ironically— falls into the poem, and the poem shuffles from "buildings" to "building," from "frame" to "framed," from "the patients" to "Patients." It sounds potentially tremendously powerful—if Lowell or someone had written within such parameters, it would have had tremendous power (say, "tops of the moving trees move helter-skelter")—yet no power accrues to it here. Rather, the miracle is that the frailty, even the lightness of the thing is not impaired. It is someone taking these tiny steps, backward and forward, and not treading on anything, not hurting anything.

However halting, impaired, almost uncommunicative the poem, I still have the perverse sense that the station to which it is tuned, as it were, however low, is merriment. The sentences may be mumbled and reluctant and short and full of wrong turnings, but there is still a kind of low ebb of wit in them—in the macabre speculation, the observation of others like or unlike himself, in the unexpectedly fluent linkage of smoke and fire. It is, in other words, and perhaps again unexpectedly, literary—and I have come to think that Schuyler is everywhere literary. It seems to me not inappropriate to be reminded of other poems and poets by "Arches," by the other "Payne Whitney Poems," by Schuyler passim. Thus, "her hair dressed with stark simplicity" (from "Let's All Hear It for Mildred Bailey!") is Horace; "Buried at Springs" anticipates Bishop's "North Haven," and there is no shortage of other "Bishop moments," such as "More litter, less clutter" from "The Master of the Golden Glow" or "The bay agitatedly tries to smooth itself out. / If it were tissue paper it would need damp and an iron," which then corpses into: "It is a good deal more than damp. / What a lot of water" ("The Edge in the Morning"); "An Almanac" is Brodsky before there was Brodsky—1969— "Shops take down their awnings; / women go south; / few streetlamp leaners; / children run with leaves running at their backs. / In cedar chests sheers and seersuckers displace flannels and wools." Rilke is a pervasive presence, "men with faces like happy fists" ("Scarlet Tanager"), or the thought in "The best, the very best roses. After learning all their names—Rose / de Rescht, Cornelia, Pax—it is important to forget them" and "When I / Was born, death kissed me. I kissed it back" (both in "Hymn to Life," which is like a stray Elegy); Frank O'Hara, Schuyler's friend and sometime flatmate, very obviously, greets—I'll keep myself therefore to one example: "Look, Mitterrand baby" ("Simone Signoret"). O'Hara aside, this is not a matter of being influenced—or influential. The quotations are not borrowings but convergences or congruences: they affirm a kind of conventionality that, with all their wacky freedoms, Schuyler's poems also satisfy. It's not that they are touchstones—something I had thought of saying about "Arches," say—but that they come up to them.

When I began reading Schuyler, I thought it wasn't possible for anyone to occupy so much of O'Hara's territory without looking pallid; then I thought I actually liked it better than O'Hara—less strenuous, less riotous, more depth and stamina in the personality, more like that "something to read in normal circumstances" (Pound) that I generally crave in poetry. After a while, I thought I hadn't liked anyone this much since Lowell; then I had the (for me) heretical thought that perhaps I even liked it better than Lowell. Still, Lowell is part of my picture of Schuyler, who is, I think, or can be, Lowell by other means. This is an inconvenient or irregular thought: a distaste for Robert Lowell and all his works seems to be axiomatic for Schuyler's admirers. There is a reflex opposition to Lowell in O'Hara and the New York School that seems to me only partly just and that I don't think they can take Schuyler with them on. Their view of Lowell seems to be stuck in around 1955—and their rather unsuccessful espousal of Schuyler, who is almost unknown in England and underappreciated in the States, rarely goes beyond perplexity and adulation. A typical sentence is Howard Moss's: "How Schuyler manages to be absolutely truthful and an obsessed romantic at the same time is his secret." Well, perhaps the critic should have tried harder to get it out of him. Lee Harwood in his afterword to Schuyler's *Last Poems* enthuses about "poems where the poet is not an isolated heroic figure but a social creature enjoying or enduring the 'ordinary' experiences of life." Harwood doesn't mention Lowell by name, but it's easy to imagine he's thinking of him in that "isolated heroic figure." But what is the speaker of "Arches," if not "an isolated heroic figure"? And how "ordinary" an experience is hospitalization anyway? I read and admire Schuyler with the same part of me that reads and admires Lowell. To make sense of "The Payne Whitney Poems," I contend that it helps to have read "For Sale," "Waking in the Blue," "Mouth of the Hudson," "Myopia: A Night," perhaps even— I provoke—"Waking Early Sunday Morning." Yes, Schuyler has a different register, his words emerge either slower or faster than Lowell's, more sparingly or more drenchingly (in "Arches," it is slow and spare), but both are in the same business of forging a written voice or making print that sounds. It doesn't seem to me justifiable to set the author of "I keep no rank nor station. / Cured, I am frizzled, stale and small" against the author of "Arches"—not to mention the fact that Elizabeth Bishop was a great admirer of both.

From "The Payne Whitney Poems," I ranged happily over the rest of *The Morning of the Poem* (1980) and then the *Selected* and *Collected Poems* of 1990 and 1993. Schuyler readers have actually fared rather well since his death, in 1993. Black Sparrow brought out *The Diary of James Schuyler* in 1997 and the *Selected Art Writings* in 1998; in 1999 Slow Dancer published as *Last Poems* those pieces that had been included in the American *Collected* but not the *Selected*; in 2009 William Corbett brought out a *Selected Letters*; and in 2001 the New York Review of Books Classics series adopted a delightful novel of Schuyler's called *Alfred and Guinevere*—his first book, from 1958—with an introduction by his friend John Ashbery.

Schuyler is first and last a poet, but the other books shed interesting light on the poetry. "For readers of his poetry, the idea of the *Diary* of James Schuyler might almost seem like too much of a good thing," begins Nathan Kernan's introduction—too much because the poems have so much of the particular and the quotidian about them. The *Art Writings*—Schuyler followed Ashbery and O'Hara to *ARTnews*, and wrote for it, off and on, from 1955 to 1978— show a well-tempered, diversely appreciative critic, with an apparently inexhaustible range of ways of saying things (on Alex Katz: "the first in the 'allegorical' style that showed the painter and his wife Ada and small son striding smiling out of a summer landscape; like the end of a Russian movie when the wheat crop has flourished") and an unexpectedly fervent commitment to a sort of minor-Ruskin aesthetic that also informs the poems (on Jane Freilicher: "that passion for prettiness that can charge a lyric gift with the greatest potency of beauty"). One thinks of the New York poets as associating with the Abstract Expressionist painters, but a lot of Schuyler's enthusiasms—not to mention his book jackets—tend to be for rather pretty and watery figurative work. O'Hara claimed not to be able to enjoy grass or trees "unless there's a subway handy"; Schuyler was a more wholehearted visitor to Long Island, a longtime resident of Vermont and Maine and upstate, and in many of his New York City poems celebrates a kind of *rus in urbe* pleasantness. The novel, finally—Schuyler wrote a couple of others, one with Ashbery, but I haven't read them—is an extraordinary piece of work, chronicling an uneasy period in the life of a brother and sister, seven-year-old Alfred and eleven-year-old Guinevere. There is no narration beyond "he said" or "she said"; the whole book is kept in speech, occasional letters (Alfred has to dictate his), and Guinevere's monstrously precocious diary entries ("When I take up smoking remember about lemon juice removing stains"). It lives in the frighteningly accurate contrast between the two voices—two ages, two sexes, but also two individuals—and, almost more, in that between written speech and writing (which, to me, is also an area where Schuyler's poetry makes a great showing). Remarkably, *Alfred and Guinevere* was originally published—mistakenly—with illustrations, as a children's book. It can be done—my cool literary eight-year-old read it aloud to me, but we both understood that wasn't properly what it was for.

Talking about the poetry of someone like Schuyler—almost devoid, I sometimes think, of any exterior mannerisms—is almost as difficult as talking about an entire person. What do you say? There is the jagged early poetry, the exceedingly narrow middle poetry—one or two words a line, in "Buttered Greens" or "Mike"—as though done with masking tape, and the wide Whitman-ish lines of the long poems, "The Crystal Lithium," "Hymn to Life," "The Morning of the Poem," "A Few Days." Over time, I suppose he became more subdued (don't we all?). A sense of style is all-pervasive, but nothing is determined or excluded, it seems, on stylistic grounds. It's as though everything has been read or played through, but also let to stand; typical of this are the geometrical line lengths, where some breaks are interesting and suggestive, and many are not.

There seems to be nothing that Schuyler cannot or will not say, but he is not a provocateur like O'Hara. Most characteristically, he is a sweet, decorous, and witty writer—but he is just as capable of being the opposite. Whichever, he seems not to have to operate under any imperative—no "I must make this charming/characteristic/peculiar/

off the wall." He often writes, as I noted of "Arches," under very low pressure, with minimal invention and exuberance—which is one of the things that make him hard to quote from. There are wonderful jokes and moments of outrage, but in a sense they are untypical, and I certainly wouldn't want to pretend he's all like that. He has that extremely rare thing, the ability to write interesting description. The "Andrew Lord Poems" is a sequence in *Last Poems* about pottery, not a subject to set the pulses racing, but the reader doesn't take against it here. Nor, conversely, is a subject used to sell a poem: "Buried at Springs" is Schuyler's elegy to O'Hara, but one almost wouldn't know it. Even irrelation, in Schuyler's hands, becomes a form of relation, just as informality is a version of formality, and inaccuracy of accuracy:

> There is a hornet in the room
> and one of us will have to go
> out the window into the late
> August midafternoon sun. I
> won. There is a certain challenge
> in being humane to hornets
> but not much ("Buried at Springs")

> Look, Mitterrand baby, your telegram
> of condolence to Yves
> Montand tells it like it is
> but just once can't some high
> placed Frenchman forget about the
> *gloire de France* while the world
> stands still a moment and all
> voices rise in mourning
> a star of stars:
> Simone Signoret was and is
> immortal
> (thanks to seeming permanence
> yes the silver screen? *l'écran?*)
> Simone Signoret, A.K.A.
> Mme Yves Montand, is dead ("Simone Signoret")

All the leaves
are down except
the few that aren't. ("Verge")

These carelessly chosen quotations—and they could be varied by hundreds, thousands of others—all have in common the idea of impermanence ("immortal" gets a line to itself). Schuyler, it seems to me, responds to the challenge of impermanence, accommodates impermanence, *sings* impermanence more than any other poet, and that's why he's a classic. In the long tangent-driven poem-fleuve "Hymn to Life," Schuyler finds himself suddenly remembering Washington, where he spent part of his boyhood: "Odd jobs, that stretch ahead, wide and mindless as / Pennsylvania Avenue or the bridge to Arlington, crossed and recrossed / And there the Lincoln Memorial crumbles. It looks so solid: it won't / Last. The impermanence of permanence, is that all there is?" There is a sort of drollery here, beginning with "crumbles." Schuyler has lost the thread of his thought, the boring vistas of odd jobs, and has allowed himself to take up—perhaps through aesthetic animus—almost a contrary position. Much dearer to his heart always is the opposite: the permanence of impermanence.

Hence, I think, the importance of tone in Schuyler (often wit), and of surface detail (prettiness). Both are secondary qualities, emanations like Yeats's "wine-breath" in "All Souls' Night," and both, in a sort of mathematical way—not change, but change in the rate of change—exhibit a kind of constancy in inconstancy, like the revolutionary "gray in which some smoke stands." Ephemeral things are sung in the most ephemeral way—and the effect is permanence (though not the dreary permanence of the Lincoln Memorial). And here too is Schuyler's literariness, *aere perennius*. Poem after poem— utterly variable, unpredictable, scatty, meandering, often on next to nothing, or on the most inconsequential things—is, in fact, a *monument*: "Milk," "Now and Then," "A blue towel," "Korean Mums." Instability of language, of level, of approach, of attention ("Dining Out with Doug and Frank" begins, "Not quite yet"; its second section begins, "Now it's tomorrow / as usual") seems to be the response, instead, of a vast style. There is no gilding or freeze-drying, no e-numbers, the perishability is in the language: you wouldn't say—I wouldn't say—Schuyler is a proponent of "the best words in the best order." And this freedom of address is actually—as I don't think it is in Ashbery and not often in O'Hara, apart from "The Day Lady Died"—responsibility.

Where this shows most, and most surprisingly, is in the endings of the poems. Again, this is hard to show by quoting, but time and again a poem that looks to be this, then that, then the other thing, will *end*—will have a proper ending. A knockout, a result, a return to the beginning, a few sixteenths of an inch along a lightmeter, a color chart, a diary or a biography. The effect is terribly moving. It unexpectedly restores the personal, the artistic, the controlling hand. It's at times as though there were one sideways genius ramifying, digressing, surprising, and then another intervened, with an implacable insistence on pushing the whole thing forward. While looking like our jumble and our aporia, a Schuyler poem is always an advance. The short poem "Closed Gentian Distances" begins—in the way dozens of Schuyler poems seem to do—"A nothing day" and ends with two lines that Heraclitus or Heaney (the pun on "stream") would have been proud of (as well as a different version of *simplex munditiis*: "crisp in elegance"): "Little fish stream / by, a river in water." So much, then, for nothing. "The Night" begins "The night is filled with indecisions / To take a downer or an upper" and ends "It's true / We do we / Love each / Other so." The first stanza of "October" goes: "Books litter the bed, / leaves the lawn. It / lightly rains. Fall has / come: unpatterned, in / the shedding leaves," and the last sentence is: "The books / of fall litter the bed," an extraordinarily slight, deft, and lovable piece of patterning. An alternative type of ending, just as conclusive and controlled, occurs when Schuyler reaches a point so bizarre, often, or so delicately foolish, that it makes further writing impossible. It sounds strange, but I can think of no better way of describing the ending of, say, the poem "The Walk": "I love / their white / scuts when they / bound away, / deer at horseplay." Or "Today": "Everything chuckles and creaks / sighs in satisfaction / reddens and ripens in tough gusts of coolness / and the sun smites." After "smites"—*rien ne va plus. Les jeux sont faits.*

ELIZABETH BISHOP

As so often, it is John Ashbery who takes the cake—the triple-decker cake with the solitary little sugar bride on top—for his description of Elizabeth Bishop (1911–1979): she is "the poets' poets' poet." It sounds well-farcical, but it's strictly true, and there's as little getting round it as there is improving on it. As I begin, therefore, I feel stirrings of a wholly impersonal desire to . . . maybe pan her? No, not really, but where else have the culture vultures not been in their charabancs, with their guides and follow-me signs?

Marianne and Mrs. Moore finished her in Brooklyn (decorum studies?) after she left Vassar. James Laughlin, founder of New Directions, publisher and friend of Ezra Pound, was so desperate to publish her that even after he accepted he wasn't going to be allowed to, he still hoped at least to be permitted to *announce* that he was, in a residual way—a sort of publisher *blanc*. The alpha males—and the alpha-beta males, and the beta-alpha males—of her generation, Lowell and Jarrell and Berryman, vied with each other to slip her the bays, though this could take strange and even injurious forms: in a Dream Song that cuts a lusty swathe through the ranks of

American poetesses, there is a tacky reference to "Miss Bishop's too noble-O," while Lowell wrote lurid, clodhopping monologues "for" her ("I would drift and hear / My genius begging for its cap and bells / And tears bedewed my flat, untasted beer"—reminding one of Jarrell's musing stricture, "but who ever saw a girl like Robert Lowell"), and poemized perfectly good short stories of hers; when he says, "'The Scream' [*sic*] owes everything to Elizabeth Bishop's beautiful, calm, story, 'In the Village,'" reader, he means it. Her standing is the more remarkable in that she didn't demand it and had no way of compelling it; no power was vested in her, she gave readings rarely, unwillingly, and not well, didn't (at least until her last decade) teach, didn't review, hardly blurbed, and her rate of production was anything but intimidating. She did have a "first read" contract with *The New Yorker* (from 1946), but even that—at that time—would have seemed more like an eccentrically coined practical arrangement by a long-term absentee than something to be envied by others, or parlayed into some advantage by herself. In the heyday of "lean quarterlies and swarthy periodicals" (Frank O'Hara), *The New Yorker* was not viewed as a particularly serious publisher of poetry. Appearing there did nothing to contradict Bishop's self-stylization as a "poet by default": "I've always felt that I've written poetry more by *not* writing it than writing it." In a generation at worst of noisemakers and grimly professional professionals, Bishop stood out like a whole thumb or a thumbs up for her unassumingness and positiveness and the reticence of her personal style.

She wasn't a player—heck, she wasn't even American, but three parts Canadian. She had spells in New York and Washington, but she didn't (as she might have said) "get on" in those places and preferred the less assertive, more hokily unregarded corners of Maine and Key West, where the United States seems, a little improbably, to fade and concede some of its identity to its neighbors; before, in 1951, taking herself off the power map altogether by accidentally immigrating to Brazil for fifteen years. Where once she had traded on absence and alienation—"the sea, desperate, / will proffer wave after wave" or *"And I shall sell you sell you / sell you of course, my dear, and you'll sell me"*—now she offered her presence—only it was her presence somewhere else: "We leave Santos at once; we are driving to the interior" she importantly/briskly/newsily ends "Arrival at Santos." She hardly needed Brazil in order to be distant, but it did provide her with the most definitively wonderful alibi (she is not above citing "Brazil, 'where the nuts come from'" in the draft of a poem). The critic David Kalstone notes, wisely: "It is rare that the imaginative possibilities of a life find so real a base." Brazil was serio-comic, excessive, tropical, garish, serendipitous, violent, unpredict-able, harmonious, and inconsequential. It was a new landscape and a different society from that in the college-bound poem-vitrines of her peers; which of them, in the 1950s, wrote about poverty, or race? Brazilians assumed she was there in disgrace, or maybe on the run. Bishop said, "They think if I was any good I'd be at home." Americans—except the few who knew—assumed much the same.

A cynical analysis of this state of affairs would suggest it was because she was so unthreatening that she was chosen for her role, and while there is probably some truth to this, there isn't much, and it was mainly her contemporaries' straightforward and never-fathomed fascination with her difference that set her up and kept her there. In the 1960s and '70s, younger American poets—James Merrill, Frank Bidart—sat at her feet; later, others, younger still, filled her classes when she taught, protestingly, at Harvard and MIT. Nor is hers at all a transatlantic reputation: she is ours as much as theirs, or should I say, theirs as much as ours. I can think of probably dozens of Brit-ish and Irish poets, men and women, younger and older, who have written about her, thought about her, commended her, invoked her example, swear by her. Nowhere else such unanimity.

When I started reading her, the book was still the *Complete Poems* of 1970, white and yellow and blue, like a Ukrainian flag and tonic. A subsequent printing of this contained her four—no more—books: *North & South* (1946), *A Cold Spring* (1955), *Questions of Travel* (1965), and *Geography III* (1976). Each book was already signifi-cantly underweight, by the standards of Larkin, let alone America. The first two were quickly republished as one, which made sense, and rang up the Pulitzer Prize in 1956; the third was bulked up by the inclusion of her story "In the Village," rather as Lowell's *Life Studies* had been by his prose memoir "91 Revere Street"; the fourth was flyaway flimsy, just ten poems in large type, none of them long, and one a translation from the unctuous Octavio Paz. We readers of the *Complete Poems* looked at each other sagaciously, with a sort of masonic wink, knowing that "complete poems" really meant "completed poems," and rolled our eyes heavenward and thought of all the ones that weren't; that waited, according to report, for years, like paintings, with primed spaces in their midst, for the right word to come along; the unseen, the unknown, the unpublished, the *unwritten* Bishop being always if not sweeter then perhaps rougher or wilder or more yielding or revealing; the typical Bishop devotee is always itching to tear the poems away from her half-done, to free them from her inner censor or inner finisher or varnisher. This is why the otherwise contentious inclusion, in *Poems*, of a selection of twenty-seven "unpublished manuscript poems" is not only salutary but also somehow inevitable; it is the way her reputation is tending. It's not that "My love, my saving grace, / your eyes are awfully blue / early and instant blue" ("Breakfast Song") is particularly deep or wonderful poetry—though it's not too shabby, in an unexpectedly kooky James Schuylerish "loving you" way (and surely the great bard of breakfast would have appreciated the way "instant" picks up the "coffee-flavored mouth" that is kissed at the beginning)—it's that we need to know she wrote it. It doesn't do her down either. Not feet of clay, just plain feet. For too long, Bishop came across as a sort of immaculate mermaid.

In 1984 there came *The Collected Prose* and *The Complete Poems* (now dated 1927–1979), with added juvenilia, more translations (more Paz), and a *klein aber fein* section of "new and uncollected poems"— all of four pieces, the *récolte* of 1978 and 1979. Since then, the post-humous publishing of Bishop has gone steroid, volumewise, but still more pagewise: a book of her watercolors, a book of uncollected poems, drafts, and fragments called *Edgar Allan Poe & The Juke-Box*, and then the letters, big books of letters, a selected letters, her correspondence with Lowell, her correspondence with her editors at *The New Yorker*, her correspondence with Marianne Moore (forthcoming), a Library of America single-volume edition of poems, stories, drafts, reviews, *and* fifty-three letters, again—it's the inescapable come-on—"many published for the first time." There is a sort of sibylline deal with Bishop, in reverse. She comes to us originally with very little, eighty or a hundred poems, and we offer her the farm; then she comes again, with a little more, and then a little more, but we have already given her everything. She has always had everything we have to give. And we stand there with our pockets turned inside out and our shoulders at half-mast, and she keeps giving more.

The poems are one-offs and all sorts. They seem to have remarkably little in the way of preset or dependable qualities to fall back on—no constancy in the way of grammar or line length or rhythm or gesture or fable or machinery. They have tics aplenty—waywardnesses, one might call them, and Bishop liked to come across as wayward—but always different ones. They repeat words, they don't repeat words; they jump, they don't jump; they widen out, they don't widen out; there are runs of questions, there are no runs of questions; there is a section in italics, there is no section in italics. It's as though each poem has to be designed separately, from scratch; there is no blueprint, no assembly line. It's hard to argue that rhyme is always important to Bishop, or a lavish way with words, or an attractive quibblingness of tone, because straightaway one can turn up examples to the contrary and find her unrhymed, parsimonious, decisive, and just as good. She was raised on psalms, studied music, was fond of singing, translated sambas, wrote Dylanesque ballads about innocent miscreants ("The Burglar of Babylon" reads to me like something that might have appeared on *Blood on the Tracks*) and blues ("Don't you call me that word, honey, / don't you call me that word. / You know it ain't very kind & it's also undeserved"), and yet the poems of hers that I go back to are composed in a straggling, spifflicated, slightly backward, Victorian-hued, indifferently musical *talk*. Others again are stiff, almost puritanically joyless, in their acceptance of menial descriptive duties. The result is that line by line, she may be as anonymous, as manifold, or, better, as *mistakable* as a great poet gets. Other poets are predictably and more or less unvaryingly themselves, like cellophane packs of cigarettes from a vending machine: With Bishop you get an unpredictable kickshaw or notion in a plastic ball for your money—sometimes purposeless and perplexing, more often flat-out exhilarating, the toy of your dreams, "an acre of cold white spray [. . .] Dancing happily by itself." Bad Lowell is just bad Lowell, it has something parodic and clanking about it, the epigrams sail bafflingly past their targets; lesser Bishop may be dis-appointing, but it is oddly inconsequential, doesn't weaken the whole, isn't demoralizing, somehow doesn't affect the whole. You stand in front of the machine, the dispenser of miniature planets, and throw in more quarters; surely you will be luckier next time; you have the obscure but possibly correct feeling that it is your fault for not understanding the toy you have been given.

It is strange, leafing through these *Poems*, that while most of the pages seem to come up in color as expected, are vibrant, gaudy, im-perishably familiar, full of lush deep-pile detail, others look utterly unfamiliar (really as though I had never seen them before)—"From the Country to the City," "Little Exercise," "Anaphora," "Letter to N.Y.," "Sunday 4 A.M.," "Night City." A book of Bishop's is a funfair, each ride or booth is its own idiom, and still there are corners back-stage where no one looks and there isn't anything much going on. She is one of those poets where you endlessly revisit the indi-vidual poem, where you gorge and glut yourself on a few individual poems—in my case, "Large Bad Picture," "Florida," "Roosters," "Seascape," "Over 2000 Illustrations and a Complete Concordance," "The Bight," "Cape Breton," "Filling Station," "Sandpiper," "Crusoe in England," "Poem," "The End of March," "Santarem," "North Haven," and as many more—without getting any closer to an encap-sulation of the poet, or perhaps—because of the way the poems abide and deflect our questioning—without even having to reach for the poet at all.

Bishop is—this isn't the same, but it may be related—a poet of "eye" and not "I," or even of "eye and tears" and not "I," and also of "we" and not "I." Both the "eye" and the "we" are ways of not say-ing "I," of getting around it or playing it down. (It's not that Bishop never says "I," but she seems almost to ration it, in a militant mod-esty, to no more than its statistically probable occurrence among the other pronouns.) She makes that very change, movingly, in the frag-ment "A Short, Slow Life":

We lived in a pocket of Time.
It was close, it was warm.
Along the dark seam of the river

the houses, the barns, the two churches,
hid like white crumbs
in a fluff of gray willows & elms,
till Time made one of his gestures;
his nails scratched the shingled roof.
Roughly his hand reached in,
and tumbled us out.

Originally, that read "I lived in a pocket of Time" (and also "and tumbled me out")—a little nightmare of scale and vulnerability and the end of coziness, alongside the pocket plays on "close" and "seam" and "fluff." But no, that wouldn't do, too much pathos, too much drama of self, too much contemplation of the ungainly blunt fingers (what is their rude gesture?), and so "I" is scratched out and becomes "we," and the poem loses its identity and its urgency (perhaps neither of them especially Bishop-like qualities anyway), and the Robert Louis Stevenson or Hans Christian Andersen idea, now gone mousy and a little folksy, fails to survive.

A Bishop poem (its watchword, "Watch it closely") goes on looking long after one thinks it should have looked away—from having seen enough, from having got or given the message, from irritation or boredom or pain. It is a type of looking, in part a quantity of looking, that sees—literally—sideshows where it looks, that specializes in distracting the reader (what is the main item here?), that disregards the conventional cut-to-the-chase grammar of looking that winnows as it sees, that is unafraid of outlandish qualifiers and similes, that continually proposes and interposes objects or scenes of probable symbolic worth (but are they?). The old man in "At the Fishhouses" sits there, "sequins on his vest and on his thumb. / He has scraped the scales, the principal beauty, / from unnumbered fish with that black old knife, / the blade of which is almost worn away." If he was in a nineteenth-century painting, he would surely have had some splendid allegorical or mythological label, but here he's just a quiet and slightly sad man (the phrases seem to proceed, too, in short hacking motions), unheroic, but also (given that he is a destroyer of beauty) unvillainous. In "Cape Breton," "A small bus comes along, in up-and-down rushes, / packed with people, even to its step." Like a sort of crowded pogo stick. Things in Bishop are not groomed and grooved and normed, but anarchically themselves. Her shoes clack in different keys. The noticing itself confers value, and is its own reward. It is worth paying attention; you will not be belabored. In "Under the Window: Ouro Preto":

> A big new truck, Mercedes-Benz, arrives
> to overawe them all. The body's painted
> with throbbing rosebuds and the bumper says

> HERE AM I FOR WHOM YOU HAVE BEEN WAITING.
> The driver and assistant driver wash
> their faces, necks, and chests. They wash their feet,

> their shoes, and put them back together again.

The awe—technology overlaid with romance overlaid with religion—disappears the moment the clapped-out huaraches make their entrance. These are just men, men in magnificent machines. Plenty of poets would have given you the Mercedes, and most the ill-translated and vainglorious annunciation (what's not to like about found poetry?); but few the rosebuds (and another truck is described as having "a syphilitic nose," though Bishop doesn't work in that designing or conniving way), and probably none the shoes. (As often in Bishop, there's a persistent, slightly mocking *tendresse* toward men.) There is a motivelessness, a plenitude, a willingness to sweep and pan as well as seize and resolve, both a petillance and a panorama, a comprehensive refusal of hierarchy and abstraction. It's a fabulous orchestra—and no conductor. The ground note is often humorous—the frantic little bus, bounding over the landscape—but never abjectly depends on being so. A passive, or latent humor.

It is not that Bishop's life was short of disturbance, or even tragedy. Quite the contrary: her father died before she was one; her mother lost her mind and was committed, leaving her to be raised by grandparents and aunts; there were accidents and suicides, ill health and alcoholism, breakups and breakdowns—all those things that were fuel and grist for her generation of American poets, and one wouldn't know it. "Although I think I have a prize 'unhappy child-hood,' almost good enough for the text-books—please don't think I dote on it," she wrote to an early biographer; the "I think" there is already heroic. To use a somewhat banal but in its empirical way unusually dependable measure, she probably suffered as many bro-ken bones in her life as John Berryman, but unlike his (the admit-tedly charming "An orange moon"), hers didn't make it into her writing. The little girl narrator of "In the Village"—a story that re-flects the last crack-up and committal of Bishop's mother—is, in her dreamy, only-child way, endlessly plucky and resolute. She both knows and doesn't know what is going on. The poems end either with a slightly unlikely exhortation—"Dress up! Dress up and dance at Carnival!" ("Pink Dog"), "Somebody loves us all" ("Filling Station"), "from Brooklyn, over the Brooklyn Bridge, on this fine morning, / please come flying" ("Invitation to Miss Marianne Moore") or with reserve and ambivalence—"faithful as enemy, or friend" ("Roosters"), "'half is enough'" ("The Gentleman of Shalott"), "again I promise to try" ("Manuelzinho"). The stereotypical form of words is "awful but cheerful" ("The Bight").

It is in rare, late poems that Bishop permits herself not a long look as much as a brief glance at the worst: "(A yesterday I find al-most impossible to lift)" ("Five Flights Up") or in "One Art" (a poem so rigid with the hieroglyphs of determination and so stifled in its compressed clamor I must admit I've never cared for it): "It's evi-dent / the art of losing's not too hard to master / though it may look like (*Write* it!) like disaster." Whether it was bravery, discretion, sto-icism, writerly morality (a refusal to pass off despondency on the reader), or a life aesthetic of no fuss, Bishop was reluctant to make herself the subject, much less the object, of her poems. Either she clapped the telescope to her blind eye—a blind I, that would be—or else she swung the thing round and minimized the hurt in that oddly inclusive and luminous context produced by looking through a telescope the wrong way. The ending of a story called "Mercedes Hospital" makes the point: "The Mercedes Hospital seems so remote and far away now, like the bed of a dried-up lake. Out of the corner of my eye I catch a glimpse of the salty glitter at its bottom, a slight mica-like residuum, the faintest trace of joyousness."

The decades have worn against the writers of disaster. They set, as one might put it in the contemporary British idiom, a rubbish example. "I am tired," Lowell wrote in *For the Union Dead*, "Everyone's tired of my turmoil." (That was in 1964; most of his moiling was still ahead of him.) Fifty years later, poetry is a card-carrying career; we are all, in Berryman's sardonic words, "Henry House," all "the steadiest man on the block," and the stronger the reaction against the so-called confessional poets, the more prominence accrued to Bishop's self-exemption, the more stark and heroic and solitary her small output, her refusal to (Berryman again) "get down in the arena," the more remarkable her finicky pursuit of accuracy, beauty, detail. She seems to be continually revising for a closer approach to the truth—"not a thought, but a mind thinking," as Bishop describes the characteristic posture of a poet perhaps unexpectedly dear to her, G. M. Hopkins—but even then it's not possible to say whether it's as a scientist twiddling a microscope, or a slightly tongue-tied trainee delivering a report to a roomful of middle managers. More and more, Bishop seems like a humble and prudent saint among self-destructive and swaggering deviltons. I was haunted, for instance, while writing this, by the notion that I had come across the plural form of the word "linoleum" somewhere, and I hadn't been reading much of anything but Bishop. Sure enough, there it was—or there they were—a couple of days later, in "A Summer's Dream": "the floors glittered with / assorted linoleums." Her grateful and somehow practical vocabulary—like a milliner's or a cabinetmaker's or a costume jeweler's—full of exquisite and *real* color distinctions (a palette like Vuillard's: "the smallest moths, like Chinese fans, / flatten themselves, silver and silver-gilt / over pale yellow, orange, or gray"), and justified flights of fancy ("impractically shaped and—who knows?—self-pitying mountains") seems increasingly immune to the ravages of time and literary inflation. There wasn't a knack, and so it couldn't be learned, you thought; whereas just possibly something like Lowell's "a red fox stain covers Blue Hill" could. One is at an extreme end of loose-mindedness—almost *Illustrious Corpses* looseness—the other is done by a sort of eye-popping exertion of will and muscle. One is contrived and synthetic—you can imagine Lowell muttering, "I want to get some color clash going, and the whole thing is to sound doomy and monosyllabic and Gothic, and I need something to deepen the color and keep everything from just sounding superficial—I know, 'fox' "—the other is beyond contrivance. Maybe there is something in those bell-curved Brazilian mountains that echoes the outline of Eeyore, but other than that I have no idea where "self-pitying" might come from. But it's absolutely right, the inturned curl, the slump, the soft steepness of it.

Perhaps one more caveat. The umami of Bishop isn't always the thing. You have to be in the mood for something that's mostly middle. She doesn't offer much to beginners and sophomores. She can seem touristic, evasive, wispy. She can seem small scale and unurgent (it's her word, I'm a little embarrassed to recall: "the pulse, / rapid but unurgent, of a motorboat"). It's a lasting puzzle that there aren't more poems (why not?), and that it's the letters that read more like a main of communication than the poems, however adorable and sinuous and unwilled these last are in their coming to being. In one letter to Lowell, she commends Anton Webern and writes about "that strange kind of modesty in almost everything contemporary one really likes—Kafka, say, or Marianne [Moore], or even Eliot and Klee and Kokoschka and Schwitters . . . Modesty, care, *space*, a sort of helplessness but determination at the same time." Attractive though the idea of modesty is, especially modern modesty, sometimes you want something a little grander, more willed, less elliptical: Shostakovich or Beckmann or Sebastiao Salgado. I remember the time I first read Bishop's "The Armadillo," excited because Lowell was said to have partly modeled his "Skunk Hour" on it, and thinking "What's this? Dystopic Beatrix Potter?" I still don't really know, and it's not a question that occurs to me with "Skunk Hour."

ROBERT LOWELL

What can I tell you about Robert Lowell? "A shilling life will give you all the facts," only the lives cost £20, and are most likely out of print. He was born Robert Traill Spence Lowell III ("Robert" and "Lowell" were the only words he could actually write—everything else he merely printed), in Boston in 1917, the son of a somewhat becalmed navy officer, who neither fought nor made it to admiral, Robert Lowell, and a high-strung mother, Charlotte Winslow. The dense-to-the-point-of-distracting prose memoir in *Life Studies*, "91 Revere Street," has a visitor to the household leaving thoughtfully, saying: "I know why young Bob is an only child."

Conventionality, privilege, and a slight Thomas Mann–ish sense of effeteness and foreboding, of being at the end of a declining line, characterize Lowell's background and youth. Art comes at the culmination of generations of public service and stainlessness—an ambassador, a president of Harvard, fully the equal of the Consular Buddenbrooks. Off to one side were poets like the Victorian beardie James Russell Lowell (it is his *Collected Poems* one sees in used-book shops everywhere) and Ezra Pound's Imagist acolyte, Amy Lowell.

Family, upbringing are held down in the scales by an unequaled memory and vividness of presentation. I have a cassette of possibly Lowell's last reading, where he mutters, off the cuff: "Memory is genius, really . . ." Whether in "91 Revere Street" or the groundbreaking childhood poems of *Life Studies*, this is what one takes away as a reader:

> To be a boy at Brimmer [his mainly-for-girls prep school] was to be small, denied, and weak. [. . .] In unison our big girls sang "America"; back and forth our amazons tramped—their brows were wooden, their dress was black and white, and their columns followed standard-bearers holding up an American flag, the white flag of the Commonwealth of Massachusetts, and the green flag of Brimmer. At basketball games against Miss Lee's or Miss Winsor's, it was our upper-school champions who rushed onto the floor, as feline and fateful in their pace as lions. This was our own immediate and daily spectacle; in comparison such masculine displays as trips to battle cruisers commanded by comrades of my father seemed eyewash—the Navy moved in a realm as ghostlike and removed from my life as the elfin acrobatics of Douglas Fairbanks or Peter Pan. I wished I were an older girl. I wrote Santa Claus for a field hockey stick.

The enfeeblement and compromise so wittily recounted here are turned into something more biological in the poem "Dunbarton":

> I borrowed Grandfather's cane
> carved with the names and altitudes
> of Norwegian mountains he had scaled—
> more a weapon than a crutch.
> I lanced it in the fauve ooze for newts.
> In a tobacco tin after capture, the umber yellow mature newts
> lost their leopard spots,
> lay grounded as numb
> as scrolls of candied grapefruit peel.
> I saw myself as a young newt,
> neurasthenic, scarlet
> and wild in the wild coffee-colored water.

This is perhaps even more like García Márquez than Mann—the scene at the very end of *One Hundred Years of Solitude*, where the last of the inbred Buendías has sprouted a tail—the counter-evolutionary, lapsed, retro-Napoleonic Lowell, a far cry, a sad falling-off from his grandfather's granite eminence.

Lowell was an unexceptional, even undistinguished schoolboy. At seventeen, he still wanted to be a footballer—he had the build for it, and the strength. Suddenly, massively, he switched his resources. The leader of a little group of three, he designated Frank Parker to be the painter, Blair Clark as the musician, and himself the poet. It's strange to think of him beginning like that—almost randomly, out of will and imagination—because he became a poet of feel and instinct, characterized by a subtlety and inwardness with words that I wouldn't have thought could be learned. The same expenditure of will characterizes him, for me, all through his twenties. He turned up to Robert Frost, with an English historical epic in couplets, and was told that it "lacked compression." He left Harvard for Kenyon, a small college in Ohio, to sit at the feet of John Crowe Ransom. He drove down to Tennessee to be with Allen Tate; when he was told there was no room at the Tates' house, and he'd have to camp on the lawn, he ignored or overrode the ironical turn of speech, bought a tent, and stayed for weeks.

The early poems, once they were publishable, have that shrillness and mastery. Contemporaries awoke to their thunderclap iambs, their menacing ambiguities ("The Lord survives the rainbow of His will," "This is the Black Widow, death"), their cold fusion of Boston and Sodom, Hiroshima and Judgment Day, their chattering alliteration, their heavily rhyming run-on lines, their disregard for ease and fluency, the word "and" (as I once put it in a review) usually the meat in a zeugma, their desperate, unlocatable religion, anywhere between Catholicism and Calvinism, their knell of an autodidact drummer applauding the end of the world. I came to them later and less willingly than I did to other, later Lowell. To appreciate them, one would have to be either powerfully religious, or else alive in the 1940s. I am moved and a little uncomprehending when I speak to my Australian poet friend Chris Wallace-Crabbe, who still seems to feel the impact of those first poems, and who can, for example, recite the very first poem of *Lord Weary's Castle*, the first trade book, "The Exile's Return"—which always struck me as a rather dusty piece—by heart. This is, by the way, a general truth in poetry: that even while you may not remember them, you are unlikely to move very far from your first impressions, and that your allegiance is probably determined by what you first read of someone.

I wish I could recover mine—my impressions. It would be like faith before fanaticism, or ritual; or the picture before many, many varnishings, because in some way reading is accretive, and you read the memory of your past readings, and nothing you reread is quite what it was when you first read it.

It was in the winter of 1976, after my first term as an undergraduate, that I borrowed a friend's copy of the omnibus edition of *Life Studies* and *For the Union Dead*, Lowell's two best-known books (1959 and 1964, respectively), and took it home with me to (then) Austria. Prose had attracted me as I think it attracts any aspiring writer—poetry in my view being a specialism, even a malformation—and then defeated me; the ability to write page after page in the same vein was beyond me, though I saw the need for it. I had begun to read quantities of poetry, rapidly, mostly at night, Yeats, Stevens, Pound. I don't know how I came upon Lowell, if it was my idea or my friend's, if I had read any before, in anthologies. Certainly, I knew nothing about him, said his name, Lowell, like vowel or towel, had no preconceptions, carried no baggage. As I say, I wish I knew what poems my reaction was based on, but whatever it was, it elicited the same response from me as Tony Harrison's poems drew from the wonderfully generous and impulsive Stephen Spender: "it seems to me I have been waiting a lifetime for this style"—which I think is the only accolade for a poet. More particularly—and this is absolutely at variance with my own predilections, and with the times, because people who went around reading and quoting such things tended to wind up at the stake in the ruthless and schismatic Cambridge of the '70s and '80s—these poems, whichever they were, struck me as, in the words of whatever French sage said it, "scriptible" even more than "lisible"—demanding to be read but, even more, to be written.

Most probably I was responding to a sort of synthesis of all of *Life Studies*, or to the atmosphere of the whole thing—especially the

title sequence in Part IV—but almost at a peradventure, I have chosen two poems from that section, which covers the *Glanz und Elend*,
the splendor and misery of three generations of Lowells and Winslows, from his infancy to the middle of his life, from the prime of his
grandfather to his own hesitant and infirm middle age (in "Skunk
Hour"). The first is "For Sale":

> Poor sheepish plaything,
> organized with prodigal animosity,
> lived in just a year—
> my Father's cottage at Beverly Farms
> was on the market the month he died.
> Empty, open, intimate,
> its town-house furniture
> had an on tiptoe air
> of waiting for the mover
> on the heels of the undertaker.
> Ready, afraid
> of living alone till eighty,
> Mother mooned in a window,
> as if she had stayed on a train
> one stop past her destination.

This is so exemplary in its limpidity and declarativeness and straight-
forwardness, it is hard to know what to say about it. The language
seems at once natural and adequate. It is immediately apprehensible
and reads as though it had been written in one go, and yet has interest and balance to nourish it through many rereadings. It, and the
poem before it, called "Father's Bedroom," I think are the two poems that William Carlos Williams—the great *simpliste*, I should like
to call him—Lowell's friend and the least likely of literary allies, particularly admired. Both are basically Imagist poems, but it is an Imagism enriched with psychological notes, with hardheadedness, with
implication. "For Sale" is static, and yet it moves (in both senses); it
is neutral but full of hurt and dread; it is palpable and factual, and
yet the things in it would not have been perceptible to—could not
have been said by—anyone else. It seems to be about a piece of real

estate, but it's actually more of a ghost story. The poem seems almost like a euphemism, so decorous, so impersonal, so well based in objectivity and fact—and yet is there anything in it that is *not* said? The worst-laid plans, it seems to say, go stray . . .

Its organization is sturdy and foursquare: fifteen lines, three—grammatically correct—sentences of five lines apiece, the lines short but flexible, four to twelve syllables. They carry rather more stresses than one might expect: "poor sheepish plaything," spondees, five stresses, aerated by unstressed syllables in the following line "organized with prodigal animosity," a pattern that repeats itself throughout the poem: "lived in just a year" (four out of five stresses), "my Father's cottage at Beverly Farms" (only five out of ten). This reassertion of heaviness lifting, almost in spite of itself, is like the moment in Peter Handke's *A Sorrow Beyond Dreams*, about his mother, who killed herself, when Handke says why make words when all he feels like doing is repeatedly tapping the same key on his typewriter again and again. There is that heaviness in "Poor sheepish plaything," the indifferent shuffling trudge through the ankle-deep consonants. As for the lightening, the consolation, that may be the consolation of articulacy, the way that each sentence is brought from appositional phrase ("Poor sheepish plaything," "Empty, open, intimate," "Ready, afraid / of living alone") to action, is quickened (Heaney's word) from noun to verb. However painful the action and the understanding of the poem may be, it still lightens the unbearable heaviness of "Poor sheepish plaything."

There is an integrity, a coherence, about "For Sale" that is one of the great virtues of Lowell's poetry, a closeness—however manufactured—to speech. As I say, it reads as though it had been written in one go. And yet the poem, for all its plainness, has something pleasurably luxuriant—or even luxurious—about it too. One doesn't doubt or disbelieve the vocabulary—it seems an absolutely natural vocabulary—nor is it exactly being flaunted, but there is something worth relishing in "mooned in a window"; in the melodious felicitous combinations of lines 1 or 6 or 11; in the play of heel and toe; in the phrase "prodigal animosity" (almost a transferred epithet, I think, the animosity *of* the prodigal, of the one who has gone forth, but suggesting also "prodigious animosity" or "prodigious animus"—a word that also means "soul," the soul that is left mooning in a window).

The luxury, the expressiveness, the ghostly skill of the poem are in large part the function of one part of speech: adjectives. Adjectives, we are told, are bad. Even such good teachers as Pound and Bunting are wary of them ("use either no ornament or good ornament," says Pound). Hughes, we are told, was such a great poet because of his way with verbs. Lowell made the adjective *salonfähig*—respectable—in modern poetry (Adam Zagajewski performs the same service for the adverb). In the context of "For Sale," this is what makes it such a maximalist poem, for all its Chinese economy. It contains nine adjectives, as well as two nouns as epithets and two past participles—almost one a line, or one word in five! The poem is slathered, stuck with adjectives, like an orange with cloves.

An adjective, an adequate adjective, is a thought or a perception. Where—as often happens in Lowell—adjectives come in twos or threes, they are constellations, distinctive and collusive, radiant with outward meaning and human prediction, and held together by inscrutable inward gravitational bonds. "Ready, afraid / of living alone till eighty," going and stopping, affirming and reluctant; "Empty, open, intimate," three complementary views of a space, the three bears, if you like, from outside, from the threshold, from within. In both instances, the contrasting or evolving meanings are underscored by similarity of sounds.

Three poems later in *Life Studies*, you encounter "Waking in the Blue," longer, better known, more anthologized, more typical. The subject by now has moved from parents and grandparents to Lowell himself. It is the first of a little minigroup, "Waking in the Blue," "Home After Three Months Away," "Memories of West Street and Lepke," that shows prismatic views of the poet against the background of three different institutions: mental hospital, what Jonathan Raban nicely dubbed "the slovenly freedom of university teaching," and prison—the reduced term of three months that Lowell did as a conscientious objector in 1943–1944. "Waking in the Blue" is hospital:

> The night attendant, a B.U. sophomore,
> rouses from the mare's-nest of his drowsy head

propped on *The Meaning of Meaning*.
He catwalks down our corridor.
Azure day
makes my agonized blue window bleaker.
Crows maunder on the petrified fairway.
Absence! My heart grows tense
as though a harpoon were sparring for the kill.
(This is the house for the "mentally ill.")

What use is my sense of humor?
I grin at Stanley, now sunk in his sixties,
once a Harvard all-American fullback,
(if such were possible!)
still hoarding the build of a boy in his twenties,
as he soaks, a ramrod
with the muscles of a seal
in his long tub,
vaguely urinous from the Victorian plumbing.
A kingly granite profile in a crimson golf-cap,
worn all day, all night,
he thinks only of his figure,
of slimming on sherbet and ginger ale—
more cut off from words than a seal.
This is the way day breaks in Bowditch Hall at McLean's;
the hooded night lights bring out "Bobbie,"
Porcellian '29,
a replica of Louis XVI
without the wig—
redolent and roly-poly as a sperm whale,
as he swashbuckles about in his birthday suit
and horses at chairs.

These victorious figures of bravado ossified young.

In between the limits of day,
hours and hours go by under the crew haircuts
and slightly too little nonsensical bachelor twinkle

of the Roman Catholic attendants.
(There are no Mayflower
screwballs in the Catholic Church.)

After a hearty New England breakfast,
I weigh two hundred pounds
this morning. Cock of the walk,
I strut in my turtle-necked French sailor's jersey
before the metal shaving mirrors,
and see the shaky future grow familiar
in the pinched, indigenous faces
of these thoroughbred mental cases,
twice my age and half my weight.
We are all old-timers,
each of us holds a locked razor.

Perhaps as with "For Sale," one's immediate reaction is: How can there be anything the matter with someone, if they express themselves so insightfully, with so much wit and joy? What is defective or deficient here? It's a pervasive, almost an all-pervading question with Lowell, and it's one of the things I grappled with—in my head, mind, never on paper—in my unwritten PhD on him a few years later. A poem begins: "I want you to see me when I have one head / again, not many, like a bunch of grapes." It's drastic and unforgettable, and partly for those reasons you're unwilling to entertain the possibility even that some sort of human hydra wrote the lines in front of you. Elsewhere, there's talk of "the kingdom of the mad— / its hackneyed speech, its homicidal eye." But when is this tailored speech ever hackneyed, and where is there a glimmer of homicide? Lowell wrote out of a condition called bipolar disorder or manic depression. From the mid-1950s, say, he suffered a manic attack pretty much annually. Typically, there's a fantastic description of it in the late book *The Dolphin*. The scene, as in "Waking in the Blue," is a bathroom:

I feel my old infection, it comes once yearly:
lowered good humor, then an ominous

rise of irritable enthusiasm . . .
Three dolphins bear our little toilet-stand,
the grin of the eyes rebukes the scowl of the lips,
they are crazy with the thirst. I soak,
examining and then examining
what I really have against myself.

Perhaps the word "crazy" stands out; if not, then perhaps "thirst" and "soak," or the "ominous / rise of irritable enthusiasm," or the Calvinist / Jesuitical "examining and then examining." That's it, anyway. I find it actually far more deeply present in Lowell's life than in his poetry and think it affected those around him—his second wife, Elizabeth Hardwick, his exceptionally devoted friends—far more than it did himself, though how is one to say that? It puts me in mind of a line from Montale: "Too many lives are needed to make one." From the mid-'60s, Lowell was prescribed lithium, which made it a little easier perhaps to control the symptoms. He was upset and bemused by the disproportionate effect of what he termed the "lack of a little salt in the brain."

I don't think there is very much for the clinician in Lowell's published poems. The drafts, yes, they are wildly, disturbingly different. Chapter 15 of Ian Hamilton's life of Robert Lowell begins with a frightening draft of "Waking in the Blue," called "To Ann Adden (Written during the first week of my voluntary stay at McLean's Mental Hospital)"—the fully circumstantial titling of a Romantic epistle—and including such lines as:

Ann, what use is my ability
for shooting the bull,
far from your Valkyrie body,
your gold-brown hair,
your robust uprightness—you, brisk
yet discrete [sic] in your conversation!

II
(a week later)

The night-attendant, a B.U. student,
rouses his cobwebby eyes
propped on his Social Relations text-book,
prowls drowsily down our corridor . . .
Soon, soon the solitude of Allah, azure day-break,
will make my agonized window bleaker.
What greater glory than recapturing the moment of glory
in *miseria*?

.   .   .   .

Your salmon lioness face is dawn.

It feels thoroughly mean to quote as much as this, and thoroughly improbable that anything worth anything could come of such writing. Here, unquestionably, *is* the kingdom of the mad with its hackneyed speech and all the rest of it. It feels strange, too, to propose that mere cutting could not just restore something to sanity but also find purpose and control and expressiveness in it. It's at this point, perhaps, that one might return to Lowell's beginnings in will and imagination. (Not the worst aspect of "To Ann Adden" is the way that the footballer seems to have returned!) But for that desire to create himself, or to create, at any rate, *something*, he might not have been able to retrieve anything at all from such—to use his word—maunderings.

In the published poem, Ann Adden, a "psychiatric fieldworker" from Bennington, is gone, and so too is the operatic exaltation that came with her. (Both, it seems, were a function of the manic phase of Lowell's disorder.) Instead, there is a canniness and craftiness and dryness and confinement—a boundedness and mildness that you could never imagine in the original draft, even where the alterations themselves are pretty tiny. Not the "cobwebby eyes" but "the mare's-nest of his drowsy head," an almost maternal note of solicitude. Not the "Social Relations text-book," dry and theoretical, but the rich joke on *The Meaning of Meaning*. Not "prowls drowsily down our corridor" but "catwalks down our corridor"—a marine ease and fitness in the verb. Not "make my agonized window bleaker" but "makes my agonized blue window bleaker," an almost unsayable blurt, the "bleaker" yearning to be "blacker."

Without the encumbrance of Ann, "massive, tawny, playful, lythe," the zany second person (the person of ode, and of poetry), the poem inhabits the comfortable third person of fiction. The "I" slips easily into the role of the little-account, lateral observer–cum–narrator figure, à la *Moby-Dick* or *Gatsby*, and leaves the stage open for the main protagonists, the "characters," Stanley and "Bobbie." ("Bobbie," of course, is not a million miles away from "Bobby," as Lowell appears elsewhere in *Life Studies*, in his mother's voice.) From this point on, what is interesting is the externality of the description of "these thoroughbred mental cases" and residual speculation on the speaker, or the person of the poet, if you prefer. Here is a poem about the mind in which, after the first four lines, the mind doesn't appear! A poem from which the reader takes blue, plumbing, sherbet, sperm whale, weight. A poem, it seems, of narcissistic self-regard and vanity, of weights and measures, of appurtenances and accoutrements. A sort of locker-room way back to health, golf caps, nudity, diet. Everything that's proposed here is physical, it's the sort of self-absorption—Mann again—of the sanatorium, of *The Magic Mountain* this time, with the Lowell figure like a sort of Hans Castorp, a visitor threatened with going native. The display of, as it were, rude health, is an effort to deny that there's anything wrong upstairs: the atmosphere is prankish, eccentric, overspecified.

"Waking in the Blue" isn't a tidy poem, with its ragged verse paragraphs, its sporadic full rhymes, its unkempt imagery. But it is precisely such looseness that allows it to accommodate so much realism. There are two main strands of imagery, one maritime and the other monumental: reading the poem puts one in mind, maybe, of a sort of Rushmore-by-the-sea. But plenty of things are not accommodated within this, and also, it doesn't seem in the least conniving or purposive. (One trusts poet and poem the more.) Scanning it, one picks up: catwalks, azure, harpoon, sunk, soaks, seal, sperm whale, crew haircuts, Mayflower, and the turtle-necked French sailor's jersey. On the monumental side, or perhaps more exactly, there where stone meets king, we have: propped, petrified, Victorian, kingly granite profile, seal (in the other sense, the royal seal, the keeper of the royal seal), Porcellian (if one allows porcelain, China shepherdesses and the like), wig, swashbuckles, ossified, Catholic, and maybe thoroughbred. Combining the two strands, one can perhaps come up with a sense of joining the crew of a ship, either voluntarily or press-ganged; stiffening—petrified, ossified—and movement or loss of movement—maunder, tense, ramrod, granite, strut, locked—are also thematized. The "mare's nest" has an overtone of the Medusa—also a word for jellyfish—suggesting a way the two types of imagery might be combined, in some sort of home for failed, Andromeda-less (Ann Adden–less?!), ossified or petrified Perseuses: "These victorious figures of bravado ossified young."

The speaker in "Waking in the Blue" perhaps agonizes—his word—over whether or not to belong. The poem begins, like Kafka's "Metamorphosis," with an awakening: out of fantasy into reality, from a personal unconscious into a shared conscious. The word "our" appears as early as line 4. "We" and "us" bring the poem to its conclusion. Lowell tries to fix his identity with recourse to other institutions, like B.U. and Harvard, to the sophomore, or "wise fool", to "Bobbie," and the "Mayflower screwballs"—the Lowells and Winslows were among the earliest American settlers. At the same time, he worries about the wisdom of throwing in his lot with these particular people—"more cut off from words than a seal"—not surprisingly. Unease is repeatedly signaled by the fishiness, the not-quite-rightness of things: "if such were possible," "vaguely urinous," the "crimson golf-cap," "without the wig," and the brilliantly suspicious "slightly too little nonsensical bachelor twinkle" of the "attendants." By the end, harrowingly, and again as in Kafka, the speaker has got himself adopted; "Bobbie" and Stanley are like monstrous parental figures, and Lowell is their son, half their age and twice their weight. The thoroughbred mental case is shut, if not "locked," and the future is settled and looks "familiar"—almost familial. The poem is at its saddest when it is most in agreement: "After a hearty New England breakfast, / I weigh two hundred pounds / this morning." It's like acceptance, or promotion. Making the grade. The locked razor is the badge of office, the scepter of this establishment.

Almost all of this is conjectural and interpretative, and some of it is not altogether serious. There must be many other ways of reading the poem. As I say, it's loose and accommodating, without ever seeming random or incoherent. Lowell was able to do this: to suggest meaning, but not insist on it or fussily encode it. I think of two lines from the lovely poem "The Old Flame": "how quivering and fierce we were, / there snowbound together, / *simmering like wasps / in our tent of books!*" (my italics) where the four words "simmering," "wasps," "tent," and "books" pull four separate ways but without exploding the image. The equivalent in "Waking in the Blue" is Lowell's use of so many different types of utterance, so that, without ever seeming to write from within madness, he is able to encompass it, or at least gesture at it. Labels and details are confidently placed; humor puts him outside the poem; the "slightly too little nonsensical bachelor twinkle" is formidably intelligent; and the sentence "These victorious figures of bravado ossified young" seems to bristle impregnably. But the closer the utterances are to the speaker, the less interrogation they will bear, and the less "prose meaning" they seem to have. Rather, they seem somehow magical, as if they'd arrived from some other language. Why: "Absence!"? What is "Crows maunder on the petrified fairway"? Why the broken-down prickly-pear rhythm of: "This is the way day breaks in Bowditch Hall at McLean's"? There is witchery here, not very far below the surface, not haplessly, or distractingly, or out of focus, but as a part of things. Lowell's poems have this way of reaching out and making meaning after meaning, but controllably always. He once said—and this seems to me to capture it very nicely—"I am not sure whether I can distinguish between intention and interpretation. I think this is what I more or less intended."

Lowell's reputation—and the poems I've brought up so far have, I suppose, comfirmed it—is for writing about and mythologizing himself. The word "confessional"—blind, involuntary, incontinent— doesn't begin to do justice to him. In 1959, when the critic M. L. Rosenthal coined it, it wasn't with any bad intention, but nowadays I can only hear it said with an implicit sneer. The "confessionalism," I think, is ours, that of our present civilization, which likes its great figures on feet of clay instead of pedestals, and would rather dismiss something than attend to it. We have become almost incapable of reading something on its own terms: it's as though we took Baudelaire's *"Au Lecteur"* too seriously, *"Hypocrite lecteur,—mon semblable,— mon frère!"* He would have been quite aghast. We strip away words and seek the underlying "reality": What's the matter with us?

In any case, even muted, that version of Lowell is inadequate to him. The other two poems I have chosen to think about—believe me, it was no very strategic choice when I made it either—go outside. The first is an elegy—though as someone said, at bottom, an elegy is always for yourself. This one is called "Alfred Corning Clark," and it's one of the best elegies I know:

> You read the *New York Times*
> every day at recess, but in its dry
> obituary, a list
> of your wives, nothing is news,
> except the ninety-five
> thousand dollar engagement ring
> you gave the sixth.
> Poor rich boy,
> you were unreasonably adult
> at taking your time,
> and died at forty-five.
> Poor Al Clark,
> behind your enlarged,
> barely recognizable photograph,
> I feel the pain.
> You were alive. You are dead.
> You wore bow-ties and dark
> blue coats, and sucked
> wintergreen or cinnamon lifesavers
> to sweeten your breath.
> There must be something—
> some one to praise
> your triumphant diffidence,
> your refusal of exertion,
> the intelligence
> that pulsed in the sensitive,
> pale concavities of your forehead.
> You never worked,
> and were third in the form.
> I owe you something—

I was befogged,
and you were too bored,
quick and cool to laugh.
You are dear to me, Alfred;
our reluctant souls united
in our unconventional
illegal games of chess
on the St. Mark's quadrangle.
You usually won—
motionless
as a lizard in the sun.

Again, how limpid and straightforward and believable this is. I don't seem to recall any of the Lowell biographers or critics even bothering to check this man out: it's all here, and they took it all for gospel, and why not. This air of truthfulness seems to me a primary quality, in no way dependent on or subservient to the "actual truth," whatever it may have been. This poem could perfectly well have been written in a way that made it unbelievable, unnecessary, or both—but you have to imagine that.

Wim Wenders said that films—fiction films, adventure films, Hollywood films—document the conditions of their own making. This poem, I think, does that. It begins with *The New York Times*, because that's where Lowell begins too: it's the messenger, it's what breaks the news to him of the death of—what to call him: not his friend, his classmate, his protector, his alter other! Lowell is clearly surprised, a little unsteady. We can't choose whom we write elegies about. (The motto, incidentally, of *The New York Times* is: "All the news that's fit to print." Hence the rather acerbic "nothing is news.")

This poem is a little drama of justification, of calling, perhaps even of attempting to refuse the call. It stutters in its little lines. It strains to swallow the vast sums and figures that arrive as the sort of advance guard of facts. It is only ever a step away from some terminal awkwardness or banality: "Poor rich boy," the bathetic oxymoron; "Poor Al Clark," the attempt at intimacy; "You were alive. You are dead," with its sophomoric full stop; the medical overtone of

"enlarged" and perhaps "pulsed"; the grisly equivocations of "lifesav-
ers" and "motionless." It's an anonymous, preppy, rather unprepos-
sessing subject that Lowell struggles and struggles to possess. The
poem can't get started, and it never flows, not even in the brilliant
Tacitean phrasing of "your triumphant diffidence, / your refusal of
exertion." It isn't, I think, until "I owe you something" that there's an
end to the false starts, and the irrelation. That's the point at which
Lowell discovers that he has that place to stand from which Archi-
medes thought he could move worlds. And the culmination is when
the poet finally possesses the subject sufficiently to risk a simile, not
even perhaps a particularly wonderful one but expressive of economy, of death in life, of a kind of classification—and Lowell was always fond of slithery creatures: newts, turtles, snakes. Until then, we
don't know how to place Clark; it's as though the poem has been
asking itself all along, "What sort of creature are you/were you?"

In the last poem, this is not in question: "Words for Muffin, a
Guinea-Pig." Muffin speaks. It's the unlikeliest of monologues,
blending the creaturely with the "human, all-too human." He speaks
in the unrhymed fourteen-line "sonnet" form that Lowell wrote and
rewrote from 1967 on, and with which he filled his late books, *Notebook*, *History*, *For Lizzie and Harriet*, and into which he threatened
to convert practically all his previous production. These fourteen-
line poems are somewhat controversial—they're Lowell's pendant to
John Berryman's Dream Song form, the sort of baggy, omnivorous
outline that would accept whatever he threw at it. It's the part of
Lowell that I've ended up nearest to myself, as a reader. It's like
nothing else. You feel no one has ever been through these hundreds
of poems, they've never been mapped, it's "here be monsters" or left
blank, and you slash your way through, finding marvelous lines that
you never see again, and sometimes whole poems that brilliantly co-
here and then disintegrate. "Words for Muffin" is one. The line by
now is everything; you have the feeling everything Lowell writes
comes out in line form. It has a kind of humility too; "somehow
never wrote something to go back to," Lowell writes in one of these
poems, "Reading Myself," and indeed he never—apart from "Quaker
Graveyard" and one or two other early poems—wrote any big, stagey
set pieces. "Why don't you lose yourself / and write a play about the

fall of Japan," he quotes the friendly/unfriendly suggestion of an ex-wife. He didn't, needless to say, but the *multum in parvo* of "Words for Muffin" makes it less of a loss:

> Of late they leave the light on in my entry,
> so I won't scare, though I never scare in the dark;
> I bless this arrow that flies from wall to window . . .
> five years and a nightlight given me to breathe—
> Heidegger said spare time is ecstasy . . .
> I am not scared, although my life was short;
> my sickly breathing sounded like dry leather.
> *Mrs. Muffin!* It clicks. I had my day.
> You'll paint me like Cromwell with all my warts:
> small mop with a tumor and eyes too popped for thought.
> I was a rhinoceros when jumped by my sons.
> I ate and bred, and then I only ate,
> my life zenithed in the Lyndon Johnson 'sixties . . .
> this short pound God threw on the scales, found wanting.

Again, for all its jaunty improbability—the guinea pig that quotes Heidegger, refers to Oliver Cromwell and Lyndon Johnson, is public figure and private citizen, recognizes *Mrs. Muffin*, sees himself effortlessly and pitilessly and punningly ("this short pound," "I ate and bred"), and even into the past tense ("I had my day")—this is a piece of real utterance. Really, it's an aria. The existence and its perspectives are mapped out with tenderness and economy and extravagance to make an alert and compendious little drama. The more things are localized and precised and adapted, the more universality they acquire. It's an odd mixture of mortal dread and mildness—a sort of buffo version of the late poems of Heine, some of which Lowell had clunkily or clankingly translated in a book called *Imitations*. "Words for Muffin" has a tender, sleepy wisdom that I don't think you can find anywhere else in poetry.

What are my "provisional conclusions" (in Montale's phrase)? That he exemplarily converted life into literature. That the range of his effects—from the most oblique, almost hermetic, feint to the plain statement of fact, to the tenderly, brassily magniloquent ("Pity the planet, all joy gone / from this sweet volcanic cone")—is unequaled. (Sometimes Lowell seems to be writing a wild interstitial English entirely his own, as with the formidably off-sounding "I lanced it in the fauve ooze for newts." At the same time, the writing never loses its inherent plausibility; it never looks like Roget's, never proliferates into verbiage, never makes mere mud.) That in his refusal as a poet to be cowed or deflected or marginalized, he, though no sort of hero, was heroic. That he is unspeakably missed by his literature and his country, and that in his absence, literary and civic life have both deteriorated. It's not that he could have done anything to prevent it, but it remains strangely haunting to read him on "Doubt, the first American virtue," or, in an astonishing Ciceronian letter addressed to *The New York Review of Books*, in the wake of the sentencing of Lieutenant Calley, the man responsible for the My Lai massacre:

> A principle may kill more than an incident. I am sick with fresh impressions. Has no one the compassion to pass judgment on William Calley? His atrocity is cleared by the President, public, polls, rank and file of the right and left. He looks almost alive; like an old song, he stirs us with the gruff poignance of the professional young soldier. He too fought under television for our place in the sun. Why should the bait be eaten when the sharks swim free? I sense a coldness under the hysteria. Our nation looks up to heaven, and puts her armies above the law. No stumbling on the downward plunge from Hiroshima. Retribution is somewhere else and we are young.

Poetry has lost so much ground in the years since Lowell started out in it, it's easy to feel a somewhat preposterous sympathy for him. There is nothing at the end of the rainbow. In Lowell's "midcentury," poetry still belonged in every well-stocked library and mind. There's really little reason to read it anymore—though apparently the queen manages a book a year. Poetry in America has declined to a civil war, a banal derby between two awful teams, and in Britain to a variety show (albeit, I suppose, a royal variety show). The last apotheosized poets are the generation of the 1910s and 1920s, Eliot and Frost and Stevens and Pound and Yeats and Bunting. They have had no successors, or the succession has not been allowed. Bishop or Lowell or Ashbery or O'Hara or Murray seem more like much-loved or eccentric or somewhat controversial deceased or elderly relatives than great poets-in-waiting. Ted Hughes already feels like a rumor. It's as though the human reef of literature was not considering any more applications, or the escalator had ground to a halt. To say that anyone who cares about poetry should read Lowell is not enough. (Can it be that they didn't know that, or haven't yet? Well, yes.) Anyone who cares about writing, or about art, or about life, should read Lowell. "Things changed to the names he gave them," he wrote, "then lost their names."

FREDERICK SEIDEL

Frederick Seidel has always been interested in taboos. Only no-nos
need apply. Everything in him is sex, politics, religion, race, and class.
A gentle giant of a black doorman remembered from childhood ("He
wore a visored cap / With a high Gestapo peak / On his impenetrably
black marble. / Waits out there in the sun to open the car door. //
My noble Negro statue's name was Heinz, / My calmly grand
George Washington") is to him a full house by any other name.

From the beginning, Seidel was always a bogeyman, a *Bürger-
schreck*, an *épateur*—a carnivore if not a cannibal in the blandly vegan
compound of contemporary poetry. He is a purveyor of "*picong*," a
Trinidadian term, from the French "*piquant*," meaning "sharp or
cutting, where the boundary between good and bad taste is deliberately blurred, and the listener is sent reeling." (This, as good a description of Seidel as inadvertence or serendipity can come up with,
is from *The World Is What It Is*, Patrick French's outstanding biography of V. S. Naipaul, and what a lot the authors of *Ooga-Booga* and
A Bend in the River have in common: both of them Insider Outsid-
ers, traveling compulsively on all five continents [though, come to

think of it, I don't recall Australia in either of them]; sharing an unspeakably deep attraction to a sort of eighteenth-century squirearchy that may or may not be England; a fascination with Africa, with Joseph Conrad, with Islam; both are students of the remorseless spread of global capital and culture, the Gulf Stream of development and the countervailing El Niño of terror; both are equally at ease in fiction and nonfiction, and in a blurring of both; and last and far from least, both exhibit, and are proud of, an insouciant erotomania. Surely Seidel, never a professional poet, never a reviewer, reciter, promoter, or teacher of poetry, could put his name to Naipaul's boast: "I have never had to work for hire; I made a vow at an early age never to work, never to become involved with people in that way. That has given me a freedom from people, from entanglements, from rivalries, from competition. I have no enemies, no rivals, no masters; I fear no one." Both are barbed, solitary, aloof, alarming figures, becoming, if anything, less mellow with age and more like their intrinsic fossil selves, jagged and serviceable, "sharp and meek," Seidel says somewhere—he does love his noses—"like the eyesight of the deaf." Thomas Mann's term *Greisen-Avantgardismus*—meaning something like "the experimental progressivism occasionally found in the very old"—suggests itself. We as readers are uneasily privileged to witness their bold, inflammatory, defamatory gestures, gestures we know there will never be time or second thought or pusillanimousness to take back.) Typically, Seidel's splendid ketchup, piccalilli, and black *Poems*—its featly five hundred pages covering fifty years of writing—runs backward, to that beginning, to the slim volume *Final Solutions*, which shared its author's initials and was published to no little controversy in 1963 when Seidel was twenty-eight and reasonably fresh out of Harvard. Now *Final Solutions* stands at the end of *Poems, 1959–2009*, as if it was always going to be there.

Nor is it just the running order that's a distinctive feature of the book. If *Poems* is a man doing a headstand, then it's a man in a bowler hat, wearing a chalk-striped four-piece suit, with a handkerchief in his top pocket and a natty carnation in his buttonhole, giving you an eyeful of his heliotrope spats. Seidel's way with poetry has always involved terribly high specifications. Try dates. If one takes the title's opening *1959* at face value, then Seidel published just one book of poems in his first twenty years of writing; his second, *Sunrise*, didn't hit the bookstores till 1980. (And how often does that happen in a poetry world characterized by facility and overproduction, by, so to speak, conspicuous production? I certainly can't think of another instance like it.) Conversely—*Greisen-Avantgardismus* again, or at the very least a late flowering—in the last ten years Seidel has published six books, three of them in the form of the three volumes of *The Cosmos Trilogy*, a Dante-based ninety-nine-canto job, with the experimental physicists' metaphor-happy concepts of Big Bang and Deep Space ("A little red / Sea horse is eleven-dimensional / Spacetime. It unicycles / Upright in space // In all directions / At once.") standing in for paradise, Seidel's familiar fast world of film shoots and Italian bespoke racebikes and tropical lagoons for Purgatorio, and Manhattan for Inferno—each canto written in a specially devised form of eight blocks of four lines that frames his poems of the early millennium in rather the same way that Robert Lowell's unrhymed sonnets or John Berryman's eighteen-line Dream Songs framed their poems of the 1960s and '70s. Very nearly two-thirds of this big book is from the last ten years, and it subsumes an opening section of almost fifty pages, *Evening Man*, that is all new.

Or try resources, style, attack. Probably one wouldn't think of going arsy-versy if one wasn't very convinced of one's newest work—but just as much of one's oldest, which of course becomes, under this dispensation, not a launching pad but a destination. And accordingly a great deal of Seidel is there from the start: the first poem in his first book is the tour de force of adolescent desires and disloyal affiliations called "Wanting to Live in Harlem" (he liked it so much he reprinted it in his second volume, so we get it twice in *Poems*, that's how far the prevailing ethos of the book, and of Seidel, is from prudence, economy, sense, concession: it's all auteurial hauteur, as if Seidel were to say "I repeat myself, very well, I repeat myself"). Later—earlier— "The Walk There" is done over as "Rilke," with the simple expedient of the protagonist's original name of "Levy" being given as "Rilke" ("You can be needed by someone / Or needy, thinks Rilke"), the poem "The Hour" is the same as "The New Woman," with one three-word sentence changed, while "Racer" loses four stanzas and a dedication, and turns into "Fog." The newspaper-fueled "The Beast Is in

Chains" has the terrific pun—and there's no shortage of awful ones elsewhere!—"The West has bombed and bombed." Seidel's aggressively schizophrenic vocabulary, old and new, Classical and Yankee, is already fully present: on the one hand, syncope, galliambic, vaginismus, vespertine, anosognosia, dysprody, pseudocyesis; on the other, loved up, Kotex pads, bluebook-blue, down-easter, fairy bars. Proper nouns and historical and news references stud the texts: the drugs Seconal and Thorazine (Seidel likes his pharmacopoeia), the rotten airplane of those days, the Electra (but no more than he likes the idea of going out in a blaze of glory, as witness the deep pun of his fifth book title, *Going Fast*), the headlines and personalities and atrocities, Kennedy, Gagarin, Oran, Spellman, Hadrian, Mather. There are acrid poem-portraits ("A Widower," "The Coalman"), monologues articulating the high-octane and emblematic misery ("Thanksgiving Day") of the decade of Eisenhower, Cheever, and Plath, notes from abroad ("Americans in Rome," "Spring"). All this Seidel had from the beginning.

What he also had was an incredibly highly developed ability to "do" his teacher, Robert Lowell—including styles Lowell in his own evolution had yet to reach. For instance, this off-kilter couplet, a sort of backward sidestep, at the end of Seidel's "After the Party" (1963), surely would have been perfect for Lowell's last book *Day by Day* (1977): "Convinced life is meaningless, / I lack the courage of my conviction." In *Final Solutions* and to some extent in *Sunrise*, published a couple of years after Lowell's death, Seidel beautifully, consummately, and mystifyingly "channels" Lowell. It's not a copy, not derivative—there's no strain, and above all no falling-off—but everything sounds as if it were Lowell writing Seidel, or Seidel writing Lowell. I know of nothing quite like it. It's as though Lowell were a fairy tale pen that had fallen into Seidel's hands, or a foreign language or birdsong in which he had attained complete mastery. The midlength female monologues would make a sort of bootleg *Mills of the Kavanaughs* (1951)—with "Thanksgiving Day" to set beside Lowell's "Thanksgiving's Over." The first "you" addressed here is Seidel's pregnant speaker's unborn child, the second is her husband. The bells and persons and relationships are overlaid in a truly nightmarish way, until in the catastrophic final image the bird, "perfect bird"—utterly Lowell, this, like his skunk with her "column of kittens"—morphs into a different bird ("goosepimpled"), and a cold and nauseating corpse takes its place at the heart of the game of happy families:

> I feel you. The oven bell
> Dings, and you call—the front door bell;
> And in the hall, Papa and your mother
> Gabble about our unborn daughter or son.
> A perfect bird. Fatty sweat
> Gleams on its bursting goosepimpled breast.

There are clumps of typically Lowellishly enjambed and mono-syllable-powered lines you can turn one way and they disappear into "Quaker Graveyard," and another way and they are "Beyond the Alps":

> Holding his breath, he watched the whole wing flex
> And flex and saw the bouncing jet pods stream
> With condensation as they plowed through clouds.
> He saw the stewardess back down the aisle
> Smiling at seat belts. ("A Year Abroad")

(Lowell I think wouldn't have been sensible enough to understand about the seat belts.) One can go through Seidel poems, ticking off Lowell features: the Saxon genitive (never more startling than in "passersby's eyes"!), the typically stretched Lowell "and," the long spelling out of names and the shorting of references (like "Jesse Owens's *putsch*"), the gangling constructions, the hyperbolic modifiers, the plangent negatives, the puns that aren't (as in "Powdered bricks had made the ground lip-red"), the short lines with heavy rhymes that do so much of the work in that bleak book *For the Union Dead* ("No violin could thaw / The rickety and raw / Purple window"), the terse, exhausted finishing sentences ("Your girlfriend shrieks with fear" or "He's coming, child, I come"). Almost all the swingeing last lines, in a blind tasting, would be attributed to Lowell, with their typical, fern-in-coal aspect of material crushed into sound and sense pattern: "Absinthe / Is now on Thorazine, the breaker of obsessions," "The obsolete slow drill that now only polishes," "Art won't forgive life, no more than life will," "The eyes of a bachelor waiting for water to boil"—sometimes with an admixture of Montale: "Still waiting! It is too late to be yourself."

After, as I see it, channeling Lowell, Seidel took to channeling— Seidel. During the 1970s and 1980s, the flavor or aura of his poems switched imperceptibly but completely from one very strong (as the French say) perfume to another, from vanilla to strawberry. Lowell is still there, as a similitude, or a point of reference, but the product itself is now pure Seidel. The difference shows in an element of excess, of taunt, of trash, of (Les Murray's word) "flaunt," a sort of F. Scott Fitzgerald that is three parts Roy Lichtenstein ("A Gallop to Farewell"):

The most underrated pleasure in the world is the takeoff
Of the Concorde and putting off the crash
Of the world's most beautiful old supersonic plane, with no
    survivors,
In an explosion of champagne.

It's the world of American attitude—"Give me Everest or give me death. Give me altitude with an attitude," Seidel says in "Climbing Everest"—from the people that gave you Marilyn and the plastic saxophone and the aluminum baseball bat, and the others that went out and played with them. What's interesting here isn't Seidel "finding his voice" as the benign cliché goes, but the fact that the poems seem to originate from somewhere as far away as ever. As I say, the writing keeps its "channeled" feel. One can't take lines or scenes or sentiments and, by adding them up, arrive at "the poet" in the way one might, with Wordsworth, say, or, for that matter, with Lowell. There is a strange distanciation—a coldness, a deliberateness, a caricatural warp and yawp, a cartoonishness—that always interposes itself, a distanciation that has grown stranger and more confident and more pronounced over the years. In an interview he gave to Wyatt

Mason in *The New York Times* in 2009, Seidel acknowledges, "Looking at these poems is sometimes an extremely strange experience, as if . . . who the hell wrote this?"

Seidel's poems go against most prevailing trends of poetry. There is nothing photographic about them, they don't home in on detail, they don't seek feeling, go in for tolerable introspection, or try to make an unassuming music. One might go so far as to say that the impulse behind their making has nothing lyrical about it. That probably is why reactions to them are so strong, why—apart from a small but persistent minority of supporters and admirers—readers and critics are so often outraged, want their money back, call Seidel all sorts of names. Where's the pissy beauty, the undemanding truth? Conditioned to the sort of poetry where the poet tries hard to be precisely the "bundle of accident and incoherence that sits down to breakfast," readers are no longer able to understand what happens when—in the rest of the Yeats tag—a phantasmagoria imposes itself. Lines like these, that come from a catalog of historical and cultural possibilities, from tall tales, from *sprezzatura*, from an exuberant, nettling Byronism, are read dully, literally, confessionally, and of course come out sounding merely obnoxious:

> Combine a far-seeing industrialist.
> With an Islamic fundamentalist.
> With an Italian premier who doesn't take bribes.
> With a pharmaceuticals CEO who loves to spread disease.
> Put them on a 916.
>
> And you get Fred Seidel.

It's important to understand that the poet is not in the lines. We're not talking advanced self-scrutiny and truth telling here. The lines are stuff, material, mortadella, it doesn't greatly matter. The poet is the meat-slicing machine. He is above all the one who insists on supplying the capitals at the beginning and the periods at the end— even though they're not proper sentences—that simpleminded and censorious readers override and disregard at their peril. In the Mason interview, Seidel says, "It's very much to do with the sense you develop, in the writing of a poem, that at a certain moment it has its separate being from you to which you have your obligations. You're you; it's it; and eventually, it really will separate from you and be absolutely not yours anymore—even if you made it. It is, of course. But it isn't. It's a thing out there." Accordingly, there is a trend in many of Seidel's newer poems of offering disclaimers. It's even less fourth wall/bourgeois theater than ever. "I'll supply the art part, he generously offers." Alternatively, he claims, "I'm a liar with a lyre," or, more confoundingly, "I am the crocodile of joy, who never lies"—if a crocodile's tears are false, does that make its smiles more or less worthy of our belief? Where he says, beautifully, "My name is Fred Seidel, / And I paid for this ad," does that accept or refuse responsibility, or is it really most like the dubious modern conflation of the two? The last two lines of *Ooga-Booga* warn the reader: "Open the mummy case of this text respectfully. / You find no one inside." And still people queue up to say what a cad Seidel is, what an unpolitically correct bounder.

I said I thought Seidel replaced Lowell's influence with his own, sometime in the '70s or '80s. In point of style, I think that's true, but Lowell continues to assert himself in one crucial way: he supplies Seidel with his structural model or blueprint. To put it another way, whatever poem Seidel is writing, it's more likely than not to be "For the Union Dead": even stanzas, uneven lines, occasional heavy rhymes, occasional heavy rhythms, coexistence of private and public themes, the poet in the poem in a cramped or slightly histrionic way ("I crouch to my television set"), the juggling of six or eight different tropes or images, like so many plates kept airborne; in "For the Union Dead" it would include, in no particular order: bulbousness, cars and machinery, the color orange, fish and the marine world, the ditch and digging, shaking, etiolation, the role or possibility of change, race relations, animation and disanimation. Seidel has written this sort of longish, ambitious, polygonal poem many times now: the first time was in the earliest poem, "Wanting to Live in Harlem," in which he makes an *Entwicklungsroman* of his own life: pictures of violins, the "colored" maid, Somerset Maughamish lusts, Jews and Romans, Lutherans and Jews, a Gauguin-like palette, a dying mother. He does it differently, less organically, more mechanically. The themes and images tend not to bleed into each other as they do in Lowell, they are checked, kept apart, the effect or the technique is more that of a collage, the lines it seems really are sliced off. With Seidel, there is something that feels machined about the writing. Even within his poems, he tends to present himself as a sort of centaur, most often an *homme-machine*: on a Ducati, in a hotel, on a Eurostar train, on a plane, on a woman (where he often sounds deliriously mechanical: "Women have a playground slide / That wraps you in monsoon and takes you for a ride"); encased in accoutrements for hunting, or tropics, or formal evening wear; always something crisp and tokenish and apart and *comme il faut*, like an Action Man figure. Lowell—"one life, one writing!"—made a sort of mulch of words, from which he himself was practically inextricable, in which he wallowed as much as worked at, the "crackled amber moonscape" left "to ripen in sunlight"; Seidel followed him neither into the obsessive revising nor the lowercase line beginnings (from *Life Studies* on). The lines are as they are: provocative, sensationalist, injurious, red top, flawed. I often have a dreamy sense of Seidel's poems being produced on a '70s (I think) gadget called a Dymo Tape, mostly used for pricing goods in stores, where letters were pressed out onto a sort of plastic tickertape, like so: "My name is Fred Seidel, / And I paid for this ad." They are printed, without being written.

At the latest in *The Cosmos Poems* (2000), form takes command. Form is valued in a Seidel poem for its externality, its invasive obtrusiveness. These poems are written from the outside. (Hence their nonlyrical and antilyrical quality.) Paradoxically, what one notices is the ever more amped-up content—the needle rarely leaves the red zone—but that is merely entailed and made possible by the hypertrophic form. Because Seidel's is not organic form, grown and traditional and moderated, sonnet, triolet, villanelle, it is poem DNA disassembled and put together in unpredictable and threatening ways. Form becomes a version of self-governance in the poem, of disobedience, a riot of primary instructions. Itself done to excess, it contributes to the poem's general air of excess. When a thing rhymes it doesn't get out of rhyme, it stutters in rhyme. Seidel's *bouts-rimés* jingle like a fruit machine spitting out coins. It's no surprise that Seidel has written at least one monorhymed poem, "Sii romantico, Seidel, tanto per cambiare," thirty lines on the syllable -*ide*. An only slightly more measured rhyme scheme (for the first fourteen-line stanza of the poem, "Do You Doha?") might go: abbbbbaaacccccc. Similarly, when a poem scans, it tramps. In trochees—no wonder "Mother Nature" segues into Longfellow—or in demented iambs ("A coconut can fall and hit you on the head, / And if it falls from high enough can kind of knock you dead"). Few poems are not built—or jerry-built—in stanzas, though stanzas may be four, five, six, seven, nine, ten, twelve, fourteen, or seventeen lines in length. "Everything in art is couplets" it says solemnly in one poem, but then the following line goes "Mine don't rhyme," and the poem, in any case, is in quatrains. Most decisive of the lot, though, and all the more effective because so rarely used outside skipping rhymes and primers, is sentence length (further emphasized because it is often coterminous with line length) ("East Hampton Airport"):

> I stand in the field opposite the airport.
> I watch the planes flying in and the planes flying out.
> My proud Irish terrier takes pills for his cardiomyopathy.
> Before we bark our last,
> Our hearts enlarge and burst.
> George Plimpton went to bed
> And woke up dead.
> I write this poem thinking of the painter David Salle
> Who wants to make a movie
> About the poet Frank O'Hara.
> A beach taxi on Fire Island hit Frank and he burst, roll credits.

The sentences are pruned back as though to prevent them from ever bursting into individual flower. (Technically speaking, it's probably the prime source of Seidel's detachment.)

Other mechanical handlings of language—interventions, one might call them—play their part: puns, repetition, word games, vocabulary stunts. Jargon and prefab phrases abound: "to die for," "metrosexual," "cremains," "stem cells," "train wreck," "total nightmare," the Yahoo-enabled six-day weather forecast, "this is a test." "Happy days are gone again," it says somewhere, crushingly, and in "A Song for Cole Porter," "Ride around, little dogies, ride around them slow," and "I knew a beauty named Dawn Green. / I used to wake at the crack of Dawn." Words and lines are swapped about between poems like hot money used to be. Intensifiers are ten a penny: "literally," "really," "utter," "incredible," "pure," "actually," "totally." Especially troubling is a derisory streak of aphasia in some poems: "A flavorful man can, and then he is not," the smuttily Shakespearean "He licks to play golf," "Winter, spring, Baghdad, fall," "Winter is wearing summer but it wants to undress for you, Fred. / Oh my God. Takes off the lovely summer frock / And lies down on the bed naked / Freezing white, so we can make death." It is epic stuff, all bleak, jaunty, scathing, and utterly contemporary ("Poem by the Bridge at Ten-shin"):

> To Ninety-second Street and Broadway I have come.
> Outside the windows is New York.
> I came here from St. Louis in a covered wagon overland
> Behind the matchless prancing pair of Eliot and Ezra Pound.
> And countless moist oases took me in along the way, and some
> I still remember when I lift my knife and fork.
> The Earth keeps turning, night and day, spit-roasting all the
>   tanned
> Tired icebergs and the polar bears, which makes white almost
>   contraband.
> The biosphere on a rotisserie emits a certain sound
> That tells the stars that Earth was moaning pleasure while it
>   drowned.
> The amorous white icebergs flash their brown teeth, hissing.
> They're watching old porn videos of melting icebergs pissing.
> The icebergs still in panty hose are lesbians and kissing.
> The rotting ocean swallows the bombed airliner that's missing.

Thank God for Fred Seidel.

TED HUGHES

I have a dim sense of how Ted Hughes may be perceived here in America. ("Stare at the monster," he wrote in the poem "Famous Poet," from the 1950s.) I have a slightly clearer sense of how he has fared in the UK, at least over the last twenty years. Neither is the slightest use in preparing one for—a word I certifiably use for the first and last time in print!—an awesome collection of poems. Hughes is at least arguably the greatest English poet since Shakespeare; what's the competition? Milton, Pope, Keats, Wordsworth, Tennyson, Hardy, (maybe) Larkin. I think such a view can be advanced. This is indeed the man with the lifelong obsession with Beethoven. The poet whose voice Seamus Heaney described as "longer and deeper and rougher." Of whom Gavin Ewart wrote his one-line poem, "Folk Hero": "The one the foreign students call Ted Huge." Unscientific though it certainly is, people who bought Ted Hughes books on Amazon UK also bought Dante, Homer, Chaucer, Shakespeare, and Heaney. Match me that.

Of course, once poets die, there's some fun cutting them down to size. *Nihil de mortuis*, unless it cuts them off at the knees. British poets particularly, because what do the British know about scale? It'll fit on a postage stamp (albeit, a stamp that isn't obliged to declare its provenance). Ask Derek Walcott about the state of British poetry, he starts brabbling about Larkin (this was when Hughes was alive but Larkin already safely dead). Ask James Schuyler for the last really good British poet, he'll send you rootling back to Swinburne, or even earlier. I have a feeling, though, that Hughes will be spared this rather Australian ("tall poppy") treatment. Not only because at above thirteen hundred pages (twelve hundred of them poems), his book handily pips even Lowell's, published just a couple of months before, but also because so many of them are wonderful, and practically unknown. And because at a time when appearance and presentation are getting to be almost everything, this onetime poet laureate (a label whose potential for comedy and obloquy has gone strangely unrecognized in the Po-Faced States) carried himself superbly. "All this, too," it says in "October Salmon," "is stitched into the torn richness, / The epic poise / That holds him so steady in his wounds, so loyal to his doom, so patient / In the machinery of heaven."

Some of it is sheer industry. Hughes applied himself to poetry for the best part of fifty years, and with barely an intermission. The list of his poetry books alone covers a large, closely set page—p. 1238, if you must know. (I suppose there are some nonentities who manage a big product, but on such a scale, one would have to be an acute graphomaniac, not merely a persistent hack, to compete.) Beyond that, there were plays, translated from Aeschylus, Euripides, Seneca, Racine, Wedekind. Poetry International at the Albert Hall in 1970, the magazine *Modern Poetry in Translation*, with his friend of fifty years, Danny Weissbort. Poetry, translated and cotranslated from János Pilinszky and Yehuda Amichai. Poetry for children, and books to stimulate children to write (a lifelong commitment). Not an exemplary editor of Plath, for the simple reason that one wouldn't wish anyone to be in that position, but I think hard to fault. Selections from Dickinson and Whitman and Keith Douglas and Coleridge and Shakespeare. Coedited two wonderful anthologies with Seamus Heaney, *The Rattle Bag* and then *The School Bag*. Work with the theater director Peter Brook as a dramaturge, and deviser of the language called Orghast. The huge experimental book on deep narrative structures in Shakespeare, called *Shakespeare and the Goddess of Complete Being*, a big selection of essays and reviews called *Winter Pollen*. (When he got the cancer that killed him, he blamed it, typically, on writing too much prose.) And all this not in some dusty monkish solitude or supportive college eyrie, but from a life in which he farmed, fished, traveled very widely, to Australia, to Africa, to Alaska, was several times honored by the Queen of England, with whom he was reputed to have got along well, and further, was—you won't need me to tell you—thrice married, and (before reading Elaine Feinstein's biography, I had no inkling of this) had many affairs, and also raised two children.

Ted Hughes's absence was one of the sad givens when I was in England in the 1980s and 1990s. One knew about him, or thought one knew about him, and knew about his work, but never had any expectation of meeting him. He was both sanctioned—the schoolmaster's poet—and under sanction. He dwelled simultaneously in a higher and a lower sphere; one thought of him as serving out some kind of punishment. Devonian relegation or house arrest. It was one of a number of revelations in Feinstein's book that he was regularly in London, and lived not quite like Aung San Suu Kyi. I saw him just twice. Once at a Faber party, where our then-editor, Craig Raine, pushed us together and we shyly gulped at each other in silence like goldfish (I saw this happening with other baby poets too), and once when he agreed to read with ten others at the London Festival Hall from the book of Ovid translations that James Lasdun and I brought out in 1992, to which he contributed four sensational pieces.

A good outcome from this partly voluntary, partly imposed seeming—partly actually illusory—withdrawal was that he kept his freedom, his dignity, his time. This extended to his personal life, his illness and death, and his work. The successive poetry editors at Fabers, Craig Raine, Christopher Reid, and Paul Keegan—who took the chair only after Hughes's death—were deeply impressed by their charge and grew close to him. The rest of us may have thought we had him down, but he retained the capacity to surprise us with his every utterance. Whether it was his wholly unexpected *Paris Review* interview with Drue Heinz in 1995, or *Birthday Letters*, which floored us, or uncollected poems in his *Selected* like "Remembering

Teheran"—who, other than the best-informed Hughes watcher would ever have guessed he'd been to Teheran (he went with Peter Brook's International Centre for Theatre Research in 1971)?—or the last printed communication I remember from him, a long, eloquent letter to the *Guardian* in 1997, pleading for foxhunting and stag-hunting to be allowed to continue, everything from him was considered and powerful and left field. Nothing less would have allowed him to be poet laureate without a considerable diminution of his prestige. (That's how things work in England.)

And that's how it is with his *Collected Poems*. Paul Keegan has taken Hughes's *New Selected Poems* of 1995 as his model and interca-lated the expected and familiar Faber texts with uncollected or small press works like a Viennese layer cake—in astonishing quantity and quality. Most *Collected Poems* merely give us what we have already. Not this one, not unless you are a wealthy book collector with access to three continents. Hughes was assiduous in sending out individual poems all his life, and he had a lifelong affinity for small presses. He had the output, too, to command this double issue. With Hughes's Hugheses, it's a little like Picasso's Picassos. Some don't fit whatever the large-press book happens to be; a few are rejects; some antici-pate or trail along after preoccupations. (There's a whole manslaugh-ter of "Crow" poems, for instance, before and after the 1970 volume.) And some—especially late—are among his most personal. It's in-teresting that these were reserved for tiny, exclusive, luxurious publications, things I never suspected existed, let alone ever saw—*Capriccio* in 1990, *Cries and Whispers* of 1998, the year Hughes died. *Capriccio* was printed in an edition of fifty copies, selling at $4,000 apiece.

As I read through this—ha—huge book, I found all my provisional findings systematically overturned. Hughes's beginnings—half a dozen or so much-anthologized pieces aside, "Wind," "Pike," "Thrushes," "View of a Pig"—were, contrary to expectation, not es-pecially impressive. (The perceived U-shape of his career.) Most of it was ordinary poetry of its time. After that, it seemed literary, dili-gently, strenuously literary. Elements of Shakespeare, a lot, of Anglo-

Saxon, of Donne, of Wallace Stevens, of Lawrence, of Hopkins. Of Plath. But when I got used to the literariness, and began looking for it, it lapsed. I felt—like Rimbaud alongside his river in "*Le Bateau Ivre*"—that I no longer had dependable guides. *Crow*, then, I read as an Eastern European book. Analytical, diminished, distended, caricatured. Like something by Holub or Herbert. Only for *Cogito* read Cuervo. Then a cosmic ferocity—always the least interesting part of Hughes to me. The hysterical, red-lit, gauge-busting style of "death-orgasm supernovae // Flood from the bitten-away gills." *Prometheus on his Rock*, no great development from its premise. (Striking, though, the number of male victim figures in the poetry.) More series: birds, fish, flowers, insects, seasons, the majestic farm diary of *Moortown* (from 1979). It's as if Rilke had written not two books of *New Poems* but seven; or not one *Duino* but more than anyone cared to keep track of. Something magnificent and medieval and also workaday about these catalog-series: each one an illuminated letter, or one of the *Très Riches Heures du Duc de Berry*. Occasional spurts of a thin but aggressive little vein of satire, like Lawrence's satire. Poems on Fay Godwin's landscape portraits of the north of England—humdrum but suddenly sensational, two or three poems in a row. Wilderness a continual preoccupation, certainly—the last chronicler of wilderness on this shrinking McPlanet. "This is the Black Rhino, the elastic boulder, coming at a gallop. / The boulder with a molten core, the animal missile, / Enlarging towards you" ("The Black Rhino"). Hughes would have known how many species and how many square miles were lost in his lifetime. He writes about things people now see on television, if at all. Things whose existence we idly assume and blithely imperil. But then the surprise of two beautiful poems on livestock auctions. Favor extended to rats. A long study, through the looking glass, of spiders mating (another male victim). A tragic view of sex (like Lawrence, the tortoise), and of poetry.

A feeling that whereas most of the best poetry of our time aims for and is distinguished by its speed (I think of Brodsky's phrase, "a highly economical form of mental acceleration"), Hughes often writes with heavy feet. Like Lawrence. Not just won't leap, but can't leap. A characteristic movement of his is the clanking, mired advance of bulldozer or caterpillar tracks. One plodding platelet at a time ("Black Hair"—a poem to Hughes's mother):

> I remember her hair as black
> Though I know it was brown.
> Dark brown. I first saw it as black.
> She was combing it. Probably it was wet.
> She was combing it out after washing it.
> Black, straight, shining hair down over her breasts.
> That's the memory.

The sentences—often, like these, noun phrases—setting themselves down, and the next one following half in its print, barely an advance. The antithesis of speed. Weight. Method. Force. Brute or main. Instruction. Like someone writing a computer program. (And then one, three or four along, will contradict it: this isn't computer programming, it's poetry. "I contradict myself? Very well, I contradict myself.") But so many wild exceptions to this. Astounding juxtapositions and swirling sentences that go miles. Perhaps one conclusion remains unoverturned: that the model and the repeated subject of Hughes's writing is Creation itself: "*Only birth matters / Say the river's whorls. And the river / Silences everything in a leaf-mouldering hush / Where sun rolls bare, and earth rolls, / And mind condenses on old haws*" ("Salmon Eggs").

When Hughes is described as a "nature poet," the effect—if not the intention—is drastically to limit him. That's what we were given at school, a vaguely reproachful litany of things with which we were unfamiliar and in which we weren't greatly interested. We didn't live in *nature*, who on earth lived in nature? But if nature, then a sort of Tinguely-cum-Brueghel *Weltmaschine* of everything-that-is-the-case. A cartoonish vitalism that saw "the phenomenal technology" inside a fox's head; to which everything, *au fond*, was wild, even house cats and daffodils, by virtue of its otherness; that outdid Marianne Moore by writing an ode to a sports car, "Flimsy-light, like a squid's funeral bone"; that offered a moorland tree as "A priest from a different land," who "Fulminated / Against heather, black stones, blown water"; that listened to a heron "cranking rusty abuse, / like an unwanted porter"; that showed us mannerly bears "eating pierced salmon off their talons"; that was incapable of seeing crabs without a nightmarish Dix or Sutherland flashback of World War I, "Giant crabs, under flat skulls, staring inland / Like a packed trench of helmets"; that deconstructed a cranefly as "Her jointed bamboo fuselage, / Her lobster shoulders, and her face / Like a pinhead dragon, with its tender moustache, / And the simple colourless church windows of her wings." Anything unhappy, ungainly, failed, or doomed enlists the poet's sympathy, whether it's a baby swallow that can't fly ("The moustached goblin savage // Nested in a scarf. [. . .] The inevitable balsa death"), an ugly, lumpy apple blossom ("A straggle of survivors, nearly all ailing"), or a dirty river ("And the Okement, nudging her detergent bottles, tugging at her nylon stockings, starting to trundle her Pepsi-Cola cans"). If this sympathy wasn't so universally extended, it might seem sentimental—a strange accusation to level at Hughes. Equally, when things work, they are celebrated for working. It is not "nature"—sky-blue and pink nature, schoolroom nature—so much as technology. A mother sheep "carries on investigating her new present and seeing how it works." A female spider's hands become cutting edge: "Far from simple, / Though, were her palps, her boxing-glove nippers— / They were like the mechanical hands / That manipulate radio-active matter / On the other side of safe screen glass." A sparrow is read as a prole: "Pin-legged urchin, he's patient. / He bathes in smoke. He towels in soot, / And with his prematurely-aged hungry street-cry / Sells his consumptive sister." All this is drama, function, it takes us to the sources of energy, character, identity. The descriptive resources of the writing match those of the creature or thing described. "The hills went on gently / shaking their sieve." Hence the allowable comparison to Shakespeare. Who other than Shakespeare would have dared the coda to "Sing the Rat," where invention and anonymous folk wit indistinguishably mingle?

O sing
Scupper-tyke, whip-lobber

Smutty-guts, pot-goblin
Garret-whacker, rick-lark
Sump-swab, cupboard-adder
Bobby-robin, knicker-knocker
Sneak-nicker, sprinty-dinty
Pintle-bum

The corollary of the "nature poet" label is that Hughes didn't "do" people. That his gift didn't extend to historical intelligence, to narrative, to psychology, to abstracting and inducing and contextualizing. It did—to all of those things, see *Birthday Letters*, see the *Tales from Ovid*—but, like Lawrence, Hughes often took animals as his way in. The *Metamorphoses* are god and man stories with animal outcomes. Animals challenged him, or commanded him unconditionally, as people did only if they struck him as exceptional, or in exceptional situations. (Old subjects, uncontemporary people, holdouts, veterans, drudges, people of a dandified strength get his praise and attention: "Sketching a Thatcher," "Dick Straightup," "Walt," "Sacrifice.") There's any amount of human intelligence and the slapstick of human incompetence ("O beggared eagle! O down-and-out falcon!") in his poem "Buzzard":

> When he treads, by chance, on a baby rabbit
> He looks like an old woman
> Trying to get her knickers off.
>
> In the end he lumbers away,
> To find some other buzzard, maybe older,
> To show him how.

(It's not just the indignity of "old woman," the covertly sexual "treads," and the ribaldry of "knickers"; it's the fact that an older buzzard might not necessarily be any more proficient.) Sometimes, a human subject will draw dignity and company from animal society, as in the early poem "The Retired Colonel": "Here's his head mounted, though only in rhymes, / Beside the head of the last English / Wolf (those starved gloomy times!) / And the last sturgeon of Thames."

("English" rhymes with "vanish," earlier.) Sometimes, it will draw further degradation, as in this short uncollected poem, "Gibraltar"—where, I'm guessing, Hughes might have visited in 1956, at the time of his Spanish honeymoon with Plath:

Empire has rotted back,
Like a man-eater
After its aeon of terror, to one fang.

Apes on their last legs—
Rearguard of insolence—
Snapping at peanuts and defecating.

The heirloom garrison's sold as a curio
With a flare of Spanish hands
And a two-way smile, wafer of insult,

Served in carefully-chipped English.
The taxi-driver talking broken American
Has this rock in his palm.

When the next Empire noses this way
Let it sniff here.

The "fang" is the Rock itself. There's a touch of Yeats about the poem, about the slightly squeamish deployment of slang (you can't help looking for the word "slouch" somewhere!), "carefully-chipped" is nice, doubling as crockery and mimicry. Overall, one might not necessarily have guessed it was Hughes, but it's very confident; had it been more widely circulated, it might have saved him from the laureateship.

"Remembering Teheran" is a terrific poem that I've written about elsewhere (see p. 112), full of heat and drought and static and theatricality and alienated intimations of prerevolutionary dread: it shows beyond a peradventure that Hughes could "do" abroad as well as anyone. "Auction at Stanbury" is a short and intense snapshot of the north of England, bleakly comic, sadly inward:

On a hillside, part farm, part stone rubble
Shitty bony cattle disconsolate
Rotten and shattered gear

Farmers resembling the gear, the animals
Resembling the strewn walls, the shabby slopes

Shivery Pakistanis
Wind pressing the whole scene towards ice

Thin black men wrapped in bits of Bradford
Waiting for a goat to come up

The auction is cleverly held off till the last two words; the scene is too miserably messy to deserve any more hierarchy or purpose than that. Shit/shat/shab/shiv. Waiting for a goat—a scapegoat, perhaps—waiting for Godot. It's a final, humbling indignity. Like the—roughly contemporaneous—devaluation of a currency. The condition of England is always something Hughes is keen to infer, sometimes ceremonially, almost magically, as in the Laureate poems, sometimes satirically in more occasional pieces. It's one of the identifications that lend a cute cultural amplitude to his poems about Plath, the fact that she's America and he's England, and much of the time he's on the receiving end: "It confirmed / Your idea of England: part / Nursing home, part morgue / For something partly dying, partly dead." By the same metonymic token, one "J.R." is identified with Australia ("your firestick-naked, billabong spirit"), his second wife Assia Wevill with an unstable amalgam of German, Jewish, Levantine, Russian, his father-in-law Jack Orchard with a gypsy Africa. It's ethnobotanical labeling.

Birthday Letters is mainly stunningly unbeautiful—it's mostly written in the bulldozer style with the short, incremental sentences—but it's still Hardy by other means. I like to think Hughes couldn't have written it without writing the *Tales from Ovid* first, to draw him into the sphere of the human and the narrative, but I'm not so sure now. It's not known whether, as the title suggests, and as I think Hughes claimed, the poems were written steadily over many years, or if they came pell-mell toward the end of his life. The latter seems likelier to me. There barely seems time to draw breath between one poem and the next; I can't imagine them being composed years apart, leisurely, or sharply, at so many separate promptings. The composition of the *Duino Elegies* strikes me as a likely parallel, some glimmerings earlier and one or two poems (there were some in the *New Selected* of 1995), but basically an abrupt tumble at the end. In the case of the *Birthday Letters*, the very notion of such a project—the narrative and publication of his version of the years with Plath—might have been the last thing to emerge.

They're not all great, or even good, poems. Partly, I think, they are pulled apart by Hughes following different, and even contradictory, purposes at the same time: to celebrate, to explain, and to mourn. The simplicity and heavy slowness of the style is almost forced upon the poet wanting to do so many different things. Third-person description, with its myriad revelations, exaggerations, and suggestions, is abandoned for a simple "I-you" mode used by Hughes for the first time, though the rest of us have been flogging it for years. Dignity and reticence, I imagine, would have meant he abhorred it. The way he uses it, it's unexpectedly capable of holding and disclosing feeling. Sometimes, it's almost a style without words. I'm thinking especially of a poem called "The Other," which it took me a while to "see," but which now looks drastic and original: "She had too much so with a smile you took some. / Of everything she had you had / Absolutely nothing, so you took some. / At first just a little." It's related to another poem from *Capriccio*, called "Folktale," but it's even more bare. Like Lawrence, it seems to break every known rule. There's not a concrete noun in the place. Not a scene. Not a recognizable event. Nothing. A few clichés are allowed to disport themselves rather grimly, but basically, it's naked arithmetic. Subtraction, to be precise. But something of the schematic style of that poem, the threadbare simplicity, an otherworldly point of view where memory and self-accusation, transgression and punishment, seem to become one thing, informs a lot of the poems of *Birthday Letters*. ("Birthday" perhaps in that rather British sense of "naked.") "Was that a happy day?" begins one poem; "Nearly happy," another. "What happened to Howard's portrait of you? / I wanted that painting." "Remember how

we picked the daffodils? / Nobody else remembers, but I remember."
It could hardly be any more straightforward. It's hard to think there
could ever be a more successful narrative—not least because we all
grew up on the story anyway. But then, "Nobody else remembers, but
I remember." It's quite a card.

Some of the poems are more furnished than others, and they are
the ones I prefer: "Fever," "Flounders," "Daffodils," "The Beach." I
read Hughes with the grain—I've learned to do that, it's wasteful not
to—and against. The one thing I'm loath to go along with is to follow him into the doomed—not just predestined, but predestinarian—
mode that he wraps a lot of the memories and episodes in. His
celebrating and mourning, in other words, I allow; I jib a little at the
explanations. Time and time again, he offers up the machinery of
doom, whether it's Ouija sessions, an offended gypsy, a dream, an
illness, Otto, poetry. There's a tense—the opposite of the future perfect, if you like, the posthumous future—where the poems like to
take you to, the tense of "I had no idea," of "if only I'd known then
what I know now," the tense of dramatic irony. "We thought they were
a windfall. / Never guessed they were a last blessing." This wears out,
and it's my one serious reservation about *Birthday Letters*. I much prefer it when Hughes coasts on the "present" of the simple past:

> You had a fever. You had a real ailment.
> You had eaten a baddie.
> You lay helpless and a little bit crazy
> With the fever. You cried for America
> And its medicine cupboard. You tossed
> On the immovable Spanish galleon of a bed
> In the shuttered Spanish house
> That the sunstruck outside glare peered into
> As into a tomb. "Help me," you whispered, "help me."

That painting over and over a scene and a situation is to me what
Hughes does best in these poems; "as into a tomb" I view as another
intrusion from the dramatic-ironical department. I like "baddie," half
condescension, half quotation. Hughes in the poem pits his amusement and his health and his good intentions against the contagion of

panic. "I bustled about. / I was nursemaid. I fancied myself at that. / I liked the crisis of the vital role." And the ending of that poem, though it has the right amplitude for an ending, is correctly deduced from the matter of the poem itself: "The stone man made soup. / The burning woman drank it."

So much of the personal drama is comic, and I bless it for that. It's "The bats had a problem"—which is right, because they're American bats from Carlsbad, as American as NASA. It's the grandiloquent, posturing timing—riding for a fall—of "We are surrounded, I said, by magnificent beaches." It's riding the long wave of remembering Plath declaiming Chaucer to an audience of cows: "It must have sounded lost. But the cows / Watched, then approached: they appreciated Chaucer." It's like a scene in Jerome K. Jerome, you wish it could go on forever. It's Plath's—justified and witty—tirades against England:

> England
> Was so poor! Was black paint cheaper? Why
> Were English cars all black?—to hide the filth?
> Or to stay respectable, like bowlers
> And umbrellas? Every vehicle a hearse.
> The traffic procession a hushing leftover
> Of Victoria's perpetual funeral Sunday—
> The funeral of colour and light and life!
> London a morgue of dinge—English dinge.
> Our sole indigenous art-form—depressionist!
> And why were everybody's
> Garments so deliberately begrimed?
> Grubby-looking, like a camouflage? "Alas!
> We have never recovered," I said, "from our fox-holes,
> Our trenches, our fatigues and our bomb-shelters."

This, for all its apparent ease, is a miraculous balance of indirect and quoted speech, of question and answer, of expansive and pithy, of detailed and universal, of naïve and informed, of drama and editorial. To throw off a phrase like "a morgue of dinge" like that, in the middle of what the fiction writers call a "riff." There's life in the old country yet. Or there was.

"REMEMBERING TEHERAN"

How it hung
In the electrical loom
Of the Himalayas—I remember
The spectre of a rose.

All day the flag on the military camp flowed South.

In the Shah's Evin Motel
The Manageress—a thunderhead Atossa—
Wept on her bed
Or struck awe. Tragic Persian
Quaked her bosom—precarious balloons of water—
But still nothing worked.

Everything hung on a prayer, in the hanging dust.

With a splash of keys
She ripped through the lock, filled my room, sulphurous,

With plumbers—
Twelve-year-olds, kneeling the fathom
A pipeless tap sunk in a blank block wall.

♦ ♦ ♦

I had a funny moment
Beside the dried-up river of boulders. A huddle of families
Were piling mulberries into wide bowls, under limp, dusty trees.
All the big males, in their white shirts,
Drifted out towards me, hands hanging—
I could see the bad connections sparking inside their heads

As I picked my way among thistles
Between dead-drop wells—open man-holes
Parched as snake-dens—

Later, three stoned-looking Mercedes,
Splitting with arms and faces, surfed past me
Warily over a bumpy sea of talc,
The uncials on their number-places like fragments of scorpions.

♦ ♦ ♦

I imagined all Persia
As a sacred scroll, humbled to powder
By the God-conducting script on it—
The lightning serifs of Zoroaster—
The primal cursive.

♦ ♦ ♦

Goats, in charred rags,
Eyes and skulls
Adapted to sunstroke, woke me
Sunbathing among the moon-clinker.
When one of them slowly straightened into a goat-herd
I knew I was in the wrong century
And wrongly dressed.

All around me stood
The tense, abnormal thistles, desert fanatics;
Politicos, in their zinc-blue combat issue;

Three-dimensional crystal theorems
For an optimum impaling of the given air;
Arsenals of pragmatic ideas—

I retreated to the motel terrace, to loll there
And watch the officers half a mile away, exercising their obso-
    lete horses.

A bleaching sun, cobalt-cored,
Played with the magnetic field of the mountains.

And prehistoric giant ants, outriders, long-shadowed,
Cast in radiation-proof metals,
Galloped through the land, lightly and unhindered,
Stormed my coffee-saucer, drinking the stain—

At sunset
The army flag rested for a few minutes
Then began to flow North

◆ ◆ ◆

I found a living thread of water
Dangling from a pipe. A snake-tongue flicker.
An incognito whisper.
It must have leaked and smuggled itself, somehow,
From the high Mother of Snows, halfway up the sky.
It wriggled these last inches to ease
A garden of pot-pourri, in a tindery shade of peach-boughs,
And played there, a fuse crackling softly—

As the whole city
Sank in the muffled drumming
Of a subterranean furnace.

And over it.
The desert's bloom of dust, the petroleum smog, the transistor
    commotion
Thickened a pink-purple thunderlight.

The pollen of the thousands of years of voices
Murmurous, radio-active, rubbing to flash-point—

♦ ♦ ♦

Scintillating through the migraine
The world-authority on Islamic Art
Sipped at a spoonful of yoghurt
And smiling at our smiles described his dancing
Among self-beheaded dancers who went on dancing with their
    heads
(But only God, he said, can create a language).

Journalists proffered, on platters of silence,
Split noses, and sliced-off ears and lips—

♦ ♦ ♦

Chastened, I listened. Then for the belly-dancer
(Who would not dance on my table, would not kiss me
Through her veil, spoke to me only
Through the mouth
Of her demon-mask
Warrior drummer)

I composed a bouquet—a tropic, effulgent
Puff of publicity, in the style of Attar,

And saw myself translated by the drummer
Into her liquid
Lashing shadow, those arabesques of God,

That thorny fount.

♦ ♦ ♦

. . . would I know there were such a place, with three old walnut trees,
near Isfahan? Is there?

—*James Buchan*

Who will dare to say to me that this is an evil foreign land.

—*Anna Akhmatova*

What follows, a little apologetically, is a microcosm of what seems to me the most important development in English letters over the last decade or so, namely, the reemergence or rediscovery of Ted Hughes. Mutatis mutandis—with different readers and different poems (although, obviously, I love "my" poem!)—it should be imagined as enacting itself thousands of times up and down the country, and abroad. The personal part of it, that which concerns me, is unimportant and accidental, and is offered with some embarrassment.

I was born in 1957, the year *The Hawk in the Rain* was published. At school in the 1970s, I was given poems of Hughes to read (never the best way—it's still put me off Auden and Larkin). I supposed for a long time that he, an Englishman of a peculiar deep Englishness and a writer on animals and elemental subjects, just didn't have much to say to me, a German of a peculiar shallow Englishness and a writer on human and anecdotal subjects. I bought his books but didn't read them much.

One day in *The Times Literary Supplement* I saw a poem that changed all that for good. I don't know what poem it was, maybe "Walt" or "For the Duration" or "The Last of the 1st/5th Lancashire Fusiliers," something about a relative who had survived World War I. Thenceforth, I read Hughes differently—as a contemporary, one of the three or four poets whose books I waited for and who made everyone else faintly superfluous. His prose—the huge book on Shakespeare, the sublimely intelligent and unconventional writing in *Winter Pollen*—the poems at the end of the 1995 *New Selected Poems*, the Ovid versions he did, first for James Lasdun and me, and then in his own *Tales from Ovid*, and the irresistible *Birthday Letters*. This tremendous surge of creative work finally and belatedly—in the eyes of my cogenerationists and me—brought Hughes out from under the everlasting 1960s and his extended tenure of the laureateship.

I haven't, in the end, chosen "Walt," or anything from Ovid, or one of the *Birthday Letters*, or that amazing poem-cum–deficit reckoning called "The Other," but one of the earlier, uncollected pieces from the *New Selected Poems*, called "Remembering Teheran." It mattered to me to get a sense of approaching something if not new, then at least disregarded or beyond the pale.

In many ways, it contradicts one's received idea of Hughes. It's not about England or about animals, it's funny and occasional (as I remember him writing somewhere that almost the whole recent output of the Western tradition has become), and exotic and diagnostic, and it deploys the poet himself in it as a kind of pawn. It is very much "my kind of poem." I wish I'd written it. More to the point, it's the kind of thing Lawrence might have written on his travels, in Germany or Italy or Australia or Ceylon or New Mexico—and perhaps did write, although I couldn't find any especially close analogy, not in Lawrence's poems, anyway. Perhaps it's not too surprising that Hughes didn't include it in any of his books of the period (if I understand the arrangement of the *New Selected Poems*, he wrote it in the 1970s): it would tend to "fall outside the frame," as you say in German. On the other hand, it would be a natural for any anthology on "abroad thoughts," of expatriation, of centrifugal musings and scrutinies. Think how well it would go with Elizabeth Bishop's poems about Brazil, Bunting's "Aus Dem Zweiten Reich," Cummings's poem about the police and the Communists in Paris, Brodsky's divertimenti from Italy, Mexico, or England, or—I think, best of all—with Robert Lowell's "Buenos Aires." It's a type of poem that comes to us from the Romantics, from Shelley's "Mont Blanc" and Goethe's "Roman Elegies," but touristically and culturally and interrogatively extended by our century; where the unsettled self takes its bearings ("In my room at the Hotel Continentál / a thousand miles from nowhere"—Lowell) and shyly or intrepidly goes out to encounter a changed world that reflects it differently, better, or perhaps not at all. "*Je*" is not "*un autre*"—perhaps, think of Bishop or Brodsky, is even more "*je*" than it ever could be "at home"—it is simply "*ailleurs*," and perhaps nowhere more so than in "Remembering Teheran."

The poem is spun out of Hughes's nerve endings. "How it hung," it starts, itself hanging, echoing Sylvia Plath's desert poem "The

Hanging Man" and, more dimly, Dylan Thomas's "I sang in my chains like the sea." Prometheus is not far to seek.

> How it hung
> In the electrical loom
> Of the Himalayas—I remember
> The spectre of a rose.

(How incredibly beautifully, by the way, Hughes writes free verse: the breaths of the first two *h*'s heavily, almost reluctantly muted into the drone of "hung," "loom" a foreshadowing of "Himalayas," "electrical" generating "spectre," the Persian picture-postcard prettiness of "rose" countermanded and finally more menacing than anything else. Isn't this tensile music Poe or Tennyson by any other means?) In another poem, that "hanging" might have been used for the structuring of the whole piece, and Hughes uses the word three more times, and maybe its presence is felt further in the army flag resting "for a few minutes," and in the water "dangling from a pipe," but the growth of the poem outstrips even such a helpless and dégagé thing as hanging. Nor is it bracketed by the flag that, at sunset, "rested for a few minutes then began to flow North" (how proud any dissident East European or South American poet would be of the two contrasting coats of the pathetic and the automatic in those glorious lines!). Instead, the poem keeps being broken open, again and again, by the pressure of its strange and abundant material. In an odd way, it gets out of sync with itself. It has its funny moment in the delicious story of the blind tap in Hughes's room and the squad of baby plumbers sent in to "fathom" it—and then an asterisk, and then "I had a funny moment." Unforgettable things crowd into the poem: the "three stoned-looking Mercedes" (a pure droll outrageous equivocation between the two senses of "stoned"—but no more than "loom" at the beginning is equivocal too: it's as though what Hughes sees and experiences is so strange he needs to call upon words in many different senses all at once) that bring back a decade of newsreel from Beirut; the gorgeous Latinity of "Eyes and skulls / Adapted to sunstroke"; the naked vulnerability of "I knew I was in the wrong century / and wrongly dressed" (a little like Lowell's "I was the worse for wear");

the Lowellian pairing of "the tense, abnormal thistles"—as indeed much of the poem is reminiscent of Lowell, and the line "In the Shah's Evin Motel" *is* Lowell just as much as "In Boston the Hancock Life Insurance Building's / beacon flared" is Lowell; the clever, helpless agglomerations of language, thickening and emulsifying, in "The desert's bloom of dust, the petroleum smog, the transistor commotion" (what a humming line!); to the beautiful line—which wouldn't look out of place in Crane (or hemicrane) or Eliot—"Scintillating through the migraine" to the final discord, "That thorny fount."

Necessarily, I think, the poem of a foreign place, or the poem of the self in a foreign place (the house that Jack didn't build), is a poem of incomplete witness. Lowell's "Buenos Aires" is an intermittent line drawn around next to nothing: leather, abrasiveness, neoclassical curves, "frowning, starch-collared crowds" (strangely both like and unlike the "cowed, compliant fish" in "For the Union Dead"). "Remembering Teheran" has an electrifying diligence about it, a continual openness to impressions, to terror, to strangeness, to awe. As it takes us through politics, religion, sex, history, technology, climate, geography, and what all else, it takes up imagery drawn from thunder, drought, electricity, music, malfunction, plants and insects, and harmonizes them, so that we lose our sense of these things originally having been distinct. It's a glorious synesthetic operetta (Hughes can be extremely funny) made from his sympathetic crackle to the crackle of the place. With his living phrasing, his imaginative connections, even his spiny dashes and asterisks, he fuses things together and himself with them, and causes the thorns of strangeness to flow, and then to sing.

HEANEY'S HAIKU

1.1.87
Dangerous pavements.
But I face the ice this year
With my father's stick.

"1.1.87" follows the title poem in *Seeing Things* (with its *Tempest*-like reference to "my undrowned father"), about an earlier near thing, and "The Ash Plant," about Patrick Heaney's last days and willing spirit ("He'll never rise again but he is ready"); and it is itself followed by the exquisite, absolving dream of "An August Night" ("August" surely stressed on the second syllable, as in "great" or "auspicious": his father's hands "two ferrets, / Playing all by themselves in a moonlit field," a charmed take on the literary trope, the hands of the dying man plucking at the hairs of a blanket) and by one of Seamus Heaney's poems about the importance of keeping on and toughness and fixity of purpose, this one called "Field of Vision." (There seem so many of these that, on reflection, this eldest son was much more delicate and suggestible than he cared to appear.)

Often the poems in Heaney's books are put together half-overlapping, like fish scales or roof tiles. The burden of a theme or an argument or (often) a geometrical conceit is taken up in poem after poem: the concentric rounds of *The Haw Lantern*; the wavy tide lines and touch lines of *Seeing Things*. The stress on any individual piece is shared among its neighbors. They bend to a common purpose.

Heaney's mother, Margaret, had died in 1984, and is commemorated in the sonnet sequence "Clearances" in *The Haw Lantern*. His father died in 1986. One of the suggested "lines" that abound in *Seeing Things* is that of moving into the senior generation, as though life were Thermopylae. (I am put in mind of the French noun *le trépas*, a poeticism or archaism, I think, meaning "death," but from stumble, or "trespass." A line too far.) Another line, another hurdle or hurtle, is the new year. "1.1.87" combines both. It marks the beginning of a new and ultimate dispensation. This is the way life is going to be from now on. Heaney is weakened, and quite possibly frightened; typically he describes himself as strengthened and emboldened: "But I face the ice this year / With my father's stick."

I am always surprised the word "armed" does not feature in the poem, so adversarial is it, so imbued with the idea of life as struggle. When I try to recite "1.1.87" from memory—not much of an ask, you'd have thought—I often put it in; I conclude, if it doesn't actually appear, it's only because it's somehow there already. The old sorcerer has gone on, the old magician, the old Prospero, but he has left his wand to the no longer young sorcerer. In breach there is continuity, in loss there is reinforcement.

I reviewed *Seeing Things* at some length when it appeared, and I was actually teaching it when a student pointed out to me that "1.1.87" is a haiku. I don't mean to advertise my impercipience, but somehow this was something that caught me entirely unawares. The great Seamus Heaney, at a great and terrible juncture of his life, writing a haiku! Reacting as (his dedicatee Derek Mahon's) Basho would have done—and if not Basho, then a schoolkid.

I am not sure if it is the humble poet of fifty—newly on his own, and into his own—trying his hand at the not-quite-serious haiku form of the beginner, or the licensed tyro ("One-off, impulsive"), crashing the summit of centuries of court tradition: "1.1.87" partakes of both.

At any rate, something in me finds it almost unbearably moving that in among the quatrains and sonnets, and facing the eleven-thirteen-eleven-syllable "August Night" (is that a supersize haiku?), Heaney slips in this inconspicuous compression of a compression, with every bit of the traditional obliqueness, every edge of implication for the future that is ascribed to the Japanese form. Gratitude for the ash plant—"Guardian of travellers and psychopomp"—is matched by gratitude to (in every sense) form.

BASIL BUNTING

Just as there are some faces that are a gift to the photographer (Artaud, Patti Smith), so certain lives are a gift to the biographer. These are, broadly, of two types: the hard and gemlike, abbreviated, compressed, intense; and the lengthy, implausible, exfoliated, whiskery, picaresque. Vehement or even violent emotion is good, overt drama, prominent contacts or associations, sudden changes of orientation, movement through different societies and settings; physical distance is helpful (the father of letter writing), marriages (more than one—important), a hint of scandal or controversy is useful, achievement and neglect, both in moderation (poverty is a great preservative, celebrity or laurels a terrible corrosive, too-obvious or excessive greatness is dreary). A late flowering is ideal, but not essential. For the former, one might nominate Trakl, Laforgue, Keats, and Shelley (I don't think I breathed while I was reading Richard Holmes's *Shelley: The Pursuit* all those years ago); for a rare, artful blending of the long and short, one can't do better than Rimbaud and Hölderlin; and for the latter, Hamsun, Yeats, Shaw—and Bunting. Incidentally, or maybe not, Bunting also shows beautifully on film and still photographs, from the waggingly imperialed steely young man ("one of Ezra's more savage disciples," Yeats called him) posing in Rapallo in 1930 or 1931 on the cover of the New Directions *Complete Poems*, to the waggingly eyebrowed, scruff-bearded, snaggletoothed, twinkling-eyed dome he presented as an old man in his eighties.

Basil Bunting—not a nom de guerre but his actual given name, as Pound hastened to assure a doubtful Harriet Monroe, long-suffering and mostly tame editor of *Poetry*—was the missing link back to the heyday and personalities of modernism. He wrote little ("The mason stirs: / Words! / Pens are too light. / Take a chisel to write"), but what he wrote ever more powerfully endures. Reading him now, there is an overpowering drench of the 1920s and 1930s, and a suggestion of how the style of progressive verse might have gone on, if Pound hadn't disappeared into funny money, the Cantos, and obloquy, or Eliot into verse drama and High Anglicanism. Bunting's *Complete Poems* are a tantalizingly small and pure uchronia—and as for his life, his model in these things was Walter Raleigh.

"A Life of Bunting," then, was for many years the most obviously "missing" book I could think of. For all the reasons—the ticked boxes—above; for a beautiful relation between the long life as old as the century (1900–1985) and the small, sharply flavored work (the *Complete Poems* are with difficulty bulked up to 240 pages: they make Elizabeth Bishop look lax if not garrulous); for the unusual way time—history—is precipitated in a literary life. "Bunting had a knack of being in the thick of things," Richard Burton observes in this first proper biography of the poet: it feels like a flagrant understatement. Adventures of the mind are two a penny; here are actual, palpable scrapes: individuals sent to kill him, crowds baying for his blood, a life spent on four continents (and at sea), never far from the bread line. In 1934, when he wasn't even halfway into it, and most of the most outlandish things still lay ahead of him, and he was stuck in the Canary Islands, William Carlos Williams wrote: "Bunting is living the life, I don't know how sufficiently to praise him for it. But it can't be very comfortable to exist that way. I feel uneasy not to be sending him his year's rent and to be backing at the same time a book of my own poems." Imagine Tintin not as a supposed journalist with a cowlick but Haddock-bearded and a rare poet, and you get

Bunting. Even if he had written nothing at all, his life would still be worth telling: as an extravagant shape, as an example of what is possible, or just to give oneself a fright.

Bunting was born the son of a progressively minded doctor in Scotswood-on-Tyne. He was not a Quaker, but was educated at Quaker boarding schools. In 1918 he was sent to prison for being a conscientious objector; this seems to have involved a certain deliberateness, even willfulness, on Bunting's part. Quite often, Bunting's life frays into uncertainty, competing versions, colorful mists of low factual density, ultimately the beguiling wraiths of myths, suitably embellished by himself or the other gifted embellishers among whom he mostly lived. (Take a bow, Ford Madox Ford, take two!) Pound tells the story (in Canto LXXIV) of "Bunting / doing six months after that war was over / as pacifist tempted by chicken but declined to approve / of war." Burton agrees that the *Sun*-worthy "Pacifist Tempted by Chicken"—when Bunting went on a hunger strike, a freshly roasted chicken was said to have been brought to his cell on several successive days by his jailers—sounds a little too good to be true. On his release, he enrolled in the newish London School of Economics, but left in 1922 without taking his degree. He was radical, brilliant, but also "a great poseur," feckless, improvident, and prone to "nerve storms": the type of individual that looks if not to poetry, then to some other reevaluative hierarchy to adjust his low standing, his perceived lack of usefulness, his reversed poles. A scalene peg. He was impatient with institutions, with convention, with medium term thinking and planning, with England. He began to go abroad: to Denmark ("on his bicycle the Dane is a beautiful creature, but off it he does not feel at home, and looks as awkward as an automaton"), to Paris, to Rapallo. In 1924 he met Pound there, supposedly—the inevitable mythopoeic embellishment—on top of a local hill. "Villon," his first long poem, was written in 1925, and published, with Pound's help—one might say, passim—in *Poetry* five years later. The poem won a $50 prize, which straightaway went to pay the expenses incurred by the birth of a daughter, Bourtai, in 1931. (Bunting's three children with his first, American wife, Marian, all had Persian names; two later children, born to his Persian wife, Sima, were called Maria and Thomas.)

Between 1925 and 1940, Bunting was really all over the place—not that that couldn't be said about the time before and much of the time after as well. He came and went between Rapallo and England, where he took a job as a music critic; he did good work, breaking lances for very old and very new music, Monteverdi and Schoenberg alike, but he was never enthusiastic about employment in general, or journalism in particular, and was always grateful when they lapsed from him. (I think of Les Murray's lovely and perplexed line, "In the midst of life, we are in employment.") His relations with London, and with "southrons" in general, were not straightforward, though not as negative as they are sometimes painted either. He acquired a temporary patron in the form of a rich American widow, Margaret de Silver. He had book plans, rather English subjects, all: one on Dickens, one on music halls, one on prisons, but he was never that sort of jobbing writer. He lived for six months in 1928 in a shepherd's cottage in Northumberland. He visited Berlin, and (perhaps the only Englishman to do so) hated it. In Venice he met Marian Culver—she was a recent Columbia graduate "doing" Europe—and married her on Long Island. He spent time in New York with his Poundian confrères Williams and Zukofsky, but (small surprise) there were no openings for him in the States; "It was better to go back and see how long we could live on nothing in Italy—rather than the very short time you can live on nothing in the United States." It is a little hard to imagine how the Buntings got by in Italy, and the biography doesn't really help. "We have very few descriptions of the Buntings' family life at this (or any other) time," Burton notes. Marian had a remittance from her family; he may have been helped by his mother (who joined them in Rapallo periodically; his father was dead); I don't think there was much paid work involved. Bunting advances the perverse and implausible claim, "It seems as though Italy were the only climate in which I can get up any energy." He sailed, he taught himself Persian, but when you look at him lolling in white ducks and singlet, an eccentric monument, ripped, evenly tanned and rather dazzling, everything about him seems to scream *dolce far niente* at you.

Then, whether it was because of the increasing expense of Italy, the disagreeable impact of fascism, the still more disagreeable relaying of Fascist and anti-Semitic paroles from his friend Pound, or just his own innate restlessness, Bunting upped sticks and the family moved to the Canary Islands, a Spanish possession sixty miles off the coast of southern Morocco: "Just got back from a visit to the local Sahara. Seven or eight miles wide and ever so many long, sand covered with loose pieces of pumice about as big as a man's head. A sort of pale grey thorn scrub, and a few camels eating it. A sort of green shrub much rarer, and a goat or two eating that." A second daughter, Roudaba, was born in Tenerife in 1934, but mostly Bunting was pretty wretched. He wrote to Pound that "the people of this island [are] so unspeakable, and the food so uneatable, they make prolonged residence impossible, in spite of great cash saving." Out of aesthetic disappointment or anthropological pique, he declined to learn Spanish. (Bunting, born during the Boer War as Ladysmith was relieved, has a rather Empire way with him: smartly dividing the world into good and bad natives, with little in between; but for the appearance of that brusque trait, he would seem to have made rather a bad expatriate.) At the end of three years and much moving around, Bunting "escaped from Tenerife," only, alas, to return to London.

Shortly thereafter, Marian, pregnant with a third child, borrowed a pound from her mother-in-law, took her daughters, and went back to Wisconsin and divorced her husband of seven years. Bunting took it unexpectedly hard. He wrote little or nothing for the best part of thirty years. Pound observed drily—in his customary horrid epistolary style—"las' I heard of Bzl his wif had left and took the chillens. It wuz preyin on his cerebrum/why? Some folks iz never satisfied." Bunting managed to buy a fishing boat and lived on it for a year—*The Thistle*: even the name is a sort of protest—cutting down on his expenses and his human contacts, drifting in self-imposed quarantine. It's a suggestive image for a man who hadn't been able to make a go of things abroad, couldn't then stand to be on his home island, and could regroup only in the changeable element. He sold the boat, went to America, achieved nothing (wasn't even able to see the children), came home again. The war came at a good time for him—as wars are apt to do for individuals in abject or complicated circumstances—though he had a hard time actually getting taken. In July 1940, he was finally accepted by the RAF, after being turned down by the army and the navy. (Having very poor sight—he wore glasses as thick as pint pots—it was said he was allowed by a sympathetic doctor to memorize the eye chart.) Bunting began in Balloon Operations in the North Sea, then was sent to Persia, fought his way from Basra to Tripoli, served in Malta, then in the Sicilian invasion, then in 1944 returned to Persia, this time as an intelligence officer. It wouldn't have been Bunting if it hadn't involved the occasional spree. Driving the lead lorry of a large convoy in Scotland and spotting a brewery, he promptly took the turning, and there resulted the inevitable free drinks all round—but it wouldn't do to overstress these Compton Mackenzie–style yarns, which seem to crop up variously at all points of Bunting's life. The astonishing thing, rather, is that he performed at all: he worked, he was reliable, he was smart, he was respectful, "all the stupid military things," as he put it. For the suspicious, antiestablishment, conscientiously objecting Quaker boy of twenty years before, it was quite a turnaround. Perhaps it was the acceptance of a higher, common cause—the defeat of totalitarianism—to which he submitted himself; perhaps the corners of the air force and intelligence in which he found himself were sufficiently unconventional and improvised and reshuffled to attract and keep his loyalty and devotion. Or again, it was the Empire, which as a sort of blend of home and abroad didn't have quite the stifling values of home. "Action is a lust," he discovered, for which it was perhaps worth abandoning the reflective life, not that it was ever a consciously taken decision. At any rate, "I learned my Wing-Commander-act."

Then of course, there was Persia. Bunting adored Persia, "a country where they still make beautiful things by hand." Isfahan was his favorite city in the world. He loved the courtliness, the hospitality, the pleasure seeking, the childlike color and drama of the Persians: after all, they sang to the same qualities in him. He delighted his hosts by having named his children after their heroes and by speaking an antique form of their language that he had learned from reading the tenth-century poet Ferdowsi; "it was as if someone came along in England speaking a Chaucerian mode." If there was a place for him anywhere, then surely it was in the wonderfully named Luristan. The tribal Bunting took tea (and much else) with the tribes of Persia. In 1947 and 1948, Bunting assisted our man in Teheran, met and married a Kurdish girl, Sima Alladadian; left the Foreign Office—a sort of sideways move—to become Teheran correspondent for the *Times*; in 1952 he was finally expelled by the nationalist—and nationalizing—Mossadeq government. It was a loss all round, because Bunting really seems to have understood and liked the place, and managed to operate in it better than most. A press colleague admitted: "He told us two years ago what was going to happen in Persia, & the Foreign Office said Pooh! & so did the oil people." He wasn't easily intimidated either. At the Ritz in Teheran there was a sanctioned demonstration that Bunting insisted on joining: "I walked into the crowd and stood amongst them and shouted DEATH TO MR. BUNTING! with the best of them, and nobody took the slightest notice of me." As I say, Tintin.

If it had happened in more recent times, Bunting would have enjoyed kudos as an expert, with his serialized memoirs and semi-detached television appearances on daytime sofas to look forward to. But in 1952, things weren't like that. He returned to England, with a new young family, to find himself basically unemployable. The Buntings moved in with his mother and braced themselves for hard times. Long absence disqualified Bunting for state assistance, and the better part of what he had done while away did not redound to his credit for the simple reason that he was not able to talk about it. He was rejected for better jobs and did badly paid clerical tasks: proofreading—if you will, a man with his eyesight—bus and train timetables, gently revising sensitive trade unionists' grammar. A man meeting him for the first time was dumbfounded by his humdrum semimilitary appearance: "the story-book image of a scout-master." In 1954, he got a job as subeditor (working nights) on the *Newcastle Daily Journal*; in 1957, he moved to the *Evening Chronicle*.

For ten years—not the dishonored prophet but the returned expat and expoet in his own country—he led a plaintive, low-key existence, grumbling about money, feeling he had missed his moment, whenever that might have been. It was from this condition that he was rescued by the young Newcastle poet Tom Pickard who, having picked up a couple of leads as to Bunting's importance and local availability, telephoned him and shortly afterward turned up on his doorstep. With Pickard's encouragement, Bunting was tied into a local writing scene in Newcastle (he read several times at the newly opened Morden Tower), he found publishers for some of his old poems, and even began writing again. His long poem "Briggflatts" was written on a commuter train; the last of his "sonatas" (it's only twenty pages), it was cut down from something apparently very much longer. It was published to widespread acclaim in 1965, and Bunting was rediscovered (mostly for the first time). He was able to retire from the *Chronicle* and parlay his continuing existence—here after all was something like the Stephen Spender of Modernism, he had known Yeats, was an associate of Pound's, could remember Eliot as a progressive—into readings and teaching jobs in America, grants from the Arts Council and Northern Arts, radio and television appearances on the BBC, and then—surely mistakenly—honorific presidencies (in the sense that he was honoring them) of the Poetry Society (at a particularly horrible time in its history) and Northern Arts. The scout master was elbowed aside by a strange new act: the Grand Old Man, the English Celt (listen to the recording of "Briggflatts," where he seems to have caught Pound's Scottish accent). Oxford published his *Collected Poems* in 1978 and a posthumous *Uncollected Poems* in 1991. He continued to be shunted around from house to house (he never seemed to find rest or comfort), wrote little, but had leisure to opine and reminisce. He didn't have much use for the work of his contemporaries and juniors (his fellow Celts David Jones and Hugh MacDiarmid were partial exceptions), but was on the whole pleasant about it. A breezy manner ("Unabashed boys and girls may enjoy them. This book is theirs"), a few eclectic names— Pound, Zukofsky, Whitman, Wordsworth, Spenser, Horace, Villon, Ferdowsi, Manuchehri—and a few ideas—poetry as music, poetry as carving and parsimony—resonated perhaps a little more after the stifling Amis-Larkin fifties and sixties. The Beatles—Northern Songs!—bought expensive limited editions of his books and took care to be seen reading them. Bunting died in hospital in Hexham in 1985; his ashes were scattered in the Quaker graveyard at Brigflatts that he had first visited as a small boy in the early century.

And the poetry? It's acquired an oddly strategic quality. So much depends on . . . Basil Bunting. Without Bunting, Pound is a greatly diminished figure, the enabler of Joyce and Eliot and Hemingway but of no one of real consequence since the '20s; with Bunting he remains central past the 1960s, and England for the first time plays in the Modernist colors alongside Ireland and the United States. Donald Davie wrote that Bunting was "very important in the literary history of the present century as just about the only accredited British member of the Anglo-American poetic avant-garde of the Twenties and Thirties." Yes, he holds the century together, but almost more important he holds the two sides of the Atlantic together as well. Richard Burton cites Martin Seymour-Smith, for whom Bunting was the only English poet to solve the problem of how to assimilate the lively spirit of American poetry without losing his own sense of identity (a nice and a true description). So somehow the persistence and adequacy of British English in the twentieth century is also dependent on Bunting. I think all of this is true, and obviously nowhere more so than in "Briggflatts," which looks across fifty years at a harsh, cold, bright reality in curt speech that is in touch with Ezra Pound's "The Seafarer." Hence, America, Modernism (the sealing couplet), the century, and England all together, with a touch of sweetness:

Stocking to stocking, jersey to jersey,
head to a hard arm,
they kiss under the rain,
bruised by their marble bed.
In Garsdale, dawn;
at Hawes, tea from the can.
Rain stops, sacks
steam in the sun, they sit up.
Copper-wire moustache,
sea-reflecting eyes
and Baltic plainsong speech
declare: By such rocks
men killed Bloodaxe.

Partly following Bunting himself, Burton is often at pains to defend Bunting from Pound. He groans when a critic remarks that you could track Bunting "everywhere in Pound's snow." But I think it's a question of the intention with which his name is brought up: Pound is not only and everywhere a menace, and in any case Bunting was never his creature: "I don't want to minimise my debt to Ezra nor my admiration for his work, which should have 'influenced' everybody, but my ideas were shaped before I met him and my technique I had to concoct for myself." Bunting gave Pound the magnificent punny formula "DICHTEN = CONDENSARE": poetry is not so much to make new as to make dense. He went through Shakespeare's sonnets cutting lines and shuffling phrases. I can't imagine a Pound reader not enjoying Bunting (the change of ear and vernacular), and vice versa. Both seemed to enjoy writing English like a foreign language, whether it's Pound's "The harsh acts of your levity! / Many and many, / I am hung here, a scare-crow for lovers" or Bunting's "You idiot! What makes you think decay will / never stink from your skin?" Both wrote many poems that are pure trope, ubi sunts and aubades and the rest of them. The distance between translation and original poem, between lyric and "mask" or "persona" is closed. You get Bunting as a Japanese hermit ("I do not enjoy being poor, / I've a passionate nature. / My tongue / clacked a few prayers"), Bunting as a Middle Eastern nymphet (in "Birthday Greeting"), Bunting as a queasy Eliotish visitor to Berlin ("Women swarm in Tauentsien-strasse. / Clients of Nollendorferplatz cafes, / shadows on sweaty glass, / hum, drum on the table"), Bunting as a splendidly tiddly businessman ("I'm not fit for a commonplace world / any longer, I'm / bound for the City, // cashregister, adding-machine, / rotary stencil. / Give me another // double whiskey and fire-extinguisher, / George. Here's / Girls! Girls!"), Bunting as an aging madam in "The Well of Lycopolis." Language becomes the sum of its possibilities. Bunting extended Pound's writ to Persian and the Queen's English. To me, it's a virtuous and a mutually reinforcing association. One reads both with the same senses and nerves and parts of one's brain, the author of *A Lume Spento* (1908) and *Lustra* (1916) and the author of *Redimiculum Matellarum* (1930) and *Loquitur* (1965), the author of *Cathay* (1915) and the author of *Chomei at Toyama* (1932), the author of *The Cantos* and the author of *Briggflatts* (1965). Both espoused a fresh, flexible, original style, the style of young men for thousands of years, assembled from beauty, learning, satire, and irreverence. The Bunting who in the early twenties and in his own early twenties first approached Ezra Pound wrote: "I believed then, as now, that his 'Propertius' was the finest of modern poems. Indeed, it was the one that gave me the notion that poetry wasn't altogether impossible in the XX century." Pound, I think, remained for Bunting the poet of "Homage to Sextus Propertius," and nothing that Bunting wrote is very far from it: the "Sonatas," the "Odes," and the "Overdrafts," as Bunting amiably called his own translations.

W. S. GRAHAM

The Scottish poet W. S. Graham—Sydney Graham, but also "Troubleyouas Greyhim," "Double Yes Gee," and "Sadknee Graham" (he had a patella removed when he fell twenty feet onto concrete, but strangely the drunken accident happened after the sobriquet), also *via* Jock (the generic name for a Scotsman) Graham, "Joke Grim," and numerous other variants—was born in 1918, and died twenty-eight years ago, in 1986. Death has treated him better than it treats most poets—the "no doubt I shall have a boom" of Pound's Propertius stands revealed as a false prospectus, a false Propertius, even—perhaps better than his life did. An outstandingly well-chosen volume of *Selected Poems* (presumably by Christopher Reid) in 1996 followed three years after what you'd have to call a book of rejected poems (drafts and manuscript pages, etc.) titled *Aimed at Nobody*, and then a book of letters from one of the more fascinating writers—and one of the more interesting lives—of twentieth-century poetry, and a large and beautiful sea-colored *Collected Poems*. Both books are lovingly and aptly edited, the one by two long-term friends and correspondents of the poet, the other by a younger British poet.

The fascination and the interest are almost completely separate in Graham; the one is stylistic, the other biographical-circumstantial; the one is in the poetry, the other in the letters—which are by no means to be described as the lesser book. Both should be read—though not necessarily together. Each is an absolutely characteristic product of the man and his life, the one a sound or texture, the other maybe a taste.

The poetry—to begin with that—seems to me to exist on the edge of many things: abstraction, mannerism, Scottishness, a whimsical, almost childish falsetto, a homemade philosophy of reading and communication. The poems were written by the sea's edge, in Cornwall, mostly at night, and on a typewriter, and I fancy that these things show too: a slightly spooked sense of one's own eccentric noise heading out into great expanses of space and time. "TAPTAP. Are you reading that taptap / I send out to you along / My element?" "The great abeyance," to use Plath's term for the sea—though it would serve as well for night, or a phantom readership—that was what Graham wrote into. Graham is a specialist, almost a technician of voice. His speech is never natural, and never quiet, but begins unexpectedly, and continues unpredictably. In letters he starts, "Yes, it is myself," or "It is indeed myself, Graham." He proposed once to begin a radio broadcast of his poetry with "Can you hear me?" He makes other writers appear as though they did without grammar, and without surprise. As he puts it, he is the "flying translator, translating / English into English." He writes as though he had invented the essential miracle of poetry, those marks that speak to us from the page, and continue to do so even after the poet's death. The mixture of detachment and address, of generosity and caginess, the loss of the "fourth wall" of conventional illusionist poetry, the harping on the strange, depleted nature of what is transacted between writer and reader—all these characterize Graham's mature work. By way of one preliminary instance of his sound and his method, here is one part of "Approaches to How They Behave," from 1970:

> The words are mine. The thoughts are all
> Yours as they occur behind
> The bat of your vast unseen eyes.
> These words are as you see them put

Down on the dead-still page. They have
No ability above their station.
Their station on silence is exact.
What you do with them is nobody's business.

I hold no special brief for the early poems of the '40s and '50s—
they strike me as having been, for almost everyone then writing, two
rank bad decades for poetry. Rather like John Berryman, his close
contemporary in America, Graham started off writing a larded id-
iolect of poemese, derived from Yeats, Hopkins, and Dylan Thomas.
The letters show him at pains to try and simplify the calamitous
diction of his peers (David Wright, Edwin Morgan), but the poems don't show too many signs that he was receptive to his own
teaching. A short poem like "Gigha"—it's the name of a tiny Hebri-
dean island—shows all the problems of a kind of second-generation
Imagism:

That firewood pale with salt and burning green
Outfloats its men who waved with a sound of drowning
Their saltcut hands over mazes of this rough bay.
Quietly this morning beside the subsided herds
Of water I walk. The children wade the shallows.
The sun with long legs wades into the sea.

I suppose our time tends to punish literary gestures as much as the
1940s rewarded them, but as far as I'm concerned, the attempted addition of drama to the Imagist recipe produces only distracting clutter. Is the poem action or contemplation? Is it waving or drowning?
It seems not to know. "Outfloats" and "saltcut" have a deadly callous
literariness, it almost defies belief that they are the words of a man
who lived among fishermen most of his life and often went out on
trawlers, "beside the subsided herds" is ghastly euphuism, "mazes" is
pointless, and the repetition of "wade" only serves to weaken the
only tolerable line—though of course I like "green"—the last. Oh for
the Coan ghost of T. E. Hulme, or, geographically closer, Eliot's lovely
and cogent "Rannoch, near Glencoe."

Similar strictures might be applied to most of the first third of the *Collected*, though, like most poets, Graham continued to have an ill-advised soft spot for his early production. Even the celebrated long poem "The Nightfishing" of 1955 (and hence a direct contemporary of Berryman's "Homage to Mistress Bradstreet"), though some sort of tour de force, doesn't have much to do with the poet that W. S. Graham became. It leaves me not exactly cold, but lukewarm, though I like Graham's ambition for it: "if it made somebody seasick (a good unliterary measurement) I would be pleased." The new emphasis on "unliterary," however, and the suggested conversion rate of poetry (the supreme fiction, remember) and reality are both salutary, and indicative of the future turn of Graham's writing. "The sea sails in. The quay opens wide its arms / And waves us loose." The sea, also, "as metaphor of the sea. The boat / Rides in its fires." Graham is at moments somewhere close to Stevens's terrain, "Imaginary Trees with Real Birds in Them."

Along with night, with language and typewriter noise, with Scottish words and Cornish place-names, with painter friends and spectral readers, with his early memories of Greenock, a sugar port west of Glasgow, the sea takes up residence in Graham's world. These things offer bearings, quiddity, scale. They accommodate the highly self-conscious movements of Graham's poems, which may be memory based (like "The Greenock Dialogues") or fictional (like the sequences "Malcolm Mooney's Land" or "Ten Shots of Mister Simpson" or "Clusters Travelling Out," about Arctic exploration, a photographer, and on communication among prisoners, respectively), or again consist almost entirely of his highly characteristic ontological maneuverings and jockeyings. But the temptation to be abstract is denied by the properties and settings of the poems. Even the writing about words and the writing and reading of them has something pragmatic and physical about it. Sometimes, it's the beautiful Scots vocabulary—surely unarguably a tender and more palpable speech, and in any case the language of his childhood, and always produced by Graham with exquisite tact and timing and naturalness. (As an "exile" in England, and, though as Scottish as anyone, a nonparticipant in the sort of Scots supremacist renaissance of the midcentury, Graham was in a difficult position with the likes of Hugh MacDiarmid, who—much as Marx saw communism as something on the way to the ultimate nirvana of socialism—proposed Scots as a way station toward the ultimate grail of writing in Gaelic. Graham for his part disdained what he called the "plastic Scots" of some of his peers—a thing, incidentally, that shows signs of returning in contemporary Scottish writing. I admire his language politics; a poet should be able to help himself to what he needs, rather than take politically inspired direction from himself or, worse, from others.)

There is something rickety and moving about these poems of the 1960s and '70s, even the most stodgy and naturalistic of them, that for me "The Nightfishing" didn't have. A Graham poem is as unconventionally homespun as a Cornell box or a Calder mobile. He writes English like someone working with coat hangers, sometimes three nouns in unpredictable concatenation, sometimes three verbs, sometimes even—certainly, it feels like it—three prepositions. The very short two- or three-stress lines that are his most characteristic form contribute to this impression of language being *bent*:

> In fact last Tuesday afternoon
> I locked myself in my coat and closed
> The door and threw myself on the mercy
> Of rainy December, a new month.
> One step two steps three step more.
> Four step five step I went falling
> Into the outofdoors world
> To give myself a shake to shake
> The words I live on up a bit.
> I see an old tin can in a hedge.
> It is not speaking. Here I am
> On Tuesday the   of December
> At five o'clock walking the road
> Between the whining, beaded hedges [...]
> Now as the blinders whistle for dusk
> And my simple sophisticated boots

Clip on the road as my metrenome
You should look out for me coming up
Soon to be seen from your side.

Every (absent) comma has been thought about. More naïvely trust-
worthy than Cummings, less learned and more dignified than Berryman, this shows what can yet be done with simple English. The poem
is made of next to nothing and takes place in real time. It reminds
me of what Graham says somewhere in the letters, that he most
likes writing when there is nothing particular requiring to be said.
There is a terrific economy of effect here, without any of the reaching
in "Gigha" or even "The Nightfishing." And yet the poem offers the
Joycean coinage of "metrenome," the echo of Horace in "simple sophisticated," the childish counting chant, the doubling of "shake," the
quiet surprises of "locked" and "falling," the beautifully supplemen-
tary (past and present, active and passive) participial adjectives
"whining" and "beaded" (the sort of thing one might hope to find in
Heaney), and the humble and still somehow grandiose last line. The
whole thing is its own envoi, exquisitely self-making and self-born. It
is characteristically self-involved, and yet its ultimate gesture is toward
the reader.

Even in this "outofdoors" poem, with its oddly rackety title "Nature Is Never Journalistic," there is something fetchingly minute and
what I would call interstitial. It is where Graham habitually exists in
his poems. It is what allows him to say—he has been all round it—
"It is not speaking" of the old tin can in the hedge, and to speak of it,
and perhaps for it. (It is his version of Whitman's "Look for me under your boot-soles.") Graham likes to cast himself nestling between
and behind the words, "Why did you choose this place / For us to
meet? Sit / With me between this word / And this, my furry queen. /
Yet not mistake this / For the real thing." In "Private Poem to Norman MacLeod," he writes: "My dear Norman, / I don't think we will
ever / See each other again / Except through the spaces / We make
occur between / The words to each other." At the end of the extraordinarily beautiful London poem, "The Night City," he writes: "Between the big buildings / I sat like a flea crouched / In the stopped

works of a watch." A recurring word in his work is the Cornish term for a wood louse: "grammarsow":

> Landlice, always my good bedfellows,
> Ride with me in my sweaty seams,
> Come bonny friendly beasts, brother
> To the grammarsow and the word-louse,
> Bite me your presence, keep me awake
> In the cold with work to do, to remember
> To put down something to take back.

It is the least likely of appeals—effortlessly outperforming the echo of Burns's mouse—the punning coinage, "the word-louse," stoutly underwriting the "grammarsow," which satisfyingly links his own name and—via grammar—the language. (The "sweaty seams" of course are also those of language.) These and other small deft creatures are the agency by which Graham obsessively imagines the benign burrowing movement of address in and out of language, through to the other side, the reader's. "To put down something to take back." "Soon to be seen from your side." Coming to a theater near you.

The miniaturism in such passagework—and I mean the Benjaminesque pun—is really why I love Graham. My word "falsetto" was a not quite adequate attempt to suggest the smallness, the tenderness, the maneuverability, and the unconventional resourcefulness of his writing. Here is a late poem from 1980, "The Fifth of May":

> This morning shaving my brain to face the world
> I thought of Love and Life and Death and wee
> Meg Macintosh who sat in front of me
> In school in Greenock blushing at her desk.
> I find under the left nostril difficult,
> Those partisans of stiff hairs holding out
> In their tender glens beneath the rampart of
> The nose and my father's long upperlip.

The subject couldn't be more banal; people exist who would put poems on shaving on the Index. It's pretty much straight *multum in parvo*, which I suppose is an increasingly important part of what I think poetry is for. Time and space—the history of the Clearances, maybe, the landscapes of "glens" and "rampart"—are, as it were, compressed or dissolved into this tiny piece. It reminds me of a poem of Zbigniew Herbert's, "Mr. Cogito's Face in the Mirror," which does much the same thing. Again, it takes place in a slightly accelerated real time, moving through past ("I thought") to present ("I find") to a sort of sostenuto or slow motion ("my father's long upperlip"), which is held at the end. It exhibits the most striking and lovely balance, between the two four-line sentences, between past and present, between large and small, between shaving and blushing. It is probably more obvious in its charm than other poems of Graham's, but I still find it impossible to take against. Repeatedly, incrementally, it defies expectation. There is a surprise (but not a calculation) in almost every line—"my brain," "wee," "I find," "partisans," "tender glens," "my father's long upperlip"—that seems to carry it effortlessly beyond itself, which again, I suppose, is poetry.

There is another class of Graham poem, which is—well, as they say in England, different class. He was anxious not to privilege them himself, but they escape his egalitarian tutelage. "Some of the poems," he wrote, "for me have more emotion in them than others. The Bryan Winter poem shatters me still although it is mine and I just made it up out of my head. Also the Hilton poem and my father's poem. That maybe is to be expected. But that is the kind of poems they are. They are not better for loosening a tear from the eye." Actually, I think they probably are, as I imagine Graham very well knew. "They" being "To Alexander Graham," "Lines on Roger Hilton's Watch," and "Dear Bryan Winter":

> This is only a note
> To say how sorry I am
> You died. You will realise
> What a position it puts
> Me in. I couldn't really
> Have died for you if so
> I were inclined. The carn
> Foxglove here on the wall

Outside your first house
Leans with me standing
In the Zennor wind.

And so on. One can understand Graham; to someone who makes things out of words, all one's successful productions are, so to speak, equivalent. They are all, as it were, one's children, and one loves them all. Everything written about is ennobled—an island, a fishing expedition, a walk, a shave, a friend. But the costliest, and perhaps the hardest of these, is the friend. It is like a jeweler standing by all of his work, even if some of it is from semiprecious materials and some from rubies. Still, it is very rare to have feeling in poetry talked about directly at all. No less an authority than Ezra Pound—and in some ways no more unlikely an authority than Ezra Pound—knew that what matters in poetry is emotion.

One of W. S. Graham's most passionate and prominent supporters was Harold Pinter. "I first read a W. S. Graham poem in 1949," he writes on the jacket of the *Collected*. "It sent a shiver down my spine. Forty-five years later nothing has changed." They are the oddest of pairings, but yet it makes fascinating sense. Both are their own creations. There is Pinter, the liberator of undertones in—especially British—English, of sinister aggression and hatreds, and Graham, who dwells in pleasantness and eerie brusqueness, who talks to himself as I suspect no one else—not even Yeats—has ever talked to himself, and who creates in words gossamer, almost theoretical attachments, to the absent, the sleeping, the dead, the speechless. It is almost Jekyll and Hyde. But none the less persuasive for that.

Pinter puts in an appearance toward the end of *The Nightfisherman*, as an admirer of Graham's work, as a public reader and supporter of it, and as a private patron. God knows Graham needed him, or needed such a figure, his life was one of the most poverty-stricken of any of the great twentieth-century British poets'. First and foremost, I think the letters should be read as a chronicle of this poverty and its effect—and indeed, lack of effect—on the man who so unquestioningly bore it. Near the beginning of the book we find

Graham in Cornwall. It is 1943, and he is twenty-five: "It's raining now on the roof. I'm living in a caravan a friend's lent me in Cornwall, lonely and by the sea. I fish and gather mushrooms and write and cook." He was to stay, under only slowly evolving circumstances, for more than forty years. The caravan, punningly, is later referred to as "my poor arkvan." Finding a usable lemon on the beach rates a couple of mentions. He writes to friends—often the painter John Minton—to borrow money or to discuss the modalities of its repayment. The sums are often tiny, and it is an indication of his poverty that he is driven to ask for loans only at some future date, to be certain that the money will be spent on whatever thing he has in mind, often bills or medicine. (If it came earlier, it would just be spent.) He seems always to be cheerful; he is, after all, at some level living the sort of uncompromised life he wants. "I'm writing every day and the good weather's begun and we have a goat." That's some sentence. To go to London or Scotland, he has to hitchhike. He asks friends for old boots and clothes. They move to a condemned coastguard house on the north coast of Cornwall. "I measure out my life in paraffin gallons," he writes in 1958. A visitor records: "We lived on flour-and-water pancakes cooked on a primus stove, and, when the paraffin was finished, over a driftwood fire. Sydney and Nessie [Nessie Dunsmuir, his wife] also used to collect limpets [mussels?] off the rocks and cook them, but only the cat would eat them, and even then not always." Graham visited Iceland in 1961, and Crete in 1964. In 1965, a friend offered them the use of a small cottage in the town of Madron, rent-free. When Graham won a literary prize in 1970, he used it to get an indoor toilet put in.

At many turns, the life of Graham reminds me of that of Malcolm Lowry (1909–1957), which is something I never thought I'd be able to say of anyone. Lowry, admittedly, was (in the British sense) middle class and occasionally received remittances from his family, but in the 1940s and '50s, his life in the squatter's shack in Dollarton, British Columbia, resembled Graham's, remote from metropolitan centers and "civilization," a life lived often outdoors, among simple people, without money. Like Lowry, Graham was heavily influenced by Joyce—again, I never thought I'd come across anyone who would match Lowry for Joycean puns, "too-loose Lowry-trek," "Lowry's and Penates," "delowryum tremens," but Graham does— and, like Lowry, he liked a drink. From time to time, I even had the ghostly sense I was reading Lowry: "Yes, somehow, Robin, assailed by our acquaintances and a friend here and there, and dodging the sometimes too-thoroughly felling arms of Bacchus and the baying slavering hounds of angst that howl from the hydrophobic dark and——" It was life in the wilderness, for the sake of writing. In Lowry's case, it was crowned with brilliant triumph and tragedy; in Graham's, a more bearable and sustained slower-burning success.

As well as this story, you get a very good set of a very good writer's letters. Graham was bracingly frank to his correspondents about their work, and, to some extent, his own. The blunt criticism of David Wright ("I find the last seven lines thin for you to be writing") and of a shoddy review of his own work, late on, by Michael Schmidt (who publishes the book, and publishes the letter, brave man) are quite shocking. The sentences are often wonderful, whether one run together on Tibet ("Tibet is a strange place and I read a lot about it") or two split off about the United States ("The drink here is fantastic. What strange people."). There are fine puns ("tritametre," "grahamiphone") and not such fine ones ("The bard will have flown"). Above all, in a group of letters to Roger Hilton, now recognized as having been among the best postwar British painters, there are some extraordinary documents of friendship and solicitude. Hilton was alcoholic and severely depressed in the mid-1960s when Graham met him, a tormented and tormenting man. In 1966, he was sent to prison for drunk driving. Graham sent him an astonishingly, almost insanely boisterous letter. It seems like bad taste at first, but then one sees in the manic punning the utmost expression of personal devotion in mimicry, distraction, banter, affection:

> Can you hold this paper with your manacled hands? Shall I parachute down to see you from the flying machine and say hello? Shall I start an underground tunnel here from Gulval? Shall I drop you a case of blondes? [. . .] What terrible drivel from so great a poet as me. Forgive me, Rog. The juices of dusk are flowing and the autumn rooks are calling like breaking stones. Lift me your eyebrows.

Count a hundred. Santa Claus is coming doon the chimney. Could you maybe get your various veins seen to and your divers wounds of your rough life and Daniel Druff and your hammer-claw toes? My fetishes are sweating in the darkened ward of my brain. I face the stretching Rogerless night. [. . .] O hogtied friend, keep the fort. I can't think how to write properly to you yet. Be tolerant. Take it easy (How easy to say). Are you allowed to write back? If you can reply reply.

When Hilton died in 1975, Graham was given his watch. He wrote "Lines on Roger Hilton's Watch." Like a lot of Graham's work, the inspiration is communication, is dialogue. Sometimes the poet speaks, sometimes the watch:

> He switches the light on
> To find a cigarette
> And pour himself a Teachers.
> He picks me up and holds me
> Near his lonely face
> To see my hands. He thinks
> He is not being watched.

The simplicity of this, the heartbreak, the jokey puns, the tenderness, the chugging *tch* sounds, the successive sentences all beginning "He," you might think of a Paul Klee drawing or something, but I don't know of anything like this in poetry. It is—was ("Tenses are everywhere")—the sound of W. S. Graham, 1918–1986.

ZBIGNIEW HERBERT

Zbigniew Herbert died in 1998. He was a very great and idiosyn-cratic poet—something in me wants to say a peerless poet—and, it is reported, a perennial Nobel bridesmaid. It was ironic—and no doubt wounding—that during the period of his expectations, in 1980 and 1996, two other Poles of, as I see it, manifestly lesser gifts and im-portance, Czesław Miłosz and Wisława Szymborska, were chosen by the academy and decorated by Carl Gustav.

I had been waiting for his *Collected Poems* from the time of Her-bert's death, if not even longer. Frankly, in view of some bruited complications (related below), I thought it would take rather longer than it did, and its eventual coming caught me by surprise—as per-haps things do when you wait for them hard. While waiting, I kept my hand in by buying up spare copies of his individual volumes, *Report from the Besieged City* (1985), *Mr. Cogito* (1993), both *Selected Poems* (the one from 1968 and, confusingly, a completely different book from 1977), and others; if nothing else, it was handy practical instruction in the ways of the price-supply curve. I have the German translations and read them. I can't read Polish, but I have Herbert wherever I go. He is the first poet I ever read. The poem was "From Antiquity"; I was eight. Probably he is as near to sacred to me as anything in or out of poetry is.

And now I have a book that I wasn't expecting at all. Herbert has a new translator, someone I have never heard of. Even that drafty, echoey thing the Internet (our very own updated version of Ovid's cave of rumor) has barely heard of Alissa Valles. This, by the way, is to register my surprise, not some snobbish impulse; Herbert, after all, is surely a sought-after commodity, somewhere near the pinnacle both of Polish poetry and the twentieth century; anyone taking him on should probably come with some sort of track record, not least for their own peace of mind—and even then of course it would be no guarantee of a successful outcome. It's pretty much the last thing I would press upon a young poet looking for a start in life or career, or a middle-aged one looking to diversify. I must now enter certain caveats. As I say, I can't ("can't" seems more honest, more regretful than "don't") read Polish. My information from the great publishing centers of London and New York is vague and unattributable and thirdhand. It's not a nice thing to bash a young—or an old, or a middle-aged—translator, least of all when one is unable to read the originals. But it remains the case that my strongest feeling about this book is a sort of helpless and bewildered regret.

Practically synonymous with Herbert in the English-speaking world are—or were?—his English translators, John and Bogdana Carpenter. Over more than twenty years and six books—all but the very first *Selected Poems*, which was done in 1968 by Miłosz (in the days when he still permitted himself to translate his sometime friend, sometime enemy, and sometime fellow Pole) and a Canadian diplomat, Peter Dale Scott—they were responsible for him in English. The noise that we think of as "Herbert" was made by them. Neither of them is known for anything else; he signs as poet and essayist, though I don't know his poems and essays; she, Polish by birth, teaches or taught in the Slavic department at the University of Michigan. A *Collected Poems* done by them would have been the logical culmination of their labors and was something they would have loved, as I understand it, to bring about. Then what? The desire—reasonable? unreasonable?—of the Carpenters to be credited as "editors" of such a book; a falling-out with Herbert's widow, Katarzyna, and his American publisher of forty years' standing (from the very outset), Dan Halpern; the appearance on the scene of an agent; and the instruction of a new translator, Alissa Valles. From the point of view of the Carpenters, I would have thought, a catastrophe; from the point of view of Herbert's English readership, little less than that. And all, I believe, for nonliterary reasons.

Such things do happen from time to time, but rarely at such a high level, rarely with so much at stake. And then there are ways of managing them so that least harm is done. This is not the case here. Obviously, the Carpenters are a hard act to follow. Readers bond with translations in an unexpectedly primary way. "New translation" is never the infallible trump that publishers sometimes wish (do they ever think it?) when they are driven to play it. Old translations hang around, even when they are notionally superseded or replaced, even when they have been discredited, which again is manifestly not the case here. Constance Garnett's Tolstoy, Scott Moncrieff's Proust, Edwin and Willa Muir's Kafka, H. T. Lowe-Porter's Thomas Mann all have their adherents. Notable instances in poetry include the Rilkes of J. B. Leishman or C. F. MacIntyre, and the Cavafy of Edmund Keeley and Philip Sherrard. As the song has it, the first cut is the deepest. It is almost unknown for a reader to change allegiance, even to a superior product, and again that is not the case here. Historic translations—like the Carpenters'—acquire their own momentum, their own specific virtue. It is an argument that, ironically, finds acceptance in the context of these *Collected Poems*, which includes all seventy-nine of the Miłosz/Dale Scott translations. (So much for the claim, on the back cover, that "this outstanding new translation by Alissa Valles brings a uniformity of voice to Zbigniew Herbert's entire poetic output"—which might actually have been worth striving for, though I would have called it something other than "uniformity of voice," which sounds unhappily monotonous.) Instead, poor Ms. Valles in her four-page Translator's Note is put to the necessity of welcoming the Miłosz/Dale Scott versions into her book, and even, a little humiliatingly, touting for them: "These fine translations were Herbert's first extensive introduction to the English-speaking world. They have been retained here." Those of the Carpenters, though, have not, and it seems to me that readers of their work over the past thirty years—and arguably also new readers, now denied the chance to acquaint themselves with it—are owed some sort of explanation. None is offered. There is silence—the airbrush.

A frank admission of what happened—if indeed, something has "happened"—the voicing of some proper gratitude to the Carpenters for their work, some regret for the past and modest trepidation for the future, a little of what used to be called glasnost, would have helped. Even some public relations claptrap along the lines of "personal and musical differences" would not have gone amiss. Instead, the Carpenters go by default. Adam Zagajewski in his short five-page introduction, doesn't mention them—well, perhaps it would have seemed strange if he had. Alissa Valles does—mention them:

> I owe a considerable debt to previous translators of Herbert—to John and Bogdana Carpenter, who not only acted as Herbert's translators over many years but contributed much to his reception and recognition in the English-speaking world—but also to all those who produced versions of individual poems for anthologies: Stanislaw Baranczak and Clare Cavanagh, Adam Czerniawski, and Robert Mezey, who included a translation of the poem "Sequoia" done in collaboration with Jacek Niecko in a recent Library of America *Poems of the American West*.

I quote the whole sentence because it is both an outrage and a disaster. The Oscar-style diminuendo or rallentando listing is an indignity; and as for "acted as"—are we to understand that the Carpenters were pretending, that they weren't really his translators, or that their engagement was temporary, a stopgap? Stuffing the translators of hundreds of poems over decades into one sentence with chancers who contributed a poem or two to an anthology here or there is hideous. God knows I can understand the translator's wish to appear invisible in such circumstances (I sometimes think there is no good news about translation, ever)—but it is precisely here, where there is another version, that invisibility is not an option. The publisher should have stepped forward at this point. And from Ms. Valles—who covers two of her four pages arguing the toss over the way to translate Marsyas' cry (should it be "A" or "Aaa"?)—I should have liked something on the actual pleasures and difficulties of translating Herbert.

Now. To brass tacks, to onions, to sheep, whatever. Herbert has always written poems with exiguous punctuation or (for the most part) none at all. He uses line breaks, spaces, indentation, dashes, and the occasional capitalization to mark sense and direct the reader. Given that he often wrote poems of some length—many of his greatest poems are two or three pages long—this made the experience of reading him unlike reading any other poet. There was a novelty, a surprise, an unpredictability, an ongoing untangling as one read. Every reading was a first reading. One could never remember what went with what. The poem remade itself—squeezed itself out as of a tube—before one's very eyes. It is like reading something still wet, not set, not combed, not furnished and furbished with signs, explanations, directives. Sense wasn't handed down in a predetermined, apodictic way but seemed to make itself as one blundered along. Authority is not assumed, but accrues. (There is something in Sartre, I seem to remember, about the quality of this uncharted, open-ended type of writing; one tends to associate it with the damaged and freshly dangerous condition of the world after World War II; certainly such a connection existed in the minds of Herbert and other Polish poets of his generation, veterans, many of them, of the Polish Underground.) Herbert's late poem "The Book"—though ostensibly on the work of a friend—describes the effect nicely: "This book is a gentle reminder it does not permit me / to run too rapidly in the rhythm of a coursing phrase / it bids me return to the beginning forever begin again."

The corollary of this absence of punctuation—and hence, if you like, a second component of an absolutely original style—is an unusually powerful, certain, unambiguous vestigial syntax. This holds the reader in place, points him in the desired direction, reveals contrast, reveals continuity, reveals consequence, makes irony possible. (Herbert studied philosophy and law, he is a logician in a way most writers—alarmingly, one begins to think after a while—aren't: Kafka the most obvious exception.) Without this very firm syntax, this series of pushes and prods, the reader—much more in translation—would be quite at sea; it would be like reading soup. A very basic testimony to Herbert's greatness is the simple fact that one never has this sensation of floundering while reading him. His always struck me as being probably a very demanding style to write—so much for playing tennis without a net—but (and I'm sorry about the backhanded compliment) until I saw Alissa Valles's versions I had no true understanding of the absolute mastery in the Carpenters' handling of it in English, where it is always taut, always sprung, never gassy, foggy, or cloudy.

Two further dimensions. The first, let's call it voice, Herbert's hectic, surprising, fervent, dry, whispering, breathless speech, whether in propria persona or as an alter ego or body (or rather mental!) double called Mr. Cogito, or again (a particular avocation of this poet's) bodied forth in some hostile, monstrous, tyrannical figure, Claudius, Damastes, Fortinbras—the words sometimes spinning their gears in formidable lists, sometimes impelling grave contents with a musing, methodical disbelief. And the second is diction or register, which I know sounds starchy and unattractive but is really anything but: this is dignified, detached, possessed of a noble stiffness, at once quiet and dramatic, jetting from the highly particular to the hugely general, from the antique to the current. And it all sounds like this (from "Elegy of Fortinbras"):

> Now that we're alone we can talk prince man to man
> though you lie on the stairs and see no more than a dead ant
> nothing but black sun with broken rays
> I could never think of your hands without smiling
> and now that they lie on the stone like fallen nests
> they are as defenceless as before The end is exactly this
> The hands lie apart The sword lies apart The head apart
> and the knight's feet in soft slippers

Or this (from "Isadora Duncan," from *Report from a Besieged City*):

> Lightheartedly she disclosed the secrets of her heart and alcove
> in a censurable book with the title "My Life"

Since then we know exactly how the actor Beregy
revealed to her the world of the senses how madly in love
was Gordon Craig Konstantin Stanislavski
hordes of musicians nabobs writers
while Paris Singer threw everything
he had at her feet—an empire
of never-failing sewing machines et cetera

Or this (from "Mr. Cogito on a Set Topic: 'Friends Depart'"):

with the inexorable
passing of years
his count of friends
shrank

they went off
in pairs
in groups
one by one

some paled like wafers
lost earthly dimensions
and suddenly
or gradually
emigrated
to the sky

The poems are in chronological sequence (from the '60s, the '80s, and the '90s), and the translations are, respectively, by Dale Scott and Miłosz, the Carpenters, and Alissa Valles. The passages are from poems I admire, and translations I regard as successful.

But now—invidious though it be—I must quote comparatively, to make it clear how much the old translations are to be preferred to the new. In a generally and increasingly monolingual culture, the importance of translation is little discussed and less understood. "What does it matter—we still have the author," runs one argument. Actually, "we" don't—that's the whole problem. Another would have it: "Well, another one can't hurt—the more the merrier—we can tri-angulate them, or something," though, given that what we have here is not addition but substitution, that doesn't apply either. Alissa Valles herself writes, a little disingenuously therefore: "Great poets deserve many translators." I don't agree—except over very long periods of time. They deserve—or rather should count themselves blessed to have—one good one, or preferably yet, a great one. Numbers, vari-ants, alternatives, while seeming to appease Choice—the great false god of our consumer age—actually only produce clutter, distraction, waste. Are two Rilkes better than one? Are seven better than two? I don't think so, not least when "choice" in this context is bound to be such an uninformed, haphazard operation. The argument for abun-dance is in fact an argument for oversupply. It is too anxious, too sentimental, and too pleased with itself to understand that even the perfect operating of choice is predicated on an endless round of re-jection, elimination, incineration. There's no getting around elitism, but this is the version for inflationary times, for self-publishers, and for those who can't bear to be told the bad news.

Still, it remains the case that some poets are more spacious, more accommodating than others. Herbert, I would have thought, is one of the least. A Herbert poem, with its unpunctuated layout, its rigid syntax, its careful collisions of diction, is like a tiptoeing through snow. There actually isn't room for competing versions. I have now read hundreds of pages of Alissa Valles's translations against the German, and against the Carpenters, and (if I am being generous) perhaps one time in twenty hers are better, six or eight about the same, and half the time they are worse. (For reasons to do with the infinitely ramifying nature of language, these kinds of comparisons rarely produce shut-outs; this result strikes me as being unusually conclusive.) From the very beginning, I don't think anyone has "got" Herbert in English the way John and Bogdana Carpenter have. In their introduction to their first engagement with Herbert, that sec-ond *Selected Poems* of 1977, they wrote: "One of the major principles of translation of these poems has been to *interpret* Herbert's mean-ings as thoroughly as possible. This is different from literalness; the translators have tried to recast Herbert's poems in English, using all the resources at their disposal." For years, I didn't believe them, I thought it was the usual translators' blarney. Now I do. They go on: "At the same time they have tried to resist any tendency to be reductive, to round off the texture or structure of a poem, or to adapt it to a particular idiom, or expectation. This has meant the creation of a new speaking voice, a voice that can be heard, in English." They have done brilliantly just that, using mostly tiny means of vast reach, pronouns, particles, tenses, word order, forms of the genitive (whether apostrophe or "of") even in their deployment of definite and indefinite articles (Polish has none). It goes a long way to explaining why Herbert in English is so bracing, so agile, so fresh, so delightful.

I have so many examples—literally hundreds—that it's a problem to know where to begin. (I sense, and perhaps you do too, that I've tried to put off the moment.) What about "Mr. Cogito Reflects on Suffering"? Valles ends—the object is suffering—"joke around with it / very solicitously / as with a sick child / cajoling in the end / with silly tricks / a wan / smile." The first two lines are mutually incompatible, and indeed both her verbs are excessive to the point of crude; using three "with" constructions is poor; and a characteristically glamorous or poeticizing diction gets in the way of what is being said. The Carpenters have: "entertain it / very cautiously / like a sick child / forcing at last / with silly tricks / a faint / smile." What about this description in the lovely early poem "Biology Teacher": "He towered over me / his long legs spread / and I saw / a gold chain / an ash-colored vest / and a scrawny neck / with a dead bow-tie / pinned on." Again, the word choice is flashy—towered, ash-colored, scrawny— but still more destructive is the unthinking word order. The Carpenters: "he stood high above me / on long spread legs / I saw / the little gold chain / the ash-grey frock coat / and the thin neck / on which was pinned / a dead necktie." The punch line is properly left to the end, not dispatched prematurely. (Even their dispensing with an "and" in the middle—just "I saw"—seems inspired, and typical of their thoughtful economy.) What about a difficult, bare passage in "Mr. Cogito and the Imagination"? Valles has: "a bird is a bird / slavery slavery / a knife a knife / death is death // he loved / a flat horizon / a straight line / earth's gravity." Here the Carpenters expand things gently, but decisively: "that a bird is a bird / slavery means slavery / a knife is a knife / death remains death // he loved / the flat horizon / a straight line / the gravity of the earth." Their version is so much more resolute, less perfunctory (Valles's sounds—"earth's gravity"—simply bored). Here is the poem "Mother," one of very few intimate or familial poems Herbert permitted himself. Valles:

> He fell from her lap like a ball of yarn. He unwound himself in a hurry and beat it into the distance. She held onto the beginning of life. She wound it on a finger hospitable as a ring; she wished to shelter it. He rolled down steep slopes, sometimes labored up mountains. He came back all tangled up and didn't say a word. He will never return to the sweet throne of her lap.
>
> Her outspread arms glow in the dark like an old town.

"Beat it" is a disaster, a sudden touch of Bukowski. The fourth sentence is blighted by the sloppy agreement—is a finger like a ring? Is a ring hospitable? And then do you shelter something by making it a ring? I would have thought a ring is rather exposed. The glow at the end—is it sodium?—is also distinctly unhappy. The poem looks routine, messy, abrupt, unaffecting, rather sentimental. The Carpenters render it (I don't know if it's prose or verse, and frankly I couldn't care a hang):

> He fell from her knees like a ball of yarn.
> He unwound in a hurry and ran blindly away.
> She held the beginning of life. She would wind it
> on her finger like a ring, she wanted to preserve him.
> He was rolling down steep slopes, sometimes
> he was climbing up. He would come back tangled, and be silent.
> Never will he return to the sweet throne of her knees.
> The stretched-out hands are alight in the darkness
> like an old town.

"Knees" is masterly, at beginning and end. "Preserve him" is endlessly more appropriate and feeling than "shelter it." The strange-sounding imperfect I think is a good idea, for time in the wilderness. The little inversion in line 7 could make you cry. The awful twanging of the Valles version is gone. The poem is suddenly bigger, gentler, softer.

In the hands of the Carpenters, we have seen that everything—be it an article or a tense or an "of"—can become an expressive resource deployed in Herbert's cause, with Valles, it's a potential liability. Reading her is an awful instruction in how even a great poet can be humbled by carelessness and thoughtlessness. She doesn't write even passably good English (and while you might be able to write a good poem by accident, I don't think you can make a good translation). She has such things as "the heel on the other hand," "some time off / outside of time." She uses "gingerly" (the care for oneself) as though it meant "carefully" (care for others), "convoluted" for "complicated," "syringe" for "injection." She has "downstream" in a poem about the sea, and the baffling "royal apple" for "orb." Her formulations are not strange and provoking but muzzy and nonsensical: "lanky shoulders," "immeasurably regular rings," "the fury of mass murderers," "the true bride / of real men," "lacks all dimension," "mundane / and slightly banal." Her writing is full of dreary prefabricated terms: "subjected to torture," "failed marriages," "riddle wrapped in a mystery," "quality poet," "mood swing." On occasional—redemptive— flights into a grander vocabulary, she makes a fool of herself: "indifferent plenitude" where the Carpenters—knowing or wisely sensing that Herbert demands a mixing of English and Latin—have "indifferent fullness"; "Mr. Cogito's Eschatological Premonitions" where they have "Eschatological Forebodings"; "detritus of an epic" where they have "scraps of a poem." Valles's version of "Damastes Nicknamed Procrustes Speaks" ends (it sounds rather like something from *Star Trek*): "I live in the undying hope that others will assume my task / and will bring a labor so boldly initiated to its completion"; "and bring the task so boldly begun to its end" is the Carpenters' version. Part of Herbert, it seems to me, is disdain for conventional poetic effects; as he puts it in "Mr. Cogito and the Imagination" (in the Carpenters' version), "the piano at the top of the Alps / played false concerts for him." Such things are literally and punningly "phoney." He shouldn't therefore come out sounding like Assonance 101: "laboratories of sorrow," "clumsy bumblebee," "irksome as eczema," "too shallow to swallow," "rebellion's well-spring," "more than able—docile stable," "step separately." There is no dignity in any of these, and there can be no dignity around them. How can a poem begin "In the life of Mr. Cogito / illustrated supplements / were a vital supplement"? How can one end "with the terrible consciousness that life is momentous"? How can you have an "abbess" in a poem, and an "abyss" in the next line, which is also the last, and the poem not be terminally silly? How can you ask God for "ability" in one strophe and "agility" in the next? How can you have "cut" as a verb in one line and as a noun in the next: "a plain cut across by a red stone quarry / like a holiday cut of meat"? How can you praise God for his "fathomless goodness," and two lines later comment on the "unfathomable bellows" of a donkey's lungs without being a sort of atheistical pendant to Hopkins?

Alissa Valles's Herbert is slack, chattersome, hysterical, full of exaggeration, complacency, and reaching for effect. The original (I'm quite sure) is none of those things. This *Collected Poems* is a hopelessly, irredeemably bad book. The only solution to its problems would be a bulk reinstatement of the old translations. These things matter so much; it would be nice if they made a difference.

ADAM ZAGAJEWSKI

For twenty years, since I first read the first poem, "To Go to Lvov"—in his first English-language book, *Tremor*—I have had a happily unexamined admiration for the work of the Polish poet Adam Zagajewski. Hence, perhaps, the inordinate difficulty—even for me, with my sluggishness and resistances—in approaching it now in a spirit of let's call it serious holism. And yet, I very much wanted to do it. Something about Zagajewski's poetry—the joyful flavors of it—seemed to me to elicit (or elicit from me) something like its dialectical opposite: something austere, grinding, agnostic, judicious.

I suppose what I always liked about Zagajewski's poetry is the sense of the poet as companion, as fellow reader and traveler, sharing his notes on books and places, in four books of essays and four collections of poems, without very much to tell them apart. (Though I've only met him half a dozen times at most, his voice is one of those I can hear absolutely at will.) The poems ramble woolgatheringly, and the essays are yet more aimlessly beautiful affairs than the now slightly old-fashioned-sounding label suggests; rarely do they have anything either forensic or brutally argumentative about them.

There is something enviably light-footed, alert, intense, and momentary about all the writing. It is adventitious, unplanned, follows its nose, goes very often sideways. It has a feline quality and puts me in mind of Zagajewski's curled purr (I don't know for a fact, but I don't have the slightest doubt he's a cat lover). Like a companion, you see it from the side as you amblingly read, its marked profile. (In addition to those essays, Zagajewski has written at least one novel, which I read in German, about a Polish painter in Berlin. The book was called *Der dünne Strich* ["The Thin Line" or "The Fine Line"], which is its protagonist's nickname: it might stand for Zagajewski himself). He teaches a term a year—a confrère!—in the States, and after living in Paris for twenty-five years has recently gone to live in Cracow, where he studied philosophy.

Somewhere, the poems are one poem, and the prose one prose—or they are even, all together, one writing. The names of poets—and, still more, of philosophers and composers—occur as naturally and profusely in the poems as the names of trees, or relatives, or types of fruit in the prose. Someone's sonatas or *pensées* are set next to a church or a square in a town, or a painting, or the scent of some flower or bush. The world—including great parts of the human-made world—is there for our study and our delectation. And amid these stimuli, sipping, musing, modestly disclaiming all forms of industry, proficiency, or diligence, sometimes mildly remonstrating with himself ("I haven't written a single poem / in months. / I've lived humbly, reading the paper, / pondering the riddle of power / and the reasons for obedience"), and sometimes voicing something more like a prayer ("Give us astonishment / and a flame, high, bright") is an engaging private "I" ("Herr Doktor, Herr Privatdozent"), bookworm, globetrotter, noticer, who seems very close to the poet himself.

The experience of reading them is very different, but the unselfconscious way Zagajewski handles this "I" brings to mind Frank O'Hara. Certainly, it wouldn't be easy to say which is the more charming, and charm is very much the issue. The difference is that in O'Hara, the "I" (as in "I do this, I do that") is the repository of all charm—the poems are, you might say, in Norman someone's phrase, "advertisements for myself"—in Zagajewski, the charm is that of all the world, and it is a little mysterious why no one else has noticed it first. One is solar, one is lunar. O'Hara, straightening his eyelids, throwing a couple of tangerines in an overnight bag, is personally and actively and often spectacularly eccentric; Zagajewski—if such a thing can be imagined—passively and haphazardly and rather demurely so. "Do you mean to say this has never occurred to you?" his poems seem to say, "Where have you been? What do you spend your time doing?" "I wasn't in this poem, /" he writes, "only gleaming pure pools, / a lizard's tiny eye, the wind / and the sounds of a harmonica / pressed to not my lips." And that's the poem.

Like O'Hara's, Zagajewski's poems often follow no marked or discernible plan. The poems are not particularly situated or directed. Their identity is more often collective than individual. Some—like "I Wasn't in This Poem"—are short, others are two or three pages, but generally speaking, it would be easy to move lines or blocks from one to another: "September approaches; war, death," "The sun, the opulent sun of September," "September kissed the hills / and tree-tops like someone leaving," "Peace, thick nothing, as full of sweet / juice as a pear in September." This requires, I think, the reader's assent to a sort of poetic carousel, where things come round repeatingly or blurred. It is a question both of mood—something about the cusp of feeling and thought particularly and almost dependably excites Zagajewski, even though he's not a poet of great feeling or profound thinking, and you could hardly get him more wrong than by claiming, say, that the essays "think," and the poems "feel"—and of a set of properties. Whether deliberately or not, a Zagajewski poem is like a holiday. It has a sense of leisure, of an optional or even a privileged agenda (a café, a museum, a friend or spouse, the meaning of life), it is not in a suit and tie, and it carries no briefcase. There is the holiday air of feeling more purely, as it were, more vividly, alive, but also the statistical improbability (two weeks in fifty-two?) of being there at all. Intensity or relishing of experience comes paired with a certain air of hovering. It is lifted out, suspended, musing ("A Morning in Vicenza"):

The sun was so fragile, so young,
that we were a little scared; a careless move
might scratch it, just a shout—if anyone

had tried—might do it harm; only the rushing swifts,
with wings hard as cast-iron,
were free to sing out loud, because they'd spent their brief,
uneasy childhoods in clay nests
alongside siblings, small, mad planets,
black as forest berries.

This looping through sensation, through layerings of metaphor and whimsy, this tracing of delicate aerial patternings, this speeding instability is what you get in Zagajewski. Contraries—hard and soft, timidity and boldness, silence and noise, light and darkness—are effortlessly fused together. It is a poetry not of manipulation but of adhesion: it is like a rodeo, but with swifts in lieu of mustangs or bulls.

A great many of Zagajewski's poems are—as here—dramas of presence and absence. "A Morning in Vicenza" goes on to become an elegy to two admired friends, Joseph Brodsky and Krzysztof Kieślowski, but it could have gone anywhere (I quoted the first of its three stanzas). This unpredictability, storylessness, geographical unattachment is a feature of Zagajewski; the *Selected Poems* (cut down from a somewhat longer American selection called *Without End*) might be subtitled "one hundred and sixty-three looks at the world." In *Two Cities* of 1995, the best of his prose books, Zagajewski writes: "If people are divided into the settled, the emigrants, and the homeless, then I certainly belong to the third category, although I understand it very soberly, without a shadow of sentimentality or self-pity. [. . .] To be homeless [. . .] means only that the person having this defect cannot indicate the streets, cities, or community that might be his home, his, as one is wont to say, miniature homeland." Zagajewski was a few months old when the Polish population of Lvov (reassigned to the Ukraine and called Lviv) was moved to Gliwice (the German Gleiwitz, whose inhabitants were similarly relocated), where he grew up in a haunting atmosphere of denial, make-believe, and shallow-rooted provisionality, utterly at variance with the grand, perduring, instaurational claims of communism. Some inhabitants out of protest never left their flats, others talked obsessively to the young Zagajewski of the beauty and the layout of their former city, others again specialized in collecting derelict "post-German" goods of rather superior workmanship. It is this drama, personal and collective, that fuels "To Go to Lvov," his longest poem (it is almost three pages) and for me still unsurpassed (but that's no disgrace: it's one of the outstanding poems of the past forty years):

> To go to Lvov. Which station
> for Lvov, if not in a dream, at dawn, when dew
> gleams on a suitcase, when express
> trains and bullet trains are being born. To leave
> in haste for Lvov, night or day, in September
> or in March. But only if Lvov exists,
> if it is to be found within the frontiers and not just
> in my new passport, if lances of trees
> —of poplar and ash—still breathe aloud
> like Indians, and if streams mumble
> their dark Esperanto, and grass snakes like soft signs
> in the Russian language disappear
> into thickets. To pack and set off, to leave
> without a trace, at noon, to vanish
> like fainting maidens. And burdocks, green
> armies of burdocks, and below, under the canvas
> of a Venetian café, the snails converse
> about eternity.

(That's the beginning: it hurts to stop quoting.) What I might call the "variorum infinitive" continues throughout the poem, to its very last half line, the finite-infinite: "It is everywhere." Plangency is transmuted into abundance, inaccessibility into a ubiquity of ghostly detail, inert substance into atomized fragrance.

Nothing thereafter has quite the clarity, the attack, the conviction, the purpose, the monumentality of "To Go to Lvov"—but then there are many poems to be written, and many ways of writing them. It reads almost like the first poem of someone beginning to write—which God knows it wasn't—such is its headlong, heedless speed, its bold impossibilist loveliness. But again, this happens: there is only one "Prufrock," one "Provincia Deserta," one "Quaker Graveyard in

Nantucket." Later poems exhibit a certain frugality, prudence, anxiety, patience, pacing, routine. They somewhat deliberately settle beside one another. Poetry becomes a habit—even "I haven't written a single poem / in months" becomes a habit—and one makes the best of it, as reader, or writer. The issue of Zagajewski's "homelessness," while hardly ever again as explicitly—Edenically—addressed as in "To Go to Lvov," nevertheless informs all his writing. It is there in the fullness and equability of his responses, the ungrammatical or unhierarchical speed—not grammaticized or hierarchized by belonging in any particular place—of his perceptions, "seeking the spot / where silence suddenly erupts in speech," whether in verse or prose ("A Small Nation Writes a Letter to God" in *Two Cities*):

> Light, translucent mists gathered over the fields, harvesters ate their dinners under a broad linden tree growing in the fencerow. It was so hot that hawks fell asleep in flight. And only a brown train patiently cut a shallow furrow through the heat. Rivers steamed. Creeks stopped in their tracks. Sap melted like a lump of snow. There was no mercy anywhere. Sometimes someone brought a little water to the station. What was this ill-formed, lazy train when compared to the beauty of a rustling wood? Thirsty snakes drank from puddles. Hurriedly buttoning their uniforms, sleepy stationmasters ran onto the platforms of small stations.

Or (a particularly lovely short poem) "Ode to Softness":

> Mornings are blind as newborn cats.
> Fingernails grow so trustfully, for a while
> they don't know what they're going to touch. Dreams
> are soft, and tenderness looms over us
> like fog, like the cathedral bell of Krakow
> before it cooled.

This benign, animating, gently humorous imagination suffuses Zagajewski's writing. Just as details are adduced that speak to the conditions of drought (in the prose), and of a tentative delicacy (in the poem), so every part of speech seems to work in these fabulous and harmonious rearrangements of the world: "furrow," "steamed," "sleepy," "hurriedly"; "blind," "trustfully," "tenderness," "cooled." It is no surprise that Zagajewski has written (again in *Two Cities*) a short "Defense of Adjectives," and probably they are his most defining words—though I must say, I have a particular weakness for his adverbs, a still more neglected part of speech in poetry; sometimes he seems to me the only poet who uses adverbs, certainly his are among the few I remember. Something about the mobility and expressiveness of this style corresponds in my eyes to Zagajewski's condition of "homelessness"; things require and acquire extra definition from the homeless poet. The fact that so much subtlety and dexterity are purveyed at such speed is probably the final, briefest, clinching argument for Zagajewski's greatness ("The Churches of France"):

> The churches of France, more welcoming than its inns and its
>   poems,
> Standing in vines like great clusters of grapes, or meekly, on
>   hilltops,
> Or drowned in valleys, on the floor of a green sea, in a dry
>   landscape,
> Abandoned buildings, deserted barns
> Of gray stone, among gray houses, within gray villages,
> But inside pink or white or painted by the sun coming through
>   stained glass.
> Little Romanesque shrines with stocky frames, like craftsmen
>   shaped by their labor,
> Pascal's invisible church, sewn into canvas,
> And slim cathedrals like herons above the cities, seen clearly
>   from the highway, the loveliest is in Chartres,
> Where stone stifles desire.

The two dangers to this type of writing are routine and sweetness. It can become either too easy, or too rich. Zagajewski has not managed to avoid either completely. The diction of some of the new poems has a hallowed, stained-glass simplicity that I don't always like, and the poems themselves are like minor revisitings of earlier tropes. It is as though Zagajewski has found a way of—no pun intended, but it just about works—"bottling it." The writing is still fresh, but a little weary in its familiar celebratoriness: "Joy is close," "the ocean's skin, on which / ships etch the lines of shining poems," "should such a splendid upright shape, a king, / be made a horizontal form, a line of print?" In 163 poems, there are 30 references to "poetry" or "poems," which, for a nonnaturally occurring form, seems to me too many. The prose, at the same time, has fallen for the dubious attractions of the word "splendid," which always struck me as a peculiarly bland and plummy and condescending bow tie of a word (and, incidentally, impossible to square with "ardor"): one of Keats's "splendid letters," Herbert as a "splendid" reader of his own poems, the "splendid" Parisian light, that "splendid" disease known as inspiration. I don't think it's a translation issue either. (But a note in any case on the translations; the various English versions of Zagajewski have a consummate identity and primacy and authority, to which to respond as to an original quite simply doesn't seem wrong. Clare Cavanagh, the translator of half the poetry and two of the prose books, is obviously a huge factor in the reception of Polish writing in English [she is also the translator of Wysława Szymborska], while Renata Gorczynski, who, with help from Robert Hass, translated *Tremor*, I like even more for her willingness to eccentricity in diction and lineation.)

The second threat is from sweetness. Here, it is interesting that in his essay "Against Poetry," Zagajewski notes that "Gombrowicz's chief complaint against poetry was its excessive 'sweetness,' the disproportionate amount of sugar in poetry." I have to say, I sympathize with Gombrowicz here, and, as for Zagajewski, he is as sweet as Keats. In his earlier work, on the run, one might imagine, from grayness (albeit from the grayness of Gomułka's and Gierek's and Jaruzelski's Poland to the grayness of Paris) to all forms of color, taste, beauty, art, Zagajewski was brilliant precisely at controlling or modifying sweetness. The sugars in his work were set off and complicated by other tastes: dryness, humor, modesty, fretfulness. The end of "Electric Elegy" is a good example of this blending of tones: "Sleep peacefully, German radio, / dream Schumann and don't waken / when the next dictator-rooster crows." Or "Wild Cherries": "Behind the soccer field, wild cherries / sprout on slim stems, tart / by day, sweet when asleep." I have a fear that an unhealthy sweetness, a corn-syrupy sweetness, may be beginning to appear in Zagajewski's work, perhaps brought on by so much time in the United States, where most of his livelihood and reputation are won. I fear poetry as a sort of preserve, praise for the sake of praise, and lushness for the love of lushness. As with Rilke—and it seems to me Zagajewski is like a continuation of Rilke by other means—a hard-edged oeuvre displays occasional saccharine patches. The poet himself probably sees it differently: "What is the spiritual life?" he asks (itself, I would say, a *zuckerverdächtig* sort of question), and replies, "It's aggravating that the question must even be raised; but whenever I pronounce these words, perhaps especially in the United States, my interlocutors look at me slightly askance, as if to say: Get thee to a monastery!" (I'd have thought myself that his question would have been better received here.) I freely concede that it's an aversion of mine, and probably Zagajewski is right that there isn't enough of that sort of thing going on in poetry, but I'm a little sorry that the proportions of the bland and the unsettling in his work have been adjusted, that there isn't as much pith, toughness, and humor in it as once there was, that there's a certain—or an uncertain—wooziness abroad, and a spirit of happy-endism.

LES MURRAY

In the beginning were speed, celerity, swiftness of thought. A poet who gabbled his poems like an auctioneer or a racing commentator, because that was the speed of his thought (how did his hand, taking dictation, keep up, even with the special make of pen my son likes to call an "autopilot"?). Adapting, as Joseph Brodsky liked to do, "bird" to "bard," Murray truly is the original "High-speed Bard," the pendant to the stunned—and stunning—kingfisher in his poem, with its "gold under-eye whiskers" and "beak closing in recovery." We, listening, managed to follow between one- and three-fifths of the action. (It was enough, thanks, it was plenty.) Speed begat range, sweep, domain. At the far end of range, there was still a full tank. A big and a great poem like "The Dream of Wearing Shorts Forever" arrives at the end of its rousingly unconventional new idyll without even breaking a sweat:

> Now that everyone who yearned to wear long pants
> has essentially achieved them,
> long pants, which have themselves been underwear

repeatedly, and underground more than once,
it is time perhaps to cherish the culture of shorts,

to moderate grim vigour
with the knobble of bare knees,
to cool bareknuckle feet in inland water,
slapping flies with a book on solar wind
or a patient bare hand, beneath the cadjiput trees,

to be walking meditatively
among green timber, through the grassy forest
towards a calm sea
and looking across to more of that great island
and the further topics.

Further topics, you think (it's not tropics, though you do the dou-ble take each time)? At the end of eighty-two majestic and exhaus-tive lines on the cultural and historical implications of wearing shorts? Whatever next? Then there was connection making. Will and imagination, two escaped convicts armed with machetes not much caring whether they followed the Queen's Highway or yomped across country. A man who knows. A continental poet. (The conti-nent in question is "that great island," *terra australis*.) Then there were delicacy ("Roman Cage Cups" on the frailest and most improb-ably enduring of glass artifacts), whimsy ("Homage to the Launch-ing Place": a poem about bed), silliness, the love of a giggle, a poem that was always ready to cross a busy street for a joke ("Lunch & Counter Lunch," the title of a book—thanks, I'll eat it here—from 1974). An absurdly small turning circle, the sixpence of yore. Writ-ing that seemed not to care if it was followed or not. That made sense in its own mind. Even when (as he put it) "driving a pen," Murray is still much faster and defter than the rest of us, unencumbered, reading him. (This is why, for all his pained noise to the contrary, he remains helplessly and unalterably an elitist; it is his mind that condemns him to that status. The author of "First Essay on Interest" ["Not usury, but interest"] isn't about to be flavor of the month anywhere—someone with a serious interest in interest?) Then there was coverage. He wrote a zoo (it was called *Translations from the Natural World*). He wrote a history of the first half of the twentieth century (it was a page-turner called *Fredy Neptune: A Novel in Verse*). He wrote anguished, eminently "confessional" autobiography (it was called *Subhuman Redneck Poems*).

As befits a gifted, energetic, and sprawling poet now well into his seventies, Murray has a publishing history to match, with three selected poems, and two collecteds (any and all of them are worth snapping up when met with). *Taller When Prone*—both a good-humored "fat" joke, and a sort of indomitably rebellious (and quasi-scriptural) beatitude—is accounted his twelfth individual volume, but I don't think anyone's seriously counting; *Killing the Black Dog* is a sort of further "selected," pairing a 1996 talk on the poet's—on the face of it, highly surprising—struggle with depression, and a cull of twenty-five of his—previously published—poems on or from or out of the subject. The books—the books in general—are maybe more *à thèse* than they were once, when they seemed to be just gloriously unpredictable and wildly compendious, anything and everything, prolific, equable, and dazzling encounters with city/country, narrative/image, sound/vision, past/present, domestic/abroad, personal/essayistic, experiential/speculative, but that's at least in part because of late the poet has been alarmingly stalked by his subject matter: the "stormy" volume (his word) *Subhuman Redneck Poems* (of 1996) was "so called in honour of my social class," a subject that roused again perhaps unexpectedly fierce passions in the poet; *Conscious and Verbal* (of 2000) related his terrifying brush with a near-fatal liver condition, described with Murray's typical cool, inimitable brio: "Some accident had released flora // who live in us and will eat us / when we stop feeding them the earth. / I'd rehearsed to private office of the grave, / ceased excreting, made corpse gases"; some of the subsequent books accordingly had something remedial, convalescent, narrow gauge about them: *Poems the Size of Photographs* (2002), *The Biplane Houses* (2006). I wonder just how much this has to do with the forsaking of large-scale formats (perhaps a residual fatigue from *Fredy Neptune*), long, wide, sprawling poems, typically (like "The Dream of Wearing Shorts Forever") of two or three pages, a loping, accommodating rhythm; and the writing of shorter poems in shorter stanzas and shorter lines, often fussily rhymed, and rather sharper or even shriller in tone. The big, wide books of the 1980s, *The Vernacular Republic*, *The People's Otherworld*, *The Daylight Moon*, offered one exuberant scintillating masterpiece after another *in sequence* in their tables of contents: for instance, "The Powerline Incarnation," "The Returnees," "Employment for the Castes in Abeyance," and "The Buladelah-Taree Holiday Song Cycle." Or: "1980 in a Street of Federation Houses," "The Butter Factory," "Bats' Ultrasound," and "Roman Cage Cups." Or again: "The Quality of Sprawl," "Shower," "Two Poems in Memory of My Mother," and "Machine Portraits with Pendant Spaceman." (There is pleasure in merely quoting such idiosyncratic titles—like going through great historic team sheets from memory—even without their evocative appeal to the instructed reader.) The inescapable and true conclusion is that for ten or twenty years around the turn of the millennium there was no better poet writing in English than Les A. Murray.

Murray remains a phenomenal poet, and if the new poems are less striking and maybe a tad less wonderful than the older ones, then it is either that we, his older readers, have long had it too good; or that he is writing smaller, though just as well; or that the new poems need a little time to unfurl in our minds before they can rival the status of their predecessors, simply because such bold and mannered things always take time to acquire resonance and familiarity—and probably all three. Contemporaries of Hopkins, reading *his* poems as they emerged, would have had cause to feel the same way. (Certainly, for new readers the imperative remains: start immediately, and start anywhere; and wonder, not where Murray has been—because for the last quarter century at least he has been waiting to be found, like an undiscovered or, rather, "undiscovered," continent—but where you have been, yourselves.)

The thing about Murray is that he needs little or nothing to run on. He is a poetical perpetual motion machine. He doesn't need, therefore, intense experience, or its mental/intellectual equivalent, something to prove—a bee in his bonnet—a cause—to write great poetry. He takes no ball, and runs with it. He doesn't actually need the Taj Mahal (with which *Taller When Prone* begins—"From a Tourist Journal"), though there is of course no one one would rather have writing about it: "In a precinct of liver stone, high / on its dais, the Taj seems bloc hail." It remains the case, though: the way there is just as good, or even a little better, "over honking roads / being built under us, past baby wheat / and undoomed beasts and walking people." The smiling attentiveness, the respect for the blur of other beings and becomings, are pure, best Murray.

Taller When Prone is like a book of late Rilke, stray personal dedications, handwritten improvisations, travel notes, set topics, and young ladies' poetry album poems (*Albumblätter*), but then tipped or armed or inflected with a memory of the reliable magic of the *New Poems* of 1907. It is indeed "further topics": brown suits and bastardy (united in the person of the former Australian prime minister, Bob Hawke); an ancient pear tree that after more than a century continues to bear fruit; a pork sandwich, its paper wrapper scrunched up in—typical Murrayism, two parts oxymoron to one of surrealism—a "greaseproof rose"; another retelling of the tragedy of his father and his uncle Archie; the poet's strange mute cat; a lunar eclipse; the night sky; the vagaries of the stock market; lavender fields in Provence; toddlers playing in a roomful of red balloons; his wife's restored eyesight following an operation for cataracts. It celebrates "Cherries from Young" ("one lip-teased drupe / or whole sweet gallop / poured out of cardboard" and "Eucalypts in Exile" ("Their suits are neater abroad, / of denser drape, un-nibbled: / they've left their parasites at home"). It keeps a weather eye out for the police—always a *bête bleue* of Murray's—(in "Croc"), and, in a splendid blizzard of estuary Saxon, proposes, Marianne Moore–style, an unlikely new name for London's fourth airport: "so savour this name: London Sexburga Airport." It hymns the new fast metaphysics of motorways ("I'll ride a slow vehicle // before cars are slow / as country was slow"—the "slow vehicle" is Murray's hearse-to-be), and recalls an ingenious way of getting across (boiling-hot) tarred roads relatively unscathed during "the barefoot age" ("The Filo Soles"). Like the *Neue Gedichte*, the poems average out at around sonnet length and sonnet punch. The cobbler's widow in "Winding Up at the Boot-maker's" ("Kneeling up in Mediterranean black, / reaching down the numbered parcels / as if returning all their wedding gifts") has something of Rilke's notes on life at the Rodins', or his Paris poem

"The Blind Man," where a blind beggar is described as extending his hand "almost formally, as if in marriage." "The Suspect Corpse," fourteen lines from "The dead man lay, nibbled, between / dark carriages of a rocky river, // a curled load of himself, in cheap / clothes crusted in dried water," down to its denouement: "After three months, he could only / generalise, and had started smiling," seems to me to be very evidently in communion with Rilke's "Washing the Corpse," at the end of which "one without a name / lay there, bare and clean, and gave orders." "Generalise"—a refusal to incriminate anyone or himself under the torture that is forensics—is unexpected and funny and canny, and "smiling"—the skull's grin—is grimly sweet; truly, in both cases, dead men talk.

As with Rilke, physical laws change direction, gestures and appearances acquire a different meaning, and power is vested in unexpected quarters. The delicate pastry makes an impermeable layering for tender feet in "The Filo Soles"; "Midi" begins with a cloudscape of exceptional firmness, "Muscles and torsos of cloud / ascended over the mountains," and ends (by agency of the blue herb, itself described as "a strange maize / deeply planted as mass javelins") as an even more solid wonder: "sweet walling breath / under far-up gables of the lavender." "The Farm Terraces" celebrates these wonders of (no pun intended) terrifying human persistence and anonymous, collective labor ("at the orders of hunger / or a pointing lord"), a form of planetary home improvement, visible from space, "Baskets of rich made soil / boosted up poor by the poor." Everywhere, there are these little, or not so little wonders, whether they meet with Murray's approval or not: "A full moon always rises at sunset / and a person is taller when prone" and the drolly conservative musing, "Soldiers now can get in the family way" are both taken from "The Conversations"; there is the blind man who says to the poet, over the phone, "I can hear you smiling," or the mute cat, "A charcoal Russian / he opens his mouth like other cats / and mimes a greeting mew." The language knots, bulges, scintillates; everywhere, organic matter is being pressed to coal, or coal to diamonds. The effect can be silly (I can see and hear Murray's cracked giggle)—"Raj-time uniforms," "plum Crimean fig," "the drunk heir-splitting / of working for parents"—but it is never arch, and is sometimes sublime: "As

bees summarise the garden," or "Chefs' knives peeled green islands /
as the climate turned bohemian / over Woop Woop of the wind
farms / and the bloodshot television" in a poem about global warm-
ing and fusion cuisine, both together (I'll confess I don't understand
the "bloodshot television"—perhaps the turbines interfere with the
reception?). An "Infinite Anthology" celebrates a sort of folk poetry
close to Murray's heart, wonderfully resourceful anonymous linguistic inventions that add, often slyly or disrespectfully, to the gaiety of
things: "daylight—second placegetter when winner is very superior
to field," "dandruff acting—the stiffest kind of Thespian art," "Bap-
tist Boilermaker—coffee and soda (an imagined Puritan cocktail),"
"limo—limousin cattle / proud—castrated but still interested."

A surprise in *Killing the Black Dog* is Murray's prose: he can really
write it, and not like Lowell, say, in "91 Revere Street" or "Near the
Unbalanced Aquarium," like the poetry, only more so—*thicker* im-
pasto of adjectives, *more* proper names, the same furtive emblems, the
same wounding, pivotal scenes—but as its own thing, with the clarity
and good order and communicativeness of prose. Murray doesn't
affect to like prose—in this he is like Ted Hughes, who thought writing so much of it (the seven hundred pages of *Shakespeare and the
Goddess of Complete Being*) was bad for him, and even ultimately hastened his death—but he is undeniably good at it, plain, brave sentences,
descriptive, not overly luxuriant language, logical connections, pur-
poseful paragraphs, effective pacing:

> Every day, though, sometimes more than once a day, sometimes all
> day, a coppery taste in my mouth, which I termed intense insipidity,
> heralded a sense of helpless, bottomless misery in which I would lie
> curled in a foetal position on the sofa with tears leaking from my
> eyes, my brain boiling with a confusion of stuff not worth calling
> thought or imagery: it was more like shredded mental kelp mari-
> naded in pure pain. During and after such attacks, I would be pros-
> trate with inertia, as if all my energy had gone into a black hole.

Murray gives an impressively clear account of his condition, its
sudden and unexpected onset—return, really—following "a well-
attended poetry reading at the bowling club" in 1988, at the end of

which one of the audience "cheerfully recalled to me one of the nicknames she had bestowed on me thirty-odd years previously, and
within a day or two I began to come apart," its roots in the physical
and sexual humiliations he was daily offered at school ("erocide" is
Murray's term for it, "deliberate destruction of a person's sexual mo-
rale"), and the early death of his mother, and the guilt of the two
grief-stricken survivors ("Burning Want"):

> From just on puberty, I lived in funeral:
> mother dead of miscarriage, father trying to be dead,
> we'd boil sweat-brown cloth; cows repossessed the garden.
> Lovemaking brought death, was the unuttered principle.

The boiling of the "sweat-brown cloth" is especially bleak: here are
two monks, Brother Les and Brother Cecil, the last of an order.

Australia, often (the "tall poppy syndrome"), and Australian womanhood in particular, reflexive left-wing politics (encoded as "1968" or
the culture of "the demo"), fashion, hippies, Nazism, "the Totalitarian
Age" of privilege, atheism, feminism, cosmopolitan chic, got whirled
up together into a sort of enemy maelstrom of desire to hurt. Their
presence as words is always a bad sign in Murray's poems—*Taller
When Prone* has a poem called "The 41st Year of 1968," dedicated to
the memory of the "173 dead in the Victorian fires of 2009"—because
the reader knows to expect a dull blast of stodgy fury. "The worst
way to have chronic depression," Murray writes in *Killing the Black
Dog*, "is to have it unconsciously, to be in a burning rage and not
know you are angry." Prose—not the prose here, other, more po-
lemical, occasional prose—cops most of the blame, for being "more
liable than poetry to be infiltrated with the colours of confusion and
obsession," but it is a strange and terrifying thing to see Murray the
poet as well—a generous, charming, equable, and accommodating
soul, who gives equal rights and equal time to feather, flower, scale,
and rock (and to the human counterparts of these things as well)—
become vicious, embattled, humorless, and vengeful. Perhaps none
of the poems in *Killing the Black Dog* are really among Murray's best,
they are too "hot," too emotional, too determinedly therapeutic. They
let the dogs out; the effect is a little like having Charles Bukowski,

say—some hero of Beat autobiography—rewritten by Marianne Moore: it's a waste of both of them, especially Moore. (Although I read them as proof that this too—the rawly personal—is among Murray's gifts.) There are poems in which he writes *about* depression, rather as Lowell writes *about* mania, from outside, from memory, from afterward ("A Torturer's Apprenticeship"):

> Those years trapped in a middling cream town
> where full-grown children hold clear views
> and can tell from his neck he's really barefoot
> though each day he endures shoes,
>
> he's what their parents escaped, the legend
> of dogchained babies on Starve Gut Creek;
> be friends with him and you will never
> be shaved or uplifted, cool or chic.
>
> He blusters shyly—poverty can't afford instincts.
> Nothing protects him, and no one.
> He must be suppressed, for modernity,
> for youth, for speed, for sexual fun.

This is a terrifyingly lucid account of bullying, and the potential for the further, downward transmission of more bullying ("this one might have made dark news") that Murray found in himself. "A Hindenburg of vast rage / rots, though, above your life"—though "rots," as if the thing had been not a blimp but a marrow, is terrifying—somehow still stacks up alongside Lowell's coolly and amiably apologetic "when I have one head / again, not many, like a bunch of grapes." "Performance" builds on Malcolm Lowry's eight-liner "After Publication of *Under the Volcano*" ("Success is like some horrible disaster"):

> I starred last night, I shone:
> I was footwork and firework in one,
>
> a rocket that wriggled up and shot
> darkness with a parasol of brilliants

and a peewee descant on a flung bit;
I was busters of glitter-bombs expanding
to mantle and aurora from a crown,
I was fouettés, falls of blazing paint,
para-flares spot-welding cloudy heaven,
loose gold off fierce toeholds of white,
a finale red-tongued as a haka leap:
that too was a butt of all right!

As usual after any triumph, I was
of course inconsolable.

But I don't know that I know anything like "Rock Music" ("Sex is a Nazi") or "A Stage in Gentrification" ("Most Culture has been an East German plastic bag / pulled over our heads") or "Demo" ("go choke on these quatrain tablets, / I grant you no claim ever")—or if I do, then, like graffiti or heckles or green vitriol, unsigned. These are poems Yeats might have theorized or promulgated in dreams but didn't write, sour outbursts of loathing and unquenchable aggression. Writing not *about* but squarely *out of* his victimhood, Murray is too hard on others, too easy on himself; poetry here shrivels to gifted labeling and sloganeering; things normally played with and toyed with are handled in deadly earnest, as weapons; all superiority disappears, except a desperate need to be superior in close combat. It was surely to punish and forestall just such writing that Yeats delivered his stricture on arguments with others making for "rhetoric." The sense of the poet as embattled and opposed acquires an unhealthy prominence, a centrality, even.

It was one part of Murray's hope that he might be able to write "the dog" out of his system; another—as witness the title of the present volume—that it might have failed to survive its host's near-fatal liver disorder in 1996. It was in that same year that he wrote the bulk of what was originally given as a talk, and with it, the sober makings of a happy ending: "My thinking is no longer jammed and sooty with resentment. I no longer wear only stretch-knit clothes and drawstring pants. I no longer come down with bouts of weeping or reasonless exhaustion. [. . .] If I have a regret, in the sudden youth and health of my mind in its fifty-eighth year, it is that I've got well so late in my life." In a brief afterword from 2009, Murray concedes he was overoptimistic: "I know now that you can't kill the Dog, and that thus my earlier account has the wrong title; it should be called *Learning the Black Dog*." Still, he sounds a little easier, and with the rest of us, and with them (his real and imagined enemies). One feels for him, and with him, in his last sentence: "What I still do mourn is the terrible waste of energy the Dog has exacted from me, over my lifetime and especially in my twenty horror years, and how much more I might have achieved if I'd owned a single, healthy mind working on my side." Poetry, in Murray's admirable practice of it, has been a function of health, of wholesome excess, a margin of clear profit. He is not some sort of John Berryman, luridly and misguidedly asking for "the worst possible ordeal that will not actually kill him"; rather, I see him as a grease monkey fiddling and tooling with language and perception, making idiosyncratic memorial word machines. Murray's crisis narrowed and crabbed his focus, and turned him in on himself—a shame in one who sees so levelly and far, and who writes so abundantly and with such generosity and fullness. The poems and prose here are accordingly—cutely—aptly—dedicated not like his other books "to the glory of God," but "to the need of God." Murray has shown such amazing, prodigious strength of character and discipline and bravery and faith, that he allowed neither himself nor his gift to be broken, but that they fought the Dog together, if not to victory—"*wer spricht von Sieg*," says Rilke—but at least to a standstill.

AUSTRALIAN POETS

Stumbling round the house at moments of absentmindedness or in the off-hours, I wonder where the economy-sized fish tank came from, or the dictionary of some unexpectedly eloquent Oceanian language, or the errant slab of copper sulfate (did some friend or enemy leave it?). Then I remember, it's the new Australian poetry anthology I am reading, the thick end of eleven hundred large pages—is it the format called royal? or republican?!—and I am in for another round of sleeplessness. It's even possible that, in the States, I've read and written about the book mostly on Australian time.

Of course, I know anthologies aren't for reading straight through, any more than cars are for test-driving or cosmetics are for lab mice, but what else can you do? The thickness *is* alarming, but the fear gradually abates, as your marker moves forward and you yourself grow stronger from toting the book around. In fact, all nonsense and whimsy aside, *Australian Poetry Since 1788* is a compelling book and a quite exemplary anthology. I wish the poetry a large domestic and a long overdue international readership in the rest of Anglophonia. Australians have been kept—or kept themselves—to themselves for too long. An anthology is a shop window, and there are some 180 styles on view here. I don't have the background to comment on individual omissions and inclusions, but let me just say that here you will find David and Elizabeth Campbell; Kevin Hart and William Hart-Smith; the Joneses Emma and Evan; Harley Matthews and Jack Mathieu; the Porter ménage of Dorothy, Hal, and Peter; Philip Neilsen and John Neilson; Adam Gordon and Lisa Gorton; Bruce Beaver and Barcroft Boake.

I approve and endorse all the formal decisions taken by the editors, who have dealt fairly, generously, interestingly, and inwardly with the material (with which, and in which, as they say, they have lived for upward of fifty years, and this is their third anthology together). An anthology edited by poets rather than academics (they get to have their say on reputations later—why should they be present at the christening as well?) is increasingly a fine thing and a good start. Despite its length, there is actually a just proportionality and progress to the book; true, there are thirty-three poets born in the 1940s—the decade of both the editors—as many as the decades before (thirteen) and after (twenty) put together and very nearly a fifth of the total, but probably that's to be expected, and more disturbing would have been something like the opposite: a blind spot or immunity to one's direct contemporaries. Though ranging across time, an anthology almost inevitably remains *of* its own time; as one curious instance of this, the first reference to computers (from Gwen Harwood) is less than half the way into the book. A general introduction is kept very short (two pages); there are detailed—and often brilliantly lively—biographical notes on each individual poet, so that even someone represented with just one or two poems is firmly and incontrovertibly *there*; and there is an unusually hospitable approach to long poems. Fifty- or hundred-line poems are ten-a-penny here (they are only a page or two in this large format), but also included are John Farrell's wowingly macabre foundation myth "My Sundowner" at over five hundred lines, twenty-two of the twenty-seven sections of the sumptuous and sexy Aboriginal "Goulburn Island Cycle," all eight pages of Les Murray's dazzling lyrical celebration of backed-up traffic, family outings, delighted dogs, and tremendous water-skiers called "Buladelah-Taree Holiday Song Cycle," and so on and so forth.

Not that short poems and light verse are neglected either: there are Harold Stewart's couplet versions of haiku, and saucy limericks by Slessor and others, the four-line anthem to "Stringy-Bark and Green-Hide," Robert Gray's "Sixteen Short Poems" (there is no falsely modest nonsense about the editors excluding themselves; they were poets before they were editors, and they are here as poets as well as editors; each selects from the work of the other; each gets twenty pages, which is plenty but not at all excessive; fair play to them). There is Jennifer Compton's winningly persistent "Electric Fan (*from* Rome)":

The obedient fan
turns his blind face
to me—with interest.
The obedient fan
turns his blind face
to me—with interest.

There are convict ballads and songs, some simple, some more sophisticated (I love the line, "we were all associated round the old keg of rum"), pages and pages where, as much as tales of titanic labor, or skullduggery, or heroism, or stupidity, rising anapaestic rhythm settles in your acoustic brain.

Banjo Paterson's heartbreaking "Waltzing Matilda" is here, as is the anonymous "Wild Colonial Boy"; there is both "The Captain of the Push" and its parody—or possibly original—version, "The Bastard from the Bush." The great literary hoax, "Ern Malley" ("I am still / The black swan of trespass on alien waters"—doesn't it sound like a confession?) figures, as does a goodly portion of C. J. Dennis's wonderful skit on *Romeo and Juliet*, affectionately known as "The Bloke." There is Vicki Raymond's sonnet "On Seeing the First Flasher" and Bruce Dawe's lament "At Shagger's Funeral." There is Kenneth Slessor's "Country Towns" and Bruce Dawe's "Provincial City" ("Saturday night, in the main street kerb, / the angle-parked cars are full of watchers, / their feet on invisible accelerators, / going nowhere *fast*"). There is Jamie Grant's "Social Behaviour of Minted Peas" and Les Murray's "The Broadbean Sermon." There are poems of flood and poems of drought, Harley Matthews's and Leon Gellert's poems of Gallipoli and Eric Rolls's poems of World War II in New Guinea; Ada Cambridge dreams of Venice, and Dorothy Hewett has complex memories of the USSR; there is Jan Harry's "Page for a Lorikeet," Caroline Caddy's "Squid," and David Campbell's peculiar and lovely macaronic "Le Wombat." C. J. Dennis celebrates "One of those great lords of language gone for ever from Out-back," while Robert Adamson (same difference?) recollects his brothers "biting the heads off words." Elizabeth Riddell and Barry Humphries both have poems about Patrick White (and I was almost surprised there weren't more). Rhyll McMaster writes about her mother's stroke ("Her brain is stripped / to its inessentials. / She's disposed of the gears"), Robert Gray—in "In Departing Light," one of the outstanding poems in the collection—tenderly details his mother's dementia, Anthony Lawrence describes his bipolar disorder, Francis Webb his schizophrenia. There is Charles Harpur's "A vagrant mass / Of sunshine, falling into some void place," and Chris Wallace-Crabbe's—corroborative, dissenting?—"We just don't live in a hard intellectual glare." David Malouf has "Brisbane ladies, rather / the worse for war" and Anthony Lawrence has things going "prickly pear-shaped." And the best (comic) rhyme? Probably a toss-up between Barry Humphries's "misery/pat-isserie" and Alan Wearne's "Werribee/aromatherapy."

In ethnosociobiographical terms, the array of Australian poets is quite astounding—perhaps unrivaled anywhere for now. What the American poet laureate Philip Levine once called "stupid jobs" are here in wonderful profusion: Bellerive "sold brooms from door to door without much success," while Roland Robinson "was a horse-trainer, jockey, fencer, dam builder, factory worker, railway fettler, cleaner, art school model, ballet dancer, dance critic" and "caught crocodiles and snakes for a menagerie." One poet is of English and Icelandic background, and there are others whose first language was Greek or Polish, or who were Hungarian and dreamed in German; one born of Irish parents in Buenos Aires and another who remained "a real Corkonian in his speech"; one failed English grammar while another "came second in the State competition"; many had next to no formal schooling, others were dux and prefect of their expensive select schools; there were solitaries and symposiarchs; Communists and Catholics; sports buffs and *Sportmuffel*; larrikins and unrepentant members of the squattocracy; some died having put together manuscripts to send halfway round the world to England, others lost their jobs when they popped a love poem instead of a business letter into an envelope; many grew up in houses without books, others were novelists, journalists, memoirists, publishers, edited anthologies, edited each other, founded Penguin Australia, founded the *Australian Book Review*; one was professor of Zulu in London, another went to Paraguay to join a utopian Socialist community called New Australia; the early work of one was destroyed by a mice plague, another was blackballed for an acrostic that read "FUCK ALL EDITORS" (a sonnet, eh, thinks the reviewer, with his best po-face on). One was advised to leave school and go into shoe repairing, another ended his days as ambassador to France; a friend's obituary of one was turned down, another's death made front-page news; one's body lay unclaimed (all his life, he had known only poverty and poetry, it was said), another was buried in Poets' Corner in Westminster Abbey.

From lively folksy balladry on one side and a slightly anxious, etiolated literariness on the other ("even though there be / Some notes that unto other lyres belong," writes Henry Kendall), Australian poetry has come not so much into its own as into everyone else's own. (Hence my previous paragraph's reveling in the historic variety of Australian poets' lives and work; nowadays, one way or another, most poems are literary, and most poets teach.) American and British, Aboriginal and Oriental influences balance out. There are the usual mutually opposed strivings to keep standards high and to carry on a live communication with a readership; one consequence of the latter is that Australia seems to have many more verse novels than other countries. An unease, almost an embarrassment, about language and a stern desire to name and describe specifically Australian realities continue to fight each other. The ballads and the two Aboriginal song cycles were a revelation to me. Those pages are certainly the most highly flavored here. And otherwise? Eric Rolls's "Bamboo" ("But I sing of the quality of bamboo") is sly and wonderful; Douglas Stewart's brilliant "Two Englishmen" is as good an anatomization of the hapless auld enemy as I have read: "But in their own small island crowded thickly, / Each with his pride of self and race and caste, / They could not help but be a little prickly / And in their wisdom they evolved at last / This simple code to save them from destruction— / One did not speak without an introduction." Robert Gray stands out to me for having devised a calmly luxuriant manner of reminiscing: "He often drank alone / at the RSL club, and had been known to wear a carefully-considered tie / to get drunk in the sandhills, watching the sea." Gig Ryan's "If I Had a Gun" is memorably ferocious, but still, in its way, in the line of Geoff Page's paean to Australian womanhood, "Grit." I was impressed by Emma Lew's spaciously dissociated lines: "Rounded forms of crockery gleam in the great hall / The Führer's pockets are always filled with chocolates." Philip Hodgins is a real loss (he died in 1995, just thirty-six years old), but before that he was an immense gain: his hard, sad, often violent poems are both plainspoken and intense: "There wasn't much else we could do / that final day on the farm. / We couldn't take them with us into town, / no-one round the district needed them / and the new people had their own. / It was one of those things" (from "Shooting the Dogs").

KAREN SOLIE

Introducing Karen Solie, I would adapt what Joseph Brodsky said some thirty years ago of the great Les Murray: "It would be as myopic to regard Mr. Murray as an Australian poet as to call Yeats an Irishman. He is, quite simply, the one by whom the language lives." Solie is Canadian (born in 1966, in Moose Jaw, Saskatchewan, of Norwegian immigrant stock), the author of three previous books of poems, *Short Haul Engine* (2001), *Modern and Normal* (2005), and *Pigeon* (2009), and now *The Living Option: Selected Poems*, and, yes, as we embark on the third millennium of our so-called Common Era, she is indeed the one by whom the language lives. I wonder, a little bitterly, what the point of English as a soi-disant world language is if our smug maps have only the UK and the US on them, and everywhere else is apocrypha or appendix, the province of specialists or pity. Enormous credit goes to Bloodaxe for commissioning and bringing out this exhilarating volume, Solie's first book publication outside Canada.

If I wanted to show someone—an agnostic—what a modern poem can do, I would show them something by Lawrence Joseph, or

Frederick Seidel, or Karen Solie, all different but all modern, all *modo hodie*, all fresh today. A poem of Solie's is sentences in unpredictable but deep sequence in unpredictable but braced lines. It seems out of control, but isn't; it exhibits grace while falling, which is perhaps what grace is. It runs the gamut from nervous, garrulous charm to the glory and shear of impersonal style: it is idiomatic splicing in one voice. It offers wisdom, fact, and bitter experience (yes, it is pessimistic, or negative, or critical, or ironic, depending on what one word one wants to use, but then so would Whitman be if he were back among us: in Musil's *The Man Without Qualities*, Ulrich says, "The man of genius is duty bound to attack," and Brecht wrote in "To Those Born Later," "Truly, I live in dark times! / A bland word is foolish. An unlined brow / Indicates impercipience. The man laughing only / Laughs because the terrible news / Has not yet reached him"). It is a noticing, a naming and a connecting, an electric errancy. It is round-the-corner knight moves in a world of pawns, or almost worse, rooks; googlies and chinamen among dobbers. It is a widening and widening optic that returns us unexpectedly ("the variable / when the outcome is unknown, / as always the outcome is unknown"—take that, Mr. Rumsfeld!) to the place we began. It may be to comic or grievous effect. It is an adventitious gallivanting movement across country that makes denser, bunched sense than any more rational or measured or predictable progress. It looks baroque, but actually it's stringent, and vice versa. (I've come to think you can't actually have poetry without dandyism, and that includes all those I've mentioned: Frederick Seidel self-evidently, but also those seemingly austere figures Whitman, Brecht, Murray, and Brodsky. As Wallace Stevens said, "It must give pleasure.") It looks random, but like Thom Gunn's "blue jay scuffling in the bushes," it "follows some hidden purpose." Other things, set beside it, look lame and tedious—like prose. It reminds me of another axiom of Brodsky's, that poetry is a function of speed: it gets there faster than prose, and goes farther.

Quoting will come, but it is hell, and you need to know that. Solie doesn't write many short poems—say, twelve lines or fewer. They are wonderful as well ("Untitled," "The Prime Minister," "Pigeon") but somehow atypical; her standard length is a full page and upward, say, thirty to fifty lines—*pace* the author, more like a medium-haul engine. So I eye up a passage in a longer poem, and before long I know neither where to stop nor where to begin. I go on to another one. Same deal. A review—a representation—of the poems is utterly beyond me if I can't even take representative bites out of them: I am left staring down at their beguiling, unassimilable teem and squirm. There is hardly a poem in *The Living Option* that I wouldn't cite with alacrity and delight. I could write out the table of contents (Solie has wonderful titles: "Your News Hour Is Now Two Hours" or "Cardio Room, Young Women's Christian Association" or "Your Premiums Will Never Increase!" As good as anything by Eno.) I am floundering. The only reservation I have about the book is that it leaves out a number of other, equally marvelous poems. Perhaps that's where I should begin: the *livre des refusés*, grief at omission? (Though please understand that there is more than enough in *The Living Option* to overwhelm any new reader—65 poems out of a total of 143 in the three books, plus 26 new pieces.)

Enough with the computations. Take the first poem in Solie's first book, a sly little shocker called "Eating Dirt." There's a home movie, it seems, of the author in infancy, a sessile toddler, "huge and white on the just-turned plot. / An early grinning vegetable / sprung up overnight, feeding / methodically, in fistfuls." Yes, dear reader, she is doing what it says in the title. With grave charm, Solie worries "at the wisdom / of this documentary, its complicity / in my vice, where it has led." "After all," she says sagely, it's not as though she doesn't know: "some cravings / are only charming when you're small." So what does she do in the poem? Knock it on the head, desist, re-form, try something else, cold turkey? Not a bit of it. She carries on, taking care to do it secretly, though she tells us about it, and it sounds worse than anything before, with "lick" and "fingers" and "private": "I've since learned, / when potting houseplants, / to lick my fingers / in private." The poem establishes Solie in her East of Eden terrain (no pun), which is the less than ideal, the less than attractive, the recidivist, the unlucky, even the cursed and doomed. The poem pushes me toward another instaurational poem, by another farm child: "Digging," the first poem in Seamus Heaney's *Death of a Naturalist*. Both are poems that lay claim to a slightly unexpected, even slightly implausible, persistence, while acknowledging that their makers have left the straight way: one digs with his pen, the other retires to eat dirt.

Or take another unadopted poem, one or two along in *Short Haul Engine*, "Boyfriend's Car," annotated by me as "such a great poem!" Every word dangerous, every word a specification: "Black Nova. Jacked up. Fast. / Rhetorical question. Naturally, / a girl would choose / the adult conspiracy / of smoked glass, darkened interiors. / Privacy. Its language / of moving parts, belts, / and unfamiliar fluids." Again, the fast puns, the spaces in the narration, the withdrawn third person, the fearless co-opting of abstractions (privacy, language, adult), the uneasy coexistence of power—or powerlessness—and glory, divine and human (surely Apollo hovers somewhere behind the poem). "Hair in the door handle, / white white arms / pretty against / the grain, the red" is as compressed and expressive as anything in Akhmatova (say, the polluted image of her braids in the man's pipe smoke). The finish is a split of pity and terror, maximized by the line breaks: "When she asked / to go home he said / *Well now that depends / on you.*" As she will go on to show in the "found" poems of *Modern and Normal* (say, the jock's monologue in "Bruce. After Last Call"), Solie has a dandy's ear for speech, others' as well as her own.

Take another excluded poem, from *Modern and Normal*, "Lines Composed a Few Miles above Duncairn Dam." A literary-, even a poetic-sounding title, one of precious few moments of suggestion or allusion (in view of the savage sneer of "reading Bly by night / Rand by day," it's probably just as well for literature!). It's one of the great things about Solie: so much is primary, hasn't been written about before, pays no dues, does without obeisances or retreading or sheepishness. And when she does quote or refer in her poems, it's not from poets but philosophers and thinkers, which are her preferred form of accelerant or authority. (Hence the unusual thinkiness of her poems, their unfashionable tolerance for abstractions, and, not coincidentally, my difficulty in quoting from them.) Here, though, a touch of Wordsworth or Coleridge in the title, a bit of Romantic pleinairism and genius loci. And where are we? A fish camp. Somewhere an aggressive type of snail has kept away moneyed visitors, though in other respects conditions are favorable. Still, the place has failed to take off in the desired way. Ergo redneck heaven. It gets wonderfully dry, factual notations: "On the north side, squatters' cabins and planted / shade trees. Further up is the dump. Burn pit, fish guts, / trash. Recall the neighbours. You can't just do / whatever you want. There are certain kinds / of boating. Gull Lake's close. We all drive." A kind of self-governance evolves, a highly specific ecosystem, the beginnings of a kind of history: "Simmie, adjacent, was a town once. The little plank church / makes a good photograph. Someone's junk is in it." It's as perfect as a Walker Evans picture.

As Brodsky says, poets like Murray give you the living language, but you get the country thrown in, extra, no charge. It gets you thinking about the supposedly uninteresting condition of being Australian or being Canadian, of patterns of settlement in these supposedly uninteresting places without much history: that of Australia is peripheral, that of Canada (where 80 percent of the population lives within a hundred miles of the US border) is south-heavy. If Australia's a beach with a pretense of no hinterland ("the bush, or as we now say the Land, / the three quarters of our continent / set aside for mystic poetry," as Les Murray caustically remarks in "Louvres"), Canada's a frontier, an enterprise zone that frays to the north and very rapidly gets very thin on top. (Australia is afraid of what it contains, Canada of what it abuts; both, setting more store by what's underneath than what's on the surface, have declared their entrails open for business.) There are edgeland atmospheres and experiences and conditions that you don't find anywhere else, settled, unsettled, resettled, unsettling:

> The store, next to the beverage room, sells smokes
> and low-end booze, rat traps, potato wedges, shampoo,
> Raid, ice cream, cribbage boards, Crazy Glue,
> buffalo wings, rubber gloves, line and lures,
> etc. Leeches can be purchased from the pop machine
> outside, a half-dozen for $1.25. A sweet life:
> Coke, Seven-Up, water, bait. You could walk from the lake
> but no one does.

"Sweet" there may look like irony, but it's nothing of the kind. The higgledy-piggledy catalog is notably unjudgmental: pure repertorial anthropology.

If I am allowed one more *lamentoso* description of an excluded poem, then perhaps the one called "Four Factories" from *Pigeon*. Like "Eating Dirt," it's what it says on the packet: one mystery software plant (?), one potato chip factory, one cement works, one abattoir. Each section is beautifully couched in its specific speak, with its individual lighting, its angle, aperture, exposure, and problems. The high-tech acquires a cloak of sumptuously neoteric blarney, "opportune spinoffs, low-slung / by-product support outfits named in functional / shorthand." The chip factory is more honest, more straightforward, and is celebrated for its simple garishness: "It's painted a bright and not entirely baffling / turquoise, for who would want / their snacks to issue from a dour scene?" (The eighteenth-century reasonableness of tone here and elsewhere is one of Solie's great inventions: a pained elevation.) The cement factory walks us through chemistry ("Pity the diatoms, first to go, trout eggs / choked by sediment in gravelly streambeds, / ducks in chloride runoff. Pity us, / we're all messed up about it") to a rapturous upland vision of commerce, again in the necessary argot: "in condos, dude ranches, / four-season resorts, the demand for improved / infrastructure and amenities in the recreational / community of Lac des Arc." The abattoir is described in fast cutup, with slabs of critical and actual promotional language slid along on conveyors: "The Canadian / Forces steps up its recruitment // campaign. Our industry's future remains / secure. Additional openings in rendering / and hides. Animals are not our friends. Sign / on the highway, *Always, 100 Jobs!*" "Four Factories" reads to me almost like a dissident Russian poem (or dissident Sophoclean chorus): how tremendous that all this exists—and how tremendously sad. "Pity us."

Solie is expert in mobility and cheap tenancy—perhaps these too are preconditions for the modern poet. The poem "Drift" ends: "This is him, going, / This is her, gone." The poems seem to have been generated in dozens of places and the distances between them: "Days Inn," "Salmon River Motel," "Java Shop, Fort MacLeod"; "In Passing, "Skid," "Driving Alone," "Rental Car," "Medicine Hat

Calgary One-Way." Solie has measured out her life in motor vehicles: "an even-tempered '68 Volvo" and "a blue Mercury parked at the edge of the continent"; "the old Ford" and "cursing ancestors and old Volkswagens"; a "mid-century Case" and the titanic "Buhler Versatile 2360," hero of the beautiful poem "Tractor"; the cute "freshly birthed Fusions" outside a Ford plant and the "rows / of wrecked cars in the junkyards, / hoods open like a choir." After Heaney and Murray, she is the great poet of driving, but she is more radical than they are. She is prey to a sort of nomadism that feels more like claustrophobia or serial eviction than tourism. She is equally adept at looking out or back, at looking, and at imagining being seen. "In the language / of local economies you are table 12, / room 105," goes the passive version in "Driving Alone," "Pure transaction. / A sure thing of money changing hands." Against that, there are passages like: "Motel the orange of an old rind, bud green / and remaindered blue for trim. Some schemes / shouldn't work, but do. A square room / with balcony two floors above the strip. Real / keys" ("Possibility"). The "real / keys" are sublime. The poems show their familiarity with the short run, the short term, the short straw: "Eight yards to the motel office, one more / to ring the bell. The ice machine means well, a grey slab / I attend with my bucket. I've been here before, / paced it off and slept beneath a sheet / forty feet from the highway" ("More Fun in the New World"). It's not a complaint (it's not a TripAdvisor review or a slumming Baedeker), this is what there is, these are our tawdry surfaces and circumstances, this is what life has unexpectedly dished up: "A doorknob // came off in my hand like a joke prosthetic. / Rooms like this have followed me around / for 20 years. It's as though I married into a bad / family of many cousins. I was the only one // who loved them. That's what I thought" ("Conversion").

I like personal poems and have mostly quoted from Solie's. But the fact is that the individual "I" and the dual "we" are just three of the figures on her carousel. (It is striking that her oeuvre as a whole is as interesting and as intricately and cleverly put together as each individual poem—those fractals that she also writes about, in action.) She has a gift for the plural, the collective scene—intelligent, ironic, scrutinized, as everything is with her—that is rare in good Western poetry. Her synoptics are wonderful, in "Alert Bay, Labour Day," in "The Girls," in "Erie." She writes about moments when the individual docks or attempts to dock or fails to dock with what I believe Heidegger called "*das man*" (the impersonal, collective "one"). The great poem "Medicine Hat Calgary One-Way" sets out with—how to describe that tone: meekness, po-faced sedition, sober hilarity: "The bus is a wreck, and passengers / respect that": one idly wonders how such respect might manifest itself. By sitting extra still, or spitting, or smoking—perhaps as in that "family restaurant in which smoking, // active or passive, was unofficially / mandatory" ("Erie"). Or take "Prayers for the Sick," where patients waiting in a Toronto emergency ward are unexpectedly taken out of themselves and given a common purpose by their fury at a short TV loop showing the detestable, record-breaking—and currently banned—Yankees' baseball star and all-round bad hat, Alex Rodriguez, and his "dirty trick on our rookie." There is a sense here of convergence, of fellowship offered and taken, of the warmth of the tribe. In other poems, like "Three in the Afternoon" ("Stalled hour. Hour / of chronics. Never / is anything not done / less so"), the speaker retains her unhappy separateness, "while across municipalities / workers stride the day toward / the dinners they deserve." The becalmed artist of three o'clock is like a "parasite" in a Soviet reality: doesn't stride, deserves no dinner, is left like (Solie's fellow Norwegian) Edvard Munch to stare into the blank eyes ("as if recently brainwashed," as Sylvia Plath wrote) of the crowd on Karl Johansgatan.

And then there are those collectives that are deaf to the siren chant of the human—because they are other species. It is to them that Solie's special respect and admiration goes out (she once studied zoology): "Sturgeon," "Toad," "Wild Horses," "Pest Song," "Mole," "Thrasher," "Gopher": "We turn / our ankles where you've been and bust your heads / for fun." Creatures that don't need us or undermine us, that live off us or against us, that are older than us, keener and subtler and better adapted. These are upsetting, gallant, Lawrentian poems ("Wild Horses"):

A few hundred remain on grizzly lands below
hanging glaciers, among Engelmann spruce, fir,

lodgepole pine, foothills of aspen and balsam poplar
in the Siffleur, White Goat and Peace Wilderness
where they're shot for sport, caught for rodeo stock,
sold for dog food at four hundred a head. Sixteen
left to rot in the forest northwest of Jasper,
two foals dumped at a gas well site by the only
animal who kills from a distance, noise for a voice
and noise for a home, for whom all places are alike.

PART TWO

"SHARP BISCUIT": SOME THOUGHTS ON TRANSLATING

NOTES FROM A GUILTY BUSINESS

A handful of lucky or gifted poets fill their lives with poetry. I'm thinking of the likes of Ashbery, Brodsky, Ted Hughes, Les Murray. They write/wrote poems, it seems to me, practically every day, the way prose writers write their novels. The date at the bottom of Mandelstam poems. Plath poems. It's a question of the force of the gift, the pounds per square inch of the Muse. Heaney, too, comes close. The rest of us strike compromises, do something else "as well," mostly teach, in a handful of cases do other, unrelated work, have "a job" in the "real world." The job is the enemy of the poetry, its successful, favored rival (the job is everything, the poem nothing; who wants the poem, and who doesn't want the job?), but may also be the dirt from which the poetry grows. Such, anyway, is my hope, translating.

◆ ◆ ◆

Meetings with remarkable translators. To coin a phrase. The first was Ralph Manheim (translator of Grass and Handke, then as now the two most prominent living German authors, but also of Brecht and Céline and Danilo Kiš and any number of others—*Mein Kampf*, anyone?), who invited me to drinks at his flat in Paris. A native of Chicago, if I remember, and one of the great generation of American translators that was produced by the war. 1980, 1982, something like that. Six o'clock. Yardarm time. I turn up, meet him and his charming wife, who has suffered a stroke and whom he is looking after. I feel a bond with him: the unusual, "thin" spellings of our names, only one *n* in his, only one *f* in mine in the same place, plus he is exactly fifty years older than me, born in 1907. We talk about the vexatious Handke, who is also living in Paris, and with whom he says, in a gallant adaptation of the German idiom (which exists in the negative form), "*ist gut Kirschen essen*," you *can* share a bowl of cherries, i.e., a companionable and generous and uncomplicated sort. I demur, but he says it, and he may after all be right. (Years later, I am with friends in Paris. Very late, long after supper, there is a knock on the door. It is Peter Handke, who only ever walks everywhere, unannounced, with his hat full of mushrooms he has picked. They are straightaway cooked and eaten, and I am surprised by Handke, who is tanned and strong and kind, and has a firm handshake, and I think about the cherries, and the Manheims.) I drink a beer, they both have whiskey. Ralph has come from his office in another building. The sense, then, of it being a job, that he keeps regular hours, locks it up, and comes home. Doesn't allow it to sprawl greedily or disfiguringly over his life. I think, if I think at all, of my father who writes at home, giving dictation—furthermore—to my mother, in what passes for our living room. His writing is everywhere, fills the airwaves, fills our family space, governs our lives like national economy.

Then Joseph Brodsky, sometime later in the eighties, in the Tufnell Park flat of a friend of his. Espresso and Vecchio Romano in a somewhat redundant, spotless kitchen. (He wrote about Auden's "real library of a kitchen" in Kirchstetten, but I guess that for him and in his life, most of the action will have been in, so to speak, the real kitchen of this or that library. As he said, "freedom is a library"; it isn't a kitchen.) "Circumcised" cigarettes. The practiced fingers pull out the sponge, pull out the fluff, discard the fluff, return the sponge. Only then is it safe to smoke. He is translating Cavafy, whom he loves. The classicism, the history, the anonymity. Into Russian. He has brought with him from New York a Russian portable typewriter. Greek into Cyrillic. In bourgeois north London. A bizarre, Conradian phenomenon. The translator as bacillus.

Maybe one more. A rare (for me) gathering of translators in New York City, perhaps some awards ceremony, I don't remember. We fill the front rows of a theater somewhere, feeling unusually effervescent, like a gathering of missionaries, or spies on day release. Optimistic. Righteous. Both full of ourselves and among ourselves, *unter uns*. Ourselves alone—Sinn Féin. The charabanc effect. To make things better/worse, Paul Auster is brought on to address us. Then someone announces that Gregory Rabassa is of the company, somewhere right and in front of us. A slight, stooped figure rises, bows. From the stage, a beam tries to pick him out, to try to somehow give him some plasticity. I don't think I would recognize him on the street. The first translator I was aware of, I read his García Márquez when I was twenty and doorstepped his London publishers. (Remember García Márquez's praise for him as "the best Latin American writer in the English language"?) A little pencil mustache, maybe? An imperial? I doubt myself, and think probably I'm making it up, extrapolating, literarizing. We applaud frantically. Such are the heroes of a secret business, a guilty business, even.

♦ ♦ ♦

I translate to try to amount to something. When I first held my first book of poems in my hands (the least extent acceptable to the British Library, forty-eight pages including prelims), I thought it would fly away. To repair a deficit of literature in my life. My ill-advised version of Cartesianism: *traduco, ergo sum*. Ill-advised because the translator has no being, should neither be seen nor heard, should be (yawn) faithful, should be (double yawn) a plate of glass. Well, *Kerrang!!!*

♦ ♦ ♦

Many, if not most, translators operate with an acquired language, or languages, and their own, which is the one, according to Christopher

Logue, they have to be really good at. (I never trust people who translate both into and out of a language: isn't there something unsanitary about that, like drinking the bathwater?) That brings a certain dispassion to their proceedings, a lab coat, tweezers, a fume cupboard. But both my languages are "my own": German, my so-called mother tongue, and English, which I have no memory of learning at the age of four and was the language I first read and wrote in. Both are lived languages, primal languages: the one of family and first namings and, now, of companionship and love; the other of decades of, I hope, undetectable and successful assimilation in England. Which should I be without?

I was happily bilingual till my midtwenties, when I began, by economic necessity, to translate. The matching of my two languages is an inner process, the setting of a broken bone, a graft, the healing of a wound. Perhaps it can even be claimed that in me German is in some way an open wound, which is soothed and brought to healing by the application of English. Translation as a psychostatic necessity. Look, there is no break in my life, no loss of Eden, no loss of childhood certainties, no discontinuity, no breach, no rupture, no expulsion. English, then, as a bandage, a splint, a salve.

♦ ♦ ♦

Late in my translation of my father's novel of small town Germany in the thirties and forties, *The Film Explainer*, about his grandfather, my great-grandfather, you may read: "Anyone who now saw Grandfather on the street, under his artist's hat, with which 'he shields his thick skull from others' ideas' (Grandmother) no longer said: Hello, Herr Hofmann! He said: Heil Hitler! Or: Another scorcher!"

Yes, this one is ontologically and humorously important to me, it's a family book, the hero's name is Hofmann, and I identify with everyone in it because they're all a part of me: the vainglorious oldster (like me, a wearer of hats), the acerbic grandmother, the anxious-to-please small boy—but even beyond that, the expressing of that history, its domestication in English, gives me immense satisfaction. Where is the rift, the breach, if it is a matter of chance whether you say the Terry-Thomas "Another scorcher!" or the truly villainous "Heil Hitler!"? It could just as well have happened to you, it implies, and: look, I am making a joke of it, and: how can you think I am different? I am putting together something in myself, and in my history.

Hence—though of course no one likes a bad review—the way I react unusually badly (it seems to me) to mistakes (I do make them) and to readers' or reviewers' rebukes. It interferes with my healing, my knitting together, my convalescence. It tears off a bandage and scrapes open my hurt, or my heart. Don't disturb my zigzags, I think.

♦ ♦ ♦

Translation is the production of words, hundreds of thousands of words, by now many millions of words. I prefer short books, I am lazy, I am a poet, one page is usually plenty for me. But even so, the long books have snuck up on me, and passed through me. *The Radetzky March* perhaps 140,000 words. Two long Falladas, two hundred thousand apiece. Fallada short stories, another hundred thousand. Ernst Jünger 130,000, and with a bunch of other war books—how did I get into that?—comfortably four hundred thousand. Seventy books, millions and millions of words, like millions and millions of numbers, like π, an unreal number. If I notice myself starting to repeat (3 point 141592 . . .), I promise myself, then I will stop.

♦ ♦ ♦

This is all distraction on an industrial scale, the "still small voice" of poetry decibeled over, my puny resources vastly overstretched, the ninety-eight-pound weakling unhappily running amok with a chest expander. In the Nietzsche/Jünger way, it will either kill me or make me strong. Again, how did it happen? Out of fealty to my novelist father: prose. Out of my German nature: *Tüchtigkeit*, energetic production, industry, diligence. Out of dissatisfaction with my own slow, woolgathering, window-gazing methods: all-consuming tasks in unbroken sequence. Out of a desire to make more—and heavier—books:

translation. Given his druthers, what does moony Narcissus take upon himself? Why, the labors of Hercules!

♦ ♦ ♦

If you want someone to look after your sentences for you, who or what better than a poet? If you want someone to regulate—enterprisingly regulate—your diction, cadence your prose, hook a beginning to an ending, jam an ending up against a beginning, drive a green fuse through the gray limbs of clauses—a poet. If you're looking for prose with dignity, with surprise, with order, with attention to detail. That's why the first item in Tom Paulin's book of electric free translations, *The Road to Inver*, is his version of the opening of Camus's *The Plague*. Prose. Well, up to a point.

♦ ♦ ♦

And the resources, the tools? Well, they can be anything at all. Sometimes, when I've liked certain expressions in German—most especially when they weren't things I knew and therefore gave me the sense that not everyone would know them in German—I let them stand. Uncommon in German, why not new in English? In *Every Man Dies Alone*, there's this: "The actor Max Harteisen had, as his friend and attorney Toll liked to remind him, plenty of butter on his head from pre-Nazi times." There is a footnote to this, but it's none of my making: I'd have let it go without. Butter on the head—isn't it an adorable expression?! Or this, from the novel *Seven Years* by Peter Stamm, a scene in which two architects are exchanging career advice: "Berlin is an El Dorado, he said, if you're half-presentable, then you can earn yourself a golden nose." Nothing easier than to have said "really fill your boots" or "earn silly money" or "a shedload of money," but I didn't want to: the golden nose—what a perfect expression of the wealth gap: such a futile, practically syphilitic protuberance!—had wowed me too much.

So, things let stand from German—but also the opposite. Things fetched from every corner of English. Someone told me a phrase in my Wassermann translation is Australian (I spent hours looking but couldn't find the reference, though I do remember once trying to use "Esky," from "Eskimo," the Australian term for a cooler, and not being allowed to). Another expression—"a kick in the slats"—is from a Dublin-born civil servant I used to know. This is translation not quite as autobiography but maybe as "autography": turning out my pockets, Schwitters-style, a bus ticket, a scrap of newspaper, a fag packet, a page torn out of a diary. The words are not just words; they are words that I've knocked around with; they reflect my continuing engagement with Lowell, with Brodsky, with Bishop, with Malcolm Lowry, words that have had some wear and tear, there is fade in them, and softness, and history, maybe not visibly so for every reader, but palpably, to some.

I use English and American more or less as they come to hand; it used to be I thought I knew the difference, and even imagined I could deliberately switch between them, but I'm no longer sure. Is it the hood or the bonnet? The boot or the trunk? Does something take the biscuit or the cake? Is it the shoe that drops or the penny? Am I pernickety or more persnickety? Inevitably, and increasingly—it's a function of my life and reading, as well as of having employers in London and New York—things in me will come out mixed, in a style you could call "universal-provincial." A molten, mongrel English (which I happen to believe is the genius and proclivity of the language anyway). What I find most resistant (and least simpatico) is the authentic and the limited and the local (but what translation is going to sit happily with those qualities: they are each the antithesis of translation). Everything expressive is possible. I fight hard for British expressions in my US translations ("on the never-never" is one that comes to mind—surely the American economy would be in a different shape if that jolly warning of the dangers of excessive credit had been understood!), and I like introducing British readers to American expressions as well. Eight boyhood years in Edinburgh—I thought they had left no trace—find a belated upsurge in a welter of Scottish-isms: "postie," "wee," "agley," "first-footing." (The main beneficiary/sufferer was Durs Grünbein; if I thought anything by it [by no means sure], perhaps that I was mapping provincialisms, Saxon onto Scottish, eighteenth-century capital onto eighteenth-century capital, his Dresden childhood onto mine in the self-styled "Athens of the North.") Words I've used in poems myself, "bimble" and others, get in on the act. It's not just that translation takes away all your words, it's more insidious than that, more neutron-bomb-like: it takes away all *my* words. Again, once I find myself repeating myself, or see a certain predictability and mannerism in the use—without much sanction from the original—of a slightly dandyish, comical, rueful register, say .888888 recurring, it'll be time for me to stop.

♦ ♦ ♦

But that's the problem: Whose words are you going to use, if not your own? Reprising Buffon, Wallace Stevens said: "A man has no choice about his style." Why shouldn't it be just as true of a translator as of John Doe, author? Is it imagined that you take a dictionary to an original, and make fifty or hundred thousand hermetically separate transactions, translating, in effect, blind, and into a language not yours and no one else's? Is that a book? Every word taken out of its association-proof shrink-wrapping? I don't see how a personal vocabulary and personal grammar and a personal rhythm—at least where they exist, in anyone evolved enough to have them—are to be excluded. Chocolates carry warnings that they may have been manufactured using equipment that has hosted peanuts; why not translations too? But then not just "has written the occasional modern poem" but also "likes punk" or "early familiarity with the works of Dickens" or even "reads the *Guardian*" or "follows the Dow" or "fan of P. G. Wodehouse." (Yes, dear reader, these are all me.) But we are all contaminated. I have awe but not much respect for people who translate with a contemporary lexicon to hand, so that a translation of an old book is "guaranteed" to contain no words that weren't in existence—albeit in the other language—at the time of writing. It is ingenious, yes; disciplined, aha; plausible, sure; but it's entirely too mechanistic. Even if you use eighteenth-century vocabulary, chances are you won't manage a single sentence that would have passed muster in the eighteenth century. (There's a difference between a pianist and a piano tuner.) Meanwhile, your twenty-first-century reader reads you with what—his eighteenth-century parson's soul? On his Nook?

◆ ◆ ◆

I want a translation to provide an experience, and I want, as a translator, to make a difference. I concede that both aims may be felt to be somewhat unusual, even inadmissible. I can see that the idea of me as writer leans into, or even blurs, the idea of me as translator (after all, I don't need someone else's book to break my silence: I am, if you like, a ventriloquist's ventriloquist). Translating a book is for me an alternative to or an extension (a multiplier!) of writing an essay or poem. A publisher friend did me the kindness of dreaming of a world where books were thought of not by author but by translator (who is after all the one who comes up with the words on the page): so, a Pevear/Volokhonsky, not a Tolstoy; a Mitchell, not a Rilke; a Lydia Davis, not a Proust.

But where is the fidelity, you may say, where is the accuracy, the self-effacement, the service? For me the service comes in writing as well and as interestingly as possible. It comes from using the full range of Englishes, the different registers, the half-forgotten words, the tricks of voice, the unexpected tightenings and loosenings of grammar. (I serve my originals, as I see it, but I am also there to serve English, hence the importations, the "finds," the dandyisms, and the collisions.) I am impatient with null or duff passages of writing, clichés, inexactitudes, even, actually, the ordinary inert. (I don't know that I would find anything more challenging than a book where the characters only ever "went" to places, and only ever "said" things: I'd find it stifling—and have done.) In his sweet-mannered but still thought-provoking *Is That a Fish in Your Ear?* David Bellos characterizes translation as liable to produce a sort of *moyen* language, clipping the extremes of an original, tending toward the accepted and the established and the center, the unexceptional and the unexceptionable. I don't mind much where my extremes come from— whether they are mine, or my authors', but I want them to be there. Extra pixels. The high resolution of a fourth or fifth decimal place, I once put it. It's the expectation of poetry: brevity, pitch, drama. The right word, or phrase, or sentence—and thereby, too, something you mightn't have got from someone else. Yes, a translator is a passenger, riding in relative safety (and deserved penury) in a vehicle that has already been built, but I would still rather he were a passenger of the bobsled kind—a converted sprinter, someone who at least puts his own bones and balance and reactions into his work.

♦ ♦ ♦

And so one ungrateful reader sees fit to complain: "He uses words not commonly seen in books and occasionally his grammar is clumsy" (which only seems to get more hilarious the more I look at it: the wonderfully aggrieved, positively denunciatory tone; the gorgeous— imitatively clumsy—hitch, a kind of commaless splice; the absurd implication that more words may be used in speech [that written English operates a rather French system of vocabulary restraint]; the rather gray little sentence that flaunts its two mealy adverbs). A reviewer describes me as "the usually reliable" (which in some moods I would see as a slur), and goes on to grumble about my use of "inelegant nonwords" like "chuntering" (to talk in a low, inarticulate way) and "squinny" (from "squint," obviously)—both of them seem to me not just perfect but perfectly good (and since when is there a universal edict on elegance, or on frequency of use?)—and intimates he would rather (sight unseen) read eighty-year-old versions by my predecessors, the wonderfully named Cedar and Eden Paul, who sound like the grandsire and grandam of the Tea Party: perhaps I should counter by denying him any of my other, "usually reliable," translations? The novelist A. S. Byatt drew up a little list of words she thought ought not to have appeared in my translation of Joseph Roth's novel, *The Emperor's Tomb* (first published in 1938): "a ways," "gussied up," "sprog," "sharp cookie," "gobsmacked," and (rather ruthlessly, I thought) "pinkie." The action of the book straddles World War I; only the first of Byatt's terms comes from "before," the others are all "after the deluge," which I think matters. Four times I shrugged my shoulders. I inclined my head a little at "sharp cookie"—if English had offered "sharp biscuit" I might indeed have used that—but the only one that had me scrambling was "gobsmacked," which is a vulgarism not in my repertoire in speech, never mind books, or so I thought. When I looked it up in Roth, I saw it was spoken by a character called von Stettenheim, a con man—*von man*—who is described as a "Prussian vulgarian." Even that, then—reaching for a word I don't use—doesn't seem wrong to me.

What all these have in common, I think, is an angry impatience with the idea of there even *being* a translator. In their cars, as they conceive of them, there is but one steering wheel, and an author is at it (in fact there are dual controls). Such readers and critics will sometimes, rather in spite of themselves, read a translation, but with an edge of apprehension, almost already under protest or under notice. Their palette of expectation is all negative: impossible to imagine such people amused, struck, impressed, or surprised by a translation. ("Trans*la*tion?!" I seem to hear, almost like Lady Bracknell's "a *hand*bag?!") Rather, woe if the translation should happen to show itself, to obtrude. There is only disfavor forthcoming. Their wrath will be terrible to behold. A translation is possible—bearable, one thinks—only so long as it remains meek, clothy, predictable, a little old-fashioned. It should wear its inadequacy on its sleeve. Whereas, to me, to sit over something purposely disappointing, necessarily doomed, and perennially half-empty would be a waste of my life (which—who knows?—perhaps I have wasted). Yes, it is impossible, but that is where we came in, it was the fall of the Tower of Babel that gave us our ground plan. Just because I am the translator of a book doesn't seem to me to rule out finesse, pleasure, initiative, even provocation. Hans Magnus Enzensberger—who dedicated one of his books to translators, to the "noble coolies" of poetry (and what a bizarre and wonderful collision of words that is)—still thinks we should have fun. Or does it always have to be like in Pope, "and ten low words oft creep in one dull line"?

♦ ♦ ♦

Something simple on method. It used to be I wrote out a draft by hand, usually at night. Then the next day I would look up words (irritatingly, they were almost always words I knew, but at that stage

I felt I still needed the corroboration: the people who don't look things up are usually the ones who don't know them), and type up what I had. In the afternoon I would go swimming, and at night I would rough out—or rough up—the next few pages. When I'd got to the end of a manuscript, I would make a large photocopy, and scribble on it, working only—or almost only—with the English. Word processing has greatly simplified and run together these stages. What remains the case is that I get some sort of draft out as quickly as possible, put the German away, and revise, endlessly. Ten times, twenty times—more. If I can get someone to listen, I like to read a book aloud. I reread old translations of mine long after they've appeared, long after they've disappeared. I can see that it is possible for an original to get away from me, but think that on the whole that doesn't happen: all my instincts—even working at speed—are for accuracy and loyalty. I know that I've dwelt on difference and play and irresponsibility, but I am overwhelmingly a careful and dutiful worker. Further, there is a benefit to working with and from English, which is that a translation doesn't get involved in a sort of linguistic tug-of-war. There's not a struggle to be born, just a fairly quick and clean separation, and the English understands that it's on its own, as it has to be. (It's self-evident but needs saying: I translate for people without German, rather than those who have the doubtful good fortune of knowing it.) When I've translated poetry, which is in the last ten years or so, the presence or threat of a parallel text has protracted negotiations with the German; I'm not sure it's always been to the benefit of the translation, but clearly it's bound to happen that way. A poem translation can feel like the bundled-up corpse of an insect that's got caught in a spider's web, an overzealous parcel, attached by a thousand threads to the thing that will wait for it to die and then eat it: not a comfortable feeling, and not recommended.

✦ ✦ ✦

Over time, I've become more sure of myself, and more taken with myself. I'm not convinced either of these is a good thing, but again they're both likely to happen. Over their careers, a doctor or stockbroker or airline pilot will have gone the same way. Partly it's generalized experience, partly a long association with particular authors and epochs—the twenties and thirties; Stamm, Roth, Fallada, my father—but it has given rise to a sense of "this is how I do things" and even "this is how I want things to come out, and you should be satisfied with that." There's nothing so exhausting as sticking up for yourself, but I can do it when put to it. I back my feel for words against just about anyone's, I know I have a degree of impatience—I don't like fussing—and then there's something impetuous and unpredictable in me as well. That's what you get. I wouldn't want it as a sort of generalized characterological dispensation, but I think in my own case it's probably okay.

GOTTFRIED BENN

Though Gottfried Benn can scarcely be said to exist in the English-speaking world, there are a surprising number of prominent mentions of him. T. S. Eliot, for instance, in his essay "The Three Voices of Poetry" goes so far as to associate one such voice—the first, "the voice of the poet talking to himself—or to nobody"—with Benn. John Berryman allows him the end of one Dream Song: "and Gottfried Benn / said:—we are using our own skins for wallpaper and we cannot win." In his novel *Plexus*, Henry Miller is careful to leave the 1927 issue of Eugene Jolas's avant-garde magazine *transition* lying around, and quotes in extenso from Benn's essay in it. Frank O'Hara has a tilt at him in one of his invariably disastrous and perplexing diatribes, when he seems to have his ill-fitting Hector the Lecturer suit on: "Poetry is not instruments / that work at times / then walk out on you / laugh at you old / get drunk on you young / poetry's part of your self" ("To Gottfried Benn").

With all these appearances, you would have thought Benn had to have some being somewhere. But it's more like that space radiation called "chatter"; there's something that leads our instruments to think there's something "out there"; we might even give it a name, but most of us remain doubtful, and few of us expect ever to see it. I don't think you could fill a room with a conversation about Benn—non-Germans and non-Germanists, that is. And yet we're talking of someone of the eminence, say, of Wallace Stevens, someone most Germans (and most German poets, too) would concede as the greatest German poet since Rilke.

Basically, Benn has appeared once in English, in E. B. Ashton's edited collection of Benn's selected writings, *Primal Vision*, published in 1960 and still in print with New Directions. The trouble with Ashton's book—and in this it perhaps betrays its origins in the postwar decade—is that it is not primarily interested in Benn the poet but the man of ideas, the German, and the "phenotype." One has to wonder at the judgment and effectiveness (not to mention the long monopoly) of a book introducing a foreign poet to an English readership that is three parts prose, and where the translations of the poems (one-eighth of the whole) are starchy, cumbrous, and muted. They have neither the attack nor the ease of Benn in German—to me he is both the hardest and the softest poet who ever lived. Thus unsuccessfully transmitted, Benn has no English admirers; unlike Brecht, he's not even unpopular. It's only stray foreign readers like Joseph Brodsky or Adam Zagajewski who read him in a third or fourth language, or in the original, who have anything like a true or a full sense of Benn.

♦ ♦ ♦

Benn called his autobiography *Doppelleben*, but for once (see "Bauxite," see "Fragments 1955," see "Summa Summarum") he perhaps wasn't interested in counting, because I can see more like four of him: the military man, the doctor, the poet, and the ladies' man. With their different rhythms and urgencies and tolerances, these four identities—four suits of cards, two black, two red, two professional alibis, two passions, two kinds of truancy, and two kinds of work—shaped and complicated his life. He ran from woman to woman, but also from woman to poem, from poem to uniform, from uniform to lab coat, and back again, and with all the possible variations. Style trumps facts, he said, and good stage management trumps fidelity. But within the constraints of his circumstances and especially his tightly drawn financial limits (very rarely in his life did he have money), he was at pains to be a gentleman (it's not a word one hears often nowadays, but it's a concept he certainly understood and tried to live by) and to lead an upright life: that is, one informed by distance and warmth and good presentation. Accordingly, the most important and longest-lasting relationship of his life was conducted largely by mail over twenty-four years with the Bremen businessman F. W. Oelze. Benn aspired—or resigned himself—to be at once an earl and a pariah. He was a brilliant and internationally acclaimed writer of poetry and prose who never came close to being able to live by it; a notably unenthusiastic doctor who nevertheless helped his "*Schmutzfinke von Patienten*" (squalid patients) as much as he could; an amorous and courtly man and an inveterate buyer of flowers for his wives and mistresses and casual liaisons; by his left eye he had the *Mensur*, the German dueling scar, and twice—during the two world wars—he fell back into the army, where, ironically, he enjoyed the periods of greatest peace and productive contentment in his life.

Benn's first publication, in 1912—a small-press pamphlet called *Morgue and Other Poems*, one of the great debuts in literary history—catches him at a typical juncture. He had recently qualified as a medical doctor in Berlin; he was having an affair with the Jewish German poet and free spirit Else Lasker-Schüler; and he was—if the reader will allow the expression, it's still more accurate than any other I can think of—moonlighting with the army, which had paid for his education. When the First World War broke out, Benn—like so many others—quickly got hitched (though not to Lasker-Schüler), conceived a daughter (Nele was born in September 1915), and joined up again. For three years he was behind the lines in Brussels as a "doctor in a whorehouse." It was one of those immensely suggestive, paradigmatic times in his life when he was at once becalmed, isolated, and productive; the nation was distracted and engorged, but Benn was reading and writing. He writes about it with grateful rapture, almost as though he were a medieval monk left to illuminate manuscripts behind stone walls a yard thick. After the war, he tried to find the same seclusion as a skin doctor and venereologist in private practice in Berlin, but that quality of "*béguinage*" (his word: a religious seclusion) remained something best provided by the army. Accordingly, in 1935, he tried the same thing again: left Berlin, re-enlisted, and, in 1938, remarried. In World War II, he fetched up at the fortress town of Landsberg an der Warthe (today the Polish town of Gorzów Wielkopolski), which he commemorated contemporaneously in the prose of "Block II, Room 66" ("Nothing so dreamy as barracks!"). There, underemployed by the army, as the senior medical man with the rank of colonel, while waiting for the German defeat, he wrote poems, essays, and prose, among them many pieces that would have cost him his liberty and most probably his life if they had been turned over to the SS.

A brief note on the vexed and controversial circumstances that restored him to the bosom of the army. Almost all his life, Benn had no expectations from governments (it's hard to imagine him voting, and impossible to guess which way); human existence was futile, progress a delusion, history a bloody mess, and the only stay against fatuity was art, was poetry. Writing should have no truck with any social or political aims. Anything less like the useful, obedient, and subsidized creature known as the "state poet" than Gottfried Benn is impossible to imagine. Then, in 1933 and 1934, Benn drifted into the Nazi orbit. For a brief while it looked to him as though his long-range ideas about the human species, his cultural pessimism, his Nietzschean and Spenglerian gloom, had somewhere to dock. He drafted the declaration of loyalty to the newly returned Nazi government that precipitated mass resignations from the Preußische Akademie der Künste, or Prussian Academy of Arts, to which he had only recently been elected; he addressed a sharp "reply to the literary émigrés" to (his adoring admirer) Klaus Mann; he gave a talk welcoming the Italian Futurist (and Fascist) poet F. T. Marinetti to Berlin; he was briefly vice president of Hitler's Union Nationaler Schriftsteller, or Union of National Writers. Mutual disenchantment was not slow in coming; the relationship's fleeting appearance of compatibility shaded into, or gave way to, its natural level of implacable—and, for Benn, extremely threatening—mutual detestation. It dawned on Benn that the Nazis were not a bunch of pessimistic aesthetes like himself but rather were imbued with a sanguinary optimism; by the time of the Night of the Long Knives in June 1934, he was fully disabused. They, meanwhile, never forgave him for his early writings and his Jewish associations, got him struck off the medical register as a suspected Jew (Benn = Ben!), and banned him from writing altogether in 1938. They could hardly fail to find his work "degenerate," as they did that of his Expressionist colleagues in the visual arts. At this point, Benn left Berlin and took refuge in the army, which in a typically stylish and abrasive phrase he described as "the aristocratic form of emigration." He wrote an analysis of suicides in the military. All this feels to me known or partly known, understood or partly understood, in the English-speaking world. It remains an anomalous and troubling interval in his life, before, so to speak, normal disservice was resumed; to use it as grounds for not reading Benn—to play the "Fascist card"—is merely lazy and a little hysterical. Few of the Modernists, after all, had the credentials of good democrats.

Most everything else in his life comes under the heading of "Herkunft, Lebenslauf—Unsinn!" (background, CV—tosh!), as he inimitably and contemptuously put it. Still, in the wake and a little in the manner of his contempt, here goes: father a clergyman, mother originally in service, from the French-speaking part of Switzerland. (In his dry, geneticist way, Benn makes as much of his mixed parentage as, say, Thomas Mann.) Born in one vicarage, grew up in another. The second of eight children and the oldest son. Sent away to school at the age of ten. He studied religion at the behest of his father before being allowed to switch to literature and medicine. In 1914, he was a ship's doctor on a transatlantic steamship; he liked to claim he was so hard up he couldn't even afford to get off and tour New York. He was the doctor who, in 1916, officiated at the execution of the British nurse Edith Cavell and her Belgian associate, who had been found guilty of treason for having helped Allied soldiers escape from German-occupied Belgium. The year 1922 saw the death of his mother from untreated breast cancer (see "Jena") and of his first wife, Edith Osterloh, from a botched appendectomy; the fact that he and Edith had lived separate lives didn't keep Benn from being deeply affected by her death. Incompetent or at least unambitious in most practical matters, he arranged to have their daughter

Nele adopted by a Danish couple; toward the end of his life, he painstakingly rebuilt a relationship with her. In 1938, he married his second wife, Herta von Wedemeyer. Amid the confusion of the ending war, in July 1945, having been sent by Benn to the West for her own safety, Herta committed suicide, convinced she would fall into the hands of the Russians. Surely the poem "Death of Orpheus" owes something to her harrowing circumstances and to Benn's grief and guilt. Following the defeat, occupation, and then partition of Germany, Benn returned to West Berlin, opened another medical practice, and married a third time: Ilse Kaul, a dentist. Because of his sometime pro-Nazi positions, he was not allowed to publish by the Allies: "undesirable then," he wrote, a little smugly, "undesirable again now." The Swiss publisher Arche brought out *Static Poems* in 1948, ushering in a great wave of Benn's late work. He was awarded the prestigious Georg Büchner Prize in 1951. In May 1956, his seventieth birthday was celebrated with the publication of a *Collected Poems*, beginning with the recently composed "Can Be No Sorrow." On July 7, 1956, at a time when the earth would indeed "yield easily to the spade," Gottfried Benn died in Berlin.

♦ ♦ ♦

Benn's name is indissolubly connected to the German, or perhaps Nordic, movement of Expressionism, like its direct contemporaries Imagism and Dadaism a protomodern movement, but fiercer than the one and less theatrical than the other. Literary Expressionism has almost as many meanings as it has practitioners, but in a general way (and certainly in Benn) it can be seen as a simultaneous boosting of both style and content. Expressionism is gaudy, neoprimitive, volatile, provocative, antirational. The brain is eclipsed by its older neighbors: the glands, the senses (including the oldest sense, the sense of smell). Expressionism is momentary, it doesn't count days or verify destinations. It might be the humdrum Baltic—shallowest and newest and saltiest of seas, sea beach to Berlin—but it feels like the Aegean, if not the South Pacific, in the poet's rhapsodic imagination. Expressionism hymns a simpler physis, the body under its own management. Down with the boardroom, away with the little pin-striped simpleton or puritan upstairs! Expressionism is an as-if, or an if only: if only the body could write or paint or think! Or not think. Poems like "Express Train" or "Caryatid" or "Asters" are literary equivalents to the brash, paradisiac canvases of Emil Nolde or Ernst Ludwig Kirchner or Ferdinand Hodler.

Benn's very first poems were offcuts of materia medica: *Morgue* and *Fleisch* were among his titles, a prose book was called *Gehirne* (Brains). As with a lot of Expressionist writing, it was hard to see how it might develop, not least because it was all already so fully and shockingly *there*: brash, confrontational, destructive, appalling. Benn wasn't sure either. In a splendidly saturnine note in his first collected works (the *Gesammelte Schriften* of 1922—he was thirty-five), he wrote: "Now these complete works, one volume, two hundred pages, thin stuff, one would be ashamed if one were still alive. No document worthy the name; I would be astonished if anyone were to read them; to me they are already very distant, I toss them behind me like Deucalion his stones; maybe human beings will emerge from the gargoyles; but whether they do or not, I shan't love them." I don't know that I have ever seen anything less self-enamored from a poet on his or her own work. In the event, something of what he so indifferently predicted did come to pass: "human beings" did emerge from the "gargoyles"—whether or not Benn loved them hardly matters. His later poems lost their ferocity, their shock, and their prankish, metallic manipulativeness; became softer, lived in, improvised, gestured at, shuffling or shambling. They still had the same principal ingredients: corpses (or mortality) and flowers; the same groping at one notion or another of a "beautiful youth." The "lavender asters" return in the form of new flower complexes, as "drooping lilac . . . narcissus color, and smelling strongly of death," as poppies, phlox, gladioli, the "old and reliable ranunculi of Ostade," hydrangeas, and finally as forsythias and lilacs again, this time "with hope of roses." The beautiful or unbeautiful, loved or unloved cadavers have turned into Benn himself, anxiously remembering the ghosts of his salad days; or hoping to hold on, into June (of the year of his death—he died on July 7); or, in one of his last poems ("Can Be No Sorrow"), thinking soberly and unflinchingly about the deaths of poets, put together from wood and tears and pain and spasm, the "sleep well" at once a close echo and a world away from the cynical "Rest easy" of "Little Aster."

During the 1920s and '30s, Benn found a way of parlaying his short explosive free verse poems into lengthier internal combustion pieces. His characteristic form became the tightly rhymed octave, often in very short two- or three-foot lines. The longings and strictures and surfeits articulated in these are often very beautiful and bizarre, but barely translatable, not even when there are equivalents—perhaps especially not when there are equivalents. What is the English, pray, for: "Banane, yes, Banane / vie méditerranée?" "Banana, yes, banana / Mediterranean life?" I don't think so. It is as though, having been done in one language (German?), it can never be done again in any other. A blizzard of neologisms, incantatory and highly personal charm words, flower names, and technical terms; sociopathic hatred; a texture of fierce and luxurious depression. Benn pines for "Mediterranean," "Palau," "Night," "Cocaine," "Anesthesia." Life is *"niederer Wahn,"* lower or lesser madness; in its place Benn calls for "thalassale Regression," for form, trance, elevation. It might seem Decadent, 1890s-style, only there is no pose about it, nothing effete. For all the Verlaine-like sonorities of the poems, there are ferocious energies at work within them. I am conscious that the poems of this period are underrepresented in the present selection of *Impromptus.* They were too difficult and idiosyncratic for me to carry them into English in any important way. I preferred to go more or less straight from the shocking early to the weary late: to those beerily misanthropic and magically beautiful mutterings of Benn's last two decades that have always particularly entranced me as a reader. Two world wars, two marriages, two bereavements, careers in the military and medicine, and forty years of writing have gone into their making. "Ausdruck und Stoffvernichtung," expressiveness and destruction of subject matter, they are. They come with their own silence and space. Like the early poems, they are as they are, are as they want to be. The opposite of art, Benn always argued, is not actually nature but a concern to please.

Thus, the hardness of the early style—the "gargoyles"—is replaced by human tenderness, empathy, puzzlement, a kind of unfocused but unavoidable sadness. It is as though the poems themselves

HANS MAGNUS ENZENSBERGER

I was pushing twenty-two. It was May or June of 1979, and it was the year, maybe the month I was graduating—*in absentia*, what else.

People I knew were putting on a Poetry Festival in Cambridge, and I went along to some of the events in the big old Corn Exchange, where the Clash had played, and Richard Hell. My relationship with poetry was that I scorned it, and felt sorry for it. I actually meant words at all times, I didn't want to be a rock star or a comedian, but poetry as it seemed to propose itself to me, or to me then, was awful. A type of crippled language that couldn't say what it meant, that was always—like Cambridge, like England—nostalgic for better times, a hopeless anachronism, little better than lavender spats. And yet it was what I was trying to write—fiction had defeated me—and, where possible, to read.

I had known poets, had had an English teacher who was one, and a geography teacher; at school older boys had worn their ties "at half-mast" when Pound died and Auden died, but probably this was my first actual experience of poets. I don't think my expectations were keyed up. I wasn't cynical so much as unhopeful.

Into this abeyance marched—well, several people, but most particularly Hans Magnus Enzensberger, who sounds like several people anyway, and certainly does the work of several people. (He writes political essays, and has translated the complete nonsense verse of Edward Lear—and I daresay one could span the arc wider than that.) Enzensberger read, in German, and in English, which I calculated might be his third? or fifth? language (after Spanish, Finnish, Italian), from his long poem *Der Untergang der Titanic* (published the previous year in Germany; *The Sinking of the Titanic*—in his own sparkling translation—appeared in 1981). It was immediately apprehensible, it was funny, he read it and talked it with grace and self-deprecation, he beat, in other words, the English at their own game. And this, *incredibile dictu*, was a countryman of Gert Fröbe's! In the ratty, rather summerproof England of the 1970s he dazzled in his part Monsieur Hulot, part *Paris 1919* John Cale white clothes—Tom Wolfe hadn't been thought of—and it was all casual. He knew how important it was—in England!—not to be trying, or not to be seen to be trying. I think he even wore plimsolls. It was—*pace* Yeats—as though he had not a sword but a Dunlop Maxply upstairs.

He read his wonderful confection of the *Titanic*, which incorporated documentary material, old blues songs, recollections of the end of his time in Havana in 1970, descriptions of famous paintings. His poem was an elegy to capitalism, accidentally—or perhaps it wasn't an accident?—twinned with a lullaby to communism. It was the *Titanic* going down—or maybe it was the ship-shaped island of Cuba, the thorn in America's side, after the failure of the sugar gamble. If cleverness had rosy cheeks and a smile on its face, it would be Hans Magnus Enzensberger. He illuminated us. He illuminated me. I didn't speak to him till many years later, but I was always grateful to him.

MAX BECKMANN

I have never thought of the German painter Max Beckmann (1884–1950) as an especially vexed or controversial or unregarded figure, but it seems I may have been unusual in that. His work—like Picasso's, which it sometimes resembles—is unmistakably his own, it displays richly individual tendencies and conflicts, an original palette that has always had my particular admiration, an eroticism both explicit and tantalizing, an epic quality that I think of as Mediterranean or Homeric. In its drama and clutter and burstingness, it regularly challenges the very idea of what can be done in a painting. Many of Beckmann's images—some of the shrewd and masterful self-portraits and portraits, the haunting night paintings, the jumbles of figures that are between dreamy and nightmarish—have become part of my mental furniture. Above all, as what nowadays is called an "icon," in his fifty-year devotion to a career through the vicissitudes of European history, he seems to me exemplary and heroic. This is based every bit as much on his writing—the World War I letters, and especially the sublime *Tagebücher 1940–50*, which is not just one of the great art books but one of the great books, *tout court*—as on his painting. A lot of the early twentieth century German painters also wrote—Gross, Kokoschka, Klee, Schwitters. Beckmann wrote better than the best of them.

It was strange, then, to come to Paris, to the Beaubourg, which owns, it seems, precisely two Beckmann canvases, and see an exhibition mounted out of rue and contrition (and only after long and triumphant conniving), to set before the agnostic and conceited and skeptical French. This show is not a straight retrospective—there was one of those in 1984, to mark the centenary of Beckmann's birth, with stations in Munich, Berlin, St. Louis, and Los Angeles—but a faintly slanted or themed exhibition, called *Max Beckmann, un peintre dans l'histoire*. What this chiefly seems to mean is that the sequence of paintings and graphics have been punctuated by three darkened video installation rooms showing World War I infantrymen, 1920s floor shows, and World War II bombing (over the top, topless and top down?) on the grounds, presumably, that all of them—the real thing, not the video—were experienced by Beckmann. It's a little pat, a little distracting, and, bluntly, a little stupid. It also has the unfortunate effect of making Beckmann, who, with the exception of a few forays into bronze casting, was a painter and draftsman of a solidly traditional kind, old-fashioned, unexciting, even inadequate. By showing us, as it were, the stimulus, it encourages us to second-guess and then even unfairly to criticize Beckmann's "response." He was absolutely not a documentary painter, and this standard footage from our "other" century—the one we made earlier—only feeds our vanity and our sense of "yes, we know," instead of helping us in any way look at the paintings, which are difficult enough. The silence of the flickering black-and-white film loops overwhelms that of the paintings—so many of which contain muted musical instruments or "speaking" theatrical scenes, *Carnival*, *The Dream*, *Self-Portrait with Trumpet*, *Begin the Beguine*—and destroys their conversation with one another.

Nor does the exhibition make it possible to "hear" Beckmann, in the way that it's possible to "hear" him from even the tiniest of the journal entries; the prose of his that has been put up on the walls next to the paintings is confined to a gimmicky and provocative series of ten statements from an "Autobiography" of 1924, the blustering assertion *"Meine Kunst kriegt hier zu fressen"* (plenty of fodder here for my art—said about his experience as an ambulance-man in World War I), and some anodyne remarks about the images from dreams. The framing of the exhibition gives little sense of the scale or the style of Beckmann's life and personality. More tendentiously, the selection of work seems heavy, portentous, vatic. There are not, for instance, many of the portraits included, or in fact many paintings that one could describe as innocent or simple or arresting—the sort of image that would do well on a playing card and of which Beckmann produced a fair number. (He had a habit, incidentally, of testing his paintings for balance by turning them on their sides and upside down.) I have in mind, in the present exhibition, pieces like the beautiful 1926 *Portrait of Quappi in Blue*, done, by Beckmann's standards, in the extremely rapid time of just three days, or *Large Fish Still Life* of 1927, or *Still Life with Fallen Candles* of 1929. Nor would one have guessed, on the basis of this exhibition, that fully one quarter of Beckmann's output—850 oil paintings, one every three weeks over fifty years—were landscapes.

Max Beckmann came from a *grand bourgeois* background—his father was an industrialist—but lost his parents early in life. He seems always to have been accomplished and was besotted with drawing and painting from an early age. He went to art school at sixteen, having persuaded his hostile uncle to let him go by sketching him. The idea of the artist as socially and financially successful was probably bred into him. (He was also one of the first artists to teach, in the contemporary sense. In 1925, a position was created for him in Frankfurt, which he held until 1932, when the Nazis hounded him out of it. He also taught in the States, at the end of his life.) Success came to him from his early twenties; it is hard even to locate his beginnings. The paintings of young men by the sea (from 1905 and 1943) that begin and end this exhibition could be varied by any number of other pairings. For instance, there is a very strange and assured and attractive *Self-Portrait in Florence* of 1907, which shows the young man as a commanding and tense, though still pleasant, figure in formal black and wing collar, smoking, against a studio window (and messily colorful Renaissance backdrop outside); the cupped hand holding the cigarette is extended toward the onlooker, part asking for money, part like Christ on the cross. It is typical of the gestural strength and expressiveness of Beckmann's figures, which seem to begin in sculpture and end in theater. That self-portrait is one of those I miss. Beckmann was never part of any grouping or movement, but he drove himself relentlessly. By the 1910s, he was specializing in large-scale paintings of catastrophes; he did a *Titanic* and a *Messina Earthquake*. One of these mass or crowd pictures again might have opened the exhibition; the interest they evince in drama and simultaneity and group dynamic remained with the artist throughout his work.

The First World War—of which the paintings seem prophetic— again changed everything. In his impressive drypoints and draw- ings—the 1915 *Bend in the Canal* and the 1916 *Assault*—the lines look like broken needles. In 1915, Beckmann suffered some sort of breakdown and was invalided out. It is as though he doesn't re- ally trust the flesh over the bones in *Self-Portrait with Red Scarf* of 1917. There is a warped and bleached quality about the work he did afterward, an element at once of pain and caricature. Figures are shrunken, molded from plasticine or carved out of soft, yellow wood, they are directly expressive of brutality, as in the horrific carnivalesque torture scene of *The Night* (which Beckmann worked for five years to bring together), with its Gothic V's and X's; or else blithely, quea- sily, eerily civilian, as in the strange landscapes and townscapes of the early 1920s: *The Synagogue, The Nizza in Frankfurt am Main*, or *Landscape Near Frankfurt (with Factory)*. These paintings seem to come out of dreams. They share a common pallor and airlessness, though one would have to go to Kafka to bring coherence to the ritualistic violence of the former and the seeming innocence of the latter.

Gradually, the zaniness and unpredictability of these pictures seem to stabilize themselves in the milieu of the circus, and in a sort of fairground palette of candy colors, pink and light green and a but- tery yellow that he favored for a time in the mid-1920s, for instance, in the very striking portrait called *The Romanian*. Beckmann's clowns are both artist and Christ. Formats lengthen to hold vertical spills of figures—like the *Aerial Acrobats* of 1928, or the *Rugby Players* of 1929. Light gradually ceases to matter as an influence or source; shadows disappear as there is little to choose between the burning and the extinguished candles that he includes in many interiors; artificial color—color symbolism too, no doubt—comes to stand in for natural light; there is a sense that many of these paintings were made by neon in the dead of night, which, for all I know, they were. (Beckmann painted in marathon stints, often at night, and he always had several paintings on the go at once, going from one to the other.)

The paintings of the late 1920s—before the onset of lab conditions and the twenty-four-hour clock and the triptychs and the obsessive pictorial code involving fishes and masks and uniforms and handcuffs—paintings that still had to be *seen* before they were painted, paintings that stand in some verifiable relation to a time and a place and a subject, are those Beckmanns I like better than any others. *Bathing Cabin (green)*, *Scheveningen at 5 a.m.*, *The Port of Genoa*, *Portrait of Quappi in Blue*, *The Theatre Box*, *Self-Portrait in Dinner Jacket*—in most instances, the titles already serve to indicate the highly specific nature of the work—are all variously expressive of privilege and glamour. ("Quappi," by the way, the nickname of Beckmann's second wife, Mathilde von Kaulbach, is derived from the syllable "Kaul," whose only other occurence is in the word *Kaulquappe*, tadpole. But I don't know if it was particularly his name for her, or if she already went by it.) In some cases, it is the time of day or night, in some the place, in some the subject or prop. There is no longer the prima facie oddity and cramping of the earlier work, nor the depleted range of colors, nor the interiority, nor the sense of having come out of a series. These are all manifestly *external* paintings, bold and full and heavy and separate. They are predominantly blue or green or red or black, but in response to a dress, or the sea, or dawn, or night. Color and form are radicalized and simplified till each painting has an almost autonomous expressive beauty. Water at night isn't ever really the jade green of *Genoa*—worse luck!—and buildings don't have that pale, pink-accented crustacean glow, with sour little yellow sparks coming from the curving railway train at the bottom of the picture as it leaves the curving white-arched station, but what a beguiling hypothesis! These are utterly sophisticated, worldly, commanding and yet still magical paintings.

Quite a few of them were exhibited in the *Degenerate Art* exhibition of 1937 in Munich (when some of the reviewers would have liked the artists to be present, so that they might spit in their faces). On July 19, the day of the opening, Beckmann left Germany, never to return. He and Quappi spent the war years in Amsterdam. Their life together is told with brilliant laconism in the *Journals*: a minimal, but vastly expressive record of work, reading, drinking. In 1947, there was an opening in the United States, as artist in residence at Washington University in St. Louis. Beckmann died in December 1950, on the pavement outside his New York apartment.

His abundant late work can only be understood as the product of the compacting process of exile. Beckmann was deep inside his own phantasmagoria, his obsessive personal imagery, his lexicon of forms, his palette of black, steel, bronze, lemon, jade, cobalt, coral red, sky blue, purple-brown, orange, lilac, and flesh tones. The paintings are airless and lightless, drawing and painting have been driven together, they have a rough, jagged, blackened lucidity like stained glass. Even the seas and mountains look like studio. Dominant, tubular women, winged things, masks and blindfolds, fishes, mutilation, musical instruments, ladders and candles, swords and spears, spiky flowers and leaves like agave and narcissus, playing cards, upside-down or falling creatures populate and overpopulate these paintings. There is a late-classical or neobarbarian feeling of discord to many of the scenes. A pessimistic plenitude, shading into surfeit. It is painting as wisdom, as cultural commentary, not easy to like but too easily dismissed. The pain and caricature and distortion and claustrophobia of the early paintings are less glaringly evident now, but they are all-pervasive. The satirical infantilism of the early twenties has grown up. The big man who drew the little figures has shrunk into the almost unbearably sad *Self-Portrait in Blue Jacket* whose preposterous padded American shoulders hang off him, whose new industrial, electric blue (most disturbing, a color that shows for the first time in Beckmann) turns his face the color of clay, and whose once vauntingly glum mouth is eclipsed by his long, reduced fingers. Even his trademark cigarette looks thinner. On January 26, 1950, he wrote in his journal: "Twice went out *op straat*, painted the first of the blue jackets in the new self-portrait, I fear there'll be many more." In the event, it saw him off.

THE PASSENGER

Dearth of action is the mother of the motion picture.

—*Joseph Brodsky*

I saw my first Antonioni films in the mid-1960s, when I was eight and nine years old, *L'Eclisse*, *La Notte*, *L'Avventura*, when I was in America, and my father, here on a Harkness, didn't seem to have anything better to do than take me to classic European films at college film clubs. Other attributes of other movies seemed to pale in my memory, grandeur, beauty, drama, mirth (Eisenstein, Fellini, Lang, Keaton) but the etiolated atmosphere of those films—further etiolated, no doubt, in my memory—survived like nothing. The sense of an unhappy couple crawling out of a party at daybreak and crawling unhappily into a bunker on an adjacent golf course (the end of *La Notte*, written with Cesare Pavese) has been with me since then. The "sound" of Antonioni, a little quieter, more composed, and more incident-packed than that of Tarkovsky, likewise. Certain feelings of rain, wind, gloom, and other conditions, also. Some of these films I waited thirty years to see again, mostly in London. (I'm not remotely technically minded, I don't have a television, and I don't really like the idea of seeing films except in cinemas.) I would look up the listings every week, under *L*, *E*, *N*, and *A*. As far as I could see, they weren't played in decades. When I read Pavese's great short novel, *Among Women Only*, I had a sense of having seen the film of that (I had, too: *Le Amiche*). The decorous social gatherings, music, and bleak intimacies of Antonioni further remind me of the German painter Max Beckmann. It seems safe to say that my sense of what a film is—and probably what life is—was substantially formed by these early experiences.

I don't remember when I first saw *The Passenger*, or where. Perhaps in 1974 or 1975, around the time it first came out, with my father again, in Austria? Most Fridays we would walk to a little downtown vitrine and see what the five cinemas (later three) in Klagenfurt were showing, with reviews from the church paper. It was called "going to see what the Catholics had to say." Perhaps I had already seen *Last Tango in Paris* (which they can't have liked very much) because Maria Schneider meant something to me, and I know I preferred her here, in that very contemporary—seventies!—unisex helmet of hair, to those Louis XIV poodle curls in *Last Tango*. Iggy Pop's great record (and song) of that name was later. 1978 or 1979. *The Passenger*, made—ha, well—mainly in English, newer and in color, seemed to be shown more often than the early Antonioni. I saw it perhaps two or three times later on. Maybe I knew it a little better than those others, which to me became almost mythical. For whatever reason, I had a sense of it as "my" film. It is the only film I can think of that occasionally "happens" to me. Not in the sense that I am pursued by an ex-wife and the operatives of some African state, but that its strange mixtures of inner and outer, boredom and tension, reveries of sound, of indeterminate things happening, are something I encounter fairly frequently.

The Passenger is either a mystery or a mystification, depending partly on your inclinations. People, it proposes, are by their nature rootless. Rootless and doomed. Locke (Jack Nicholson) is an English TV journalist who grew up in America. His neighbor in a hotel somewhere perhaps in Morocco or Mauritania (remember Polisario?), David Robertson, has no wife or family but "commitments": a list of girls' names in a diary weeks ahead that cloak commercial transactions. The girl (Schneider) he sees once in London, then in Barcelona; she is an architecture student, presumably she can go anywhere there are buildings: her small bag moves in on the backseat of his car before you can say David Robertson. The settings are old *meubles luisants* (think of Baudelaire's "L'Invitation au voyage," *luxe, calme et volupté*) interiors of paradores in Spain, some incredibly new-looking roads (the steamrollers barely off them), and tight white towns in North Africa. Flashbacks and simultaneous goings-on in England are sprinkled in, in an often hard to follow way. The story and the feeling and the geography of the whole are very like Paul Bowles.

There is something quite desultory (I think, wonderfully desultory) about the film. The whole thing is a sort of *Nachspiel*, an epilogue. It takes Locke two hours in the film, and maybe a week or two in real time, to reach the condition of his neighbor, whom he finds dead of a sudden heart attack. Probably it was never going anywhere else. It begins with a sudden end, and ends with Locke having shot his bolt—or perhaps someone has shot his fox. Locke has come out on the other side of being a serviceable human being. His wife is carrying on with Steven Berkoff; an adopted daughter is referred to but not, I think, seen. He asks questions—of others, it seems, not to himself—as a journalist. He is probably not far from saying, with Villiers de l'Isle-Adam's Axël, a hero of decadence (if that's not too much of a contradiction in terms): "Living—let our servants do that for us!" Or he's going the other way, the way of Axël's near contemporary, Arthur Rimbaud, poet turned gunrunner. Curiously, there's very little in it. Stories like this ask us to take a certain amount on trust. We don't know—in *The Sheltering Sky*—what has made America such an intolerable proposition to Port Moresby, but he is in Africa now, and we had better get on with it. It is a little like that with Locke. A few encounters with Africans that are more enigmatic and emblematic than expressive—they make cigarette gestures to him, he gives them cigarettes, they run off somewhere—leave him banging his hand on the rocks and smashing the side of his sanded-up jeep with the shovel he could probably dig himself out with without too much bother. But his story is that of a man past digging. This part of things one could justifiably call self-indulgent—if one were of a censorious cast of mind.

Probably one is supposed to take Locke's decision as one arrived at seriously. A dignified and honorable life choice. *Du musst dein*

Leben ändern—or maybe *Du musst dein Leben enden*. He goes next door to borrow soap from his white neighbor, the man he surreptitiously interrogated the day before, over whiskey, and finds him dead on his bed. The fan is whirring, the water in his own room is running, but Robertson's heart is no longer beating. Locke sits with the body, goes through the dead man's effects. Perhaps he is struck by the fact that he wears clean, pressed clothes; perhaps that they're roughly the same size; perhaps that their passport pictures are fairly alike. (It puzzled me when I saw the film first that he works with razor blade and glue on exchanging the passport pictures. Why bother?) The exchange seems to me unprepared for, whimsical, opportunistic. A plane doesn't leave for another three days. What does he do in them; what happens to the body? The film makes a show of being in the hard world—there is a car rental, a false mustache, and a scene around a left-luggage locker, which is about as hard as the world gets in the movies—but really it only pretends. So it is more whimsy. Presumably Locke envies Robertson's condition more than he covets his life. He wants simplification rather than a fresh set of complications. He really isn't Rimbaud, turning in words and images, to do something of greater consequence and carry in the world. But Antonioni has to get Nicholson to the point where anything he does and sees must be interesting. (It is the point, I would say, where Bruno Ganz becomes human in *Wings of Desire*; in a much more general way, the point from which—if you'll excuse the generalization—Chinese poems got written. Someone has died, someone banished or abandoned, at the very least got drunk, and anything subsequent is ennobled, expressive, worthy of recording. "By the gate now, the moss is grown, the different mosses, / Too deep to clear them away!" from Pound's version of Li Po.)

That's the donnée. A little elaborate, a little crude, a little superfluous. In a film, if someone proposes themselves to you, and invites you into their life, you go. In fact, it doesn't happen enough. There's really no need for them to become somebody else first. A film about the journalist David Locke, his wife, and their adopted child, in London, is a perfectly respectable proposition. Or again, it could have happened the other way round: if Locke had died, and Robertson had slipped into his unpressed combats and madras plaid shirt, and gone to talk to the next dictator on *his* list. But the way this has permed out, it is Locke who is in a borrowed state, an altered state, a temporary and a terminal state.

Everything thereafter is aleatory and somehow doesn't claim to be the whole story. Locke is living on the edge of his—or rather someone else's—life. His condition is exemplary rather than literal or exhaustive. He is like a crab or a snail who has moved into new premises. Not only does he not have the stamina or the curiosity to make a go of this over time—we don't see him poring over a copy of *Teach Yourself Gunrunning*—he also finds (it comes with the territory) that he has involuntarily acquired a fresh set of enemies. He has to keep on the move, but even that is no guarantee of anything. The film is an interval. It is only a longer version of one shot of the rearview mirror, looking down a long tree-lined avenue, waiting for the police car to come into view. Watching it, we feel an equal threat from Locke's wife and boss, hunting for him, as from the African government's heavies. There is no difference between hostile and benign. It is less like suspense than waiting. He has stepped into another life, from which, one way or another, he is certain to be expelled. The film is called *The Passenger*—which is strange in itself, as Locke is mostly at the wheel, and one can't seriously claim it's about Schneider, the passenger therefore already is a sort of metaphor and a metaphysical label—but anyway, it might as well have been called *The Lodger* (but there's another claimant for that one).

The film, then, is just something of a certain length. A piece of string. Scenes are knots along it. It is easy to imagine other ones, or different ones, much easier than it is with most films. Equally, finding fault with them doesn't seem to be the point. They aren't load bearing. Other cafés, other roads, other hotels. Other dialogues. It doesn't matter. What matters is the limited time, the threat against it, the foreign ambience, the brief *Aufleben* of two strangers. You make up your own film, with yourself, in your own time. It's not so much *The Passenger* as *Passaggerismo*, so to speak. Not a tiptoeing, but a whole field and set of atmospheres. It's rare to see a film that appears so touristic. Set abroad—for a long time, for some reason, I supposed it was Portugal, but it's largely Spain, Barcelona, and points south—no subtitles, hotels and cafés, *amours de voyage*. It's a limited structure—call it a lean-to—but all the more durable for that.

When Bruno Ganz "falls" and becomes human in *Wings of Desire*, he is subjected to intense scrutiny by Wim Wenders. He shows us it. He is passionately, rapturously human, a kind of grown-up child. He is thrilled by everything, he is transfigured, he shines. Nicholson and Antonioni don't do anything of the kind. There is nothing coming from the inside to the outside, or the outside to the inside, for that matter. I don't know what happened to Locke's journalist's gift of observation; he doesn't show many signs of it. Everything is external and oddly impercipient or affectless. There is no "Robertson moment," where he shows us his new self and his pleasure or panic at finding himself in it. Nicholson and Schneider must be two of the more sour-looking actors around. They range from petulant cool to cool petulance. Antonioni doesn't investigate them or produce them in any striking way. Nor does Nicholson acquire any new optics. He is as deep as his pile of dollars, as wide as his *eau de nil*—or is it greenback?—car. He is neither competent nor incompetent. Nothing, then, attaches itself to the basic predicament, or detracts or distracts from it, the idea is just to be a globetrotter, and for a time. It remains a pure and almost unembodied idea. There is no particular intensity, no particularity.

Perhaps the best ways to characterize the film are negative. It is neutral, without anguish, without any voiced despair or hope, without any gravity or clinging. A tiny shot shows Nicholson and Schneider sitting at an outdoor table. Cars pass in front of them, from the left, from the right. The conversation isn't particularly scintillating or revealing. They talk throughout like strangers on a train, in a mixture of reckless banality, occasional posturing, and reckless confession. It's the tiny, shallow space—not especially well used—for the human in among the mechanical and the functional that speaks from the scene, and perhaps from the whole film. It's the macrocosm from the microcosm.

When we get to the celebrated last shot, that's another microcosm. It's another hotel room. Like the first, back in Africa, it's ground level (which in this film becomes associated with death). There has

been another desultory, unimpressive conversation between the principals, this time about blindness. Nicholson is telling a story, very
woodenly, the way people only ever tell stories in films—one feels
sure it's about *him*, but it isn't even that—about a blind friend of his
who regained his sight and who noticed ugliness everywhere. "What
can you see?" Nicholson asks Schneider. A little boy and an old
woman. A man scratching his shoulder. A kid throwing stones.
Dust. "It's very dusty here." It's true. He tells her to go. She leaves. The
shot begins—I think—with his chinos. (There is a wonderful disregard for the integral or the important in this film.) He's suddenly lain
facedown on the bed, to sleep. The camera then moves, terribly slowly
toward the metal grille in front of the French windows, which are
open. (It's an echo of the corridor of the African hotel, which is similarly open.) It pushes through, sliding and zooming. Someone is having a driving lesson on the plaza outside. A boy throws a stone at an
old man, who shouts at him. There's a large closed structure, a bullring perhaps. Schneider appears, mooching and moody. A gaggle of
children. A Vespa, or perhaps I've added that. Trumpet music, in
Spanish semitones, gallant and fading. A car stops. A black Citroën. A
black man gets out. The driver, meanwhile, gets into conversation
with Schneider, moves her away toward the bullring, and then on to
the old man. The camera all the time moving forward, perhaps beginning to pan right. Nicholson forgotten. A backfire from the Fiat,
and another noise. The Citroën leaves. Another car, a police car,
comes to a dusty stop. Policemen get out of it, Locke's flame-haired
wife too. The camera, having already turned 180 degrees, shows them
entering the hotel, tracks them past the open windows. Schneider,
back in her adjacent room. Nicholson flat on his bed, dead. The camera noses back into the room. Hotel manager, policeman, Rachel
Locke, and Schneider, standing in a line behind the body, facing forward, like last respects blocking at the end of *Hamlet*. "We have never
lived so long, nor known so much." "Did you know him?" The last
word is Schneider's "Yes." A cut, an hour or two later, and a still
camera observes the hotel manager step outside, his wife sit down on
the stoop with her knitting, the L-Fiat, driving off into the sunset,
and the low hotel frontage beside the dying sun. Something of New
Mexico, perhaps. New Spain. Credits roll.

This is *The Passenger* to me. Something happening, though—as in Auden's "Musée des Beaux Arts"—one wouldn't necessarily know it, much less what it was. A flowing together of private and public space, the hotel room and the plaza. A sense of resonant emptiness, as in De Chirico. The painstaking putting together of Mediterranean noise. You can smell these sounds. Dust and children and rattly cars. The South. Being a stranger in a place. Spanish without subtitles. Knowledge is in the air, but one doesn't have much of it oneself. The camera—the eye, not Nicholson's, but a kind of impersonal, ambient, übereye—unavailing. Getting everywhere too late. The outward look foiled and turning into an inward look back. (The people in such places see infinitely more of you than you do of them.) And hearing, the undirectional sense, knowing more than sight. In the shot, I suppose I am with Schneider, I am at large and clueless, distracted, moving, rapt. I am taking in more than I could ever want. I can feel myself being filled like a beaker. It is something to do with life lived in public, in the open, and the visitor getting only a scrambled, kaleidoscopic sense of it. It is waiting, while nothing and everything happens.

KURT SCHWITTERS

Kurt Schwitters (1887–1948) loved to play with expressive or artistic systems of every type, whether they were alphabets, numbers, colors, languages, or music. He composed sonatas out of sounds (including a sneeze), poems out of letters and numerals, paintings out of Dutch tram tickets, farmyard illustrations out of type fonts. His poems made shapes trailed across paper, while his paintings were words nailed onto card or board. "A play with serious problems," he wrote later, in his manifestly imperfect English—drama critic wasn't among his avocations—"that is art." The walls of the house he lived in with his parents in the deeply provincial German town of Hanover developed strange plaster extrusions and stalactites and angular outgrowths in room after room, and turned into a sort of Expressionistic Caligari grotto: somewhere in its windings was what he called the Cathedral of Erotic Misery, where a snail might scratch its back and appease an itch. That was the original "Merzbau." "Merz"—itself a neologism chiseled out of the name of a bank: the Kommerz- und Privatbank—became synonymous with Schwitters. Sometimes he signed himself "Merz" or incorporated it into his name—even though, as the only son of well-heeled parents, he had five perfectly good ones of his own: Kurt Hermann Eduard Karl Julius and then Schwitters. (When his own son came to be born, he named him, with a straight face, Ernst.) From 1919 on, Merz was everything he did. Merz sculptures, Merz towers, Merz drawings, Merz poems. It was, you might say, a Merz life. Schwitters is an instance of a primary creative type; had he taken a different turning, it is easy to imagine him an inventor, like Leonardo. He loved pseudonyms, heteronyms, caressive deformations, and nicknames. Was "Hanover" insufficiently exciting as an address? Well, try "Revon"! The painter and poet Hans Arp was only ever "pra" to him; wacky postcards were addressed not to "geliebter Arp" (beloved Arp—strange enough, one might think) but "beleibter pra" (portly pra). The wife of another friend, one Morf, was referred to as "die Morphinistin." Edith Thomas, the English nurse of his last years, was "Wantee," surely—though I've never seen it commented upon—an eccentric personal extension of the Anglo-French passive (like desiree or trainee or amputee). Running together the beginning of his first name and the end of his second, he called himself "Kuwitter"—cow weather, yes, but also cow whiff. When Kate Steinitz paid her first visit to the artist in 1918, it was Schwitters's parents who came to the door:

> First they showed me round their own apartment with its comfortable velour furniture and lace doilies. They were especially proud of their winter garden, which even in wartime looked to be flourishing: well-tended herbs and vegetables, among ornamental rubber trees and ferns. Then Schwitters *père* escorted me to the staircase. A strange smell greeted me there, not quite sculptor's studio, not kitchen, not zoo. But the smell, or should I say, the characteristic whiff of Schwitters, was put together from all of these components: the boiled glue or starch that Schwitters used in his collages and other works. [. . .] The sculpture smell came from the clay and plaster of Paris that he used in his subsequently celebrated Merz Column. Kitchen and baby smells were ubiquitous at the end of the war, when coal was in short supply, and people didn't like to air their rooms. And then there was the zoo smell. "Kurt keeps guinea pigs," said his father, and rang the bell.

It is a beautifully literal and for once rather benign instance of the uneasy cohabitation of art and bourgeoisie. Not the poet in the attic (as in the famous Spitzweg caricature, the pinched scribbling figure sitting up in bed in a sort of kayak posture, under an open umbrella on account of the leaking roof) so much as the irrepressible genius all-rounder slumming it in the *belle étage*. Not the standard bohemian scruff but a tall, handsome figure, as conventionally turned out in stiff collar (*Vatermörder!*) and tie as any banker or diplomat, but whose relations with Mercury—commerce, *Merz*—were alas less well ordered; whose living was trying to sell people things they didn't want made from things they *really* didn't want—i.e., rubbish off the street!—and from shouting and burbling shamelessly at "poetry readings" and public "lectures"; ever so slightly smelly, and given to displays of unpredictable behavior like growling at pretty girls in the street. *Arr*, was his word for them, in the plural, *Arren*. Then again, the man collected stamps. Schwitters signed himself once in Steinitz's guest book as "bourgeois and idiot."

In 1940, when, having fled from Germany to Norway with his now grown-up son, he scraped into Scotland on the last icebreaker that got through after the German invasion and found himself promptly interned as an "enemy alien" on the Isle of Man, it was said that Schwitters unsettled his fellows with his unstable and unpredictable blend of clown and sobersides and unabashed romantic. Probably it was ever thus. Early and often he was characterized as being of "melancholy" disposition. There was some epilepsy in the family. When he was fourteen, a nervous ailment laid him low for two years. (One thinks of something similar happening to the young Hardenberg—the future Novalis—in Penelope Fitzgerald's brilliant novel *The Blue Flower* and wonders if that wasn't genius making its presence felt in his life.) "My illness," Schwitters relates, "changed my outlook. I became aware of my love of art. First I knocked off couplets in the style of music hall comedy. One autumn evening, I noticed the cold, clear moon. Instantly, my poetry turned lyrical-sentimental. Then it was music. I learned notation, and spent one entire afternoon composing. In 1906 in Isernhagen I saw a landscape bathed in moonlight, and started to paint. One hundred watercolors of moonlit scenes. Done by candlelight. I decided to be a painter."

It may not have happened quite like this, or in such short order, but one gets a sense of the burgeoning powers within him, the vehement changeable enthusiasms, the bewildering array of possible goals for his endeavors. After his *Abitur* in 1908, Schwitters spent the best part of ten years studying commercial art (this is such a characteristic and unsolved division in him: for a couple of spells in the 1920s he worked as a typographer and an advertiser; somehow he had to alternate work and play) and academic painting, which he did in another provincial capital, Dresden. (The Expressionist painters of the *Brücke*—Kirchner, Schmidt-Rottluff, and the others, little older than Schwitters—were based in Dresden at the time, but our apparently wholly conventional young painter remained unaware of them.) In 1917, after a short, inept spell in the army, he was doing technical drawing in an iron foundry; they were glad to have him and would have kept him; he quit. As late as 1919 and married with a son, he was studying again—architecture, this time—and back in Hanover. But by then he had had a first show of his abstracts in Berlin, and nothing would be quite the same again.

It's always hard to know how and why things happen in the lives of productive people; our culinary or brewing models—combination of ingredients, temperature, time—don't quite work. Why Schwitters at the ripe old age of thirty, following an exhaustive and old-fashioned and rather blinkered grounding, having recently started a family, and in a period of uncertainty and upheaval affecting not just Germany but much of Europe, would turn his hand to making his charmed little abstract collages of scraps of paper and found materials, without the benefit of any of the usual factors-cum-clichés—extreme youth, stewing in a metropolitan hotbed of ideas, examples of others, decisive personal experience—is indeed a puzzle. We are led back to the unsatisfactory but irreducible quality of "primary creativity" and the evidence for it: those dozens of poems, articles, manifestos, sculptures, drawings, and paintings made by Schwitters in the crucial years from 1918 to 1921, and the invention of Merz as "an absolutely individual hat, that fits only one person," namely, Kurt Merz Schwitters. The only other sort of "answer" I can offer is not really an answer at all but the name of a fictional character: what of Don Quixote de la Mancha, a man in the best years, having lived hitherto in comfortable, provincial obscurity, an assiduous reader of no longer fashionable, at best somewhat specialist literature, and blessed with a character that was the familiar mixture of the romantic, the playful, and the soberly resolute, who one day took it upon himself to do battle with the whole world and became a knighterrant for the good name of Dulcinea del Toboso?

Schwitters—like Quixote—is a maximalist, a Nietzschean "revaluer of all values," who has come down to us as a minimalist (we remember scuffles with windmills). As I understand it, Merz was born out of the feeling that the world as of 1918 was trash but that it might be possible to redeem it by taking those things it said were trash and making art out of them; and meanwhile and in any case by overturning all its set opinions and priorities on all subjects. The being a generalist—disregarding the separations and jurisdictions of specialists—was part of the point. This Schwitters did, with all his divers energies: writing, painting, drawing, gluing, building. He designed a Merz stage and wished he knew music well enough to make more of a fist of composing. He left installations wherever he went: the Merzbau in Hanover (1923–1937) was followed by another in Norway (1937–1940) and a third in the English Lake District (begun in 1947 and now the only one to have survived in some sort). He wrote a short novel. He wrote a play. He wrote poems that are all over the map. He wrote some dozens of "grotesques" and some rather conventional, though "treated" fairy tales. The German edition of his extraordinarily varied collected writings comes to five stately volumes. Merz was one man's salvationist movement, nothing less. In that way it differed from its slightly older stablemate, Dada (né 1916, at the Cabaret Voltaire, Zurich). According to Merz, everything could or should be art; Dada, though coming out of much the same disgust with the war and the world and the world war, opined that art was finished, and, with more or less of a sneer, offered something else: a bicycle wheel, a urinal. Schwitters's friend Raoul Hausmann described it nicely as "satirical surrealism." Schwitters accordingly failed his audition for Club Dada, the Bolshevist Berlin branch of the chaotic movement. There is a story about Schwitters going to pay a call on George Grosz, at the time (1920) a leading member of Club

Dada. He rang the bell and said: "I'd like to speak to George Grosz. My name is Schwitters." "I'm not Grosz," said Grosz, and slammed the door in his face. A little later, there was a second ring. This time, before Grosz could get a word out, Schwitters quickly said: "And I'm not Schwitters either," and stalked off. The leader of Club Dada, Richard Huelsenbeck, was an enemy for life. He never got over the contradictions of class that Schwitters represented: to him Schwitters was a Romantic, a one-off, a dilettante, the "Kaspar David Friedrich of the Dadaist revolution"—"Kaspar" as in Kasper the clown, not Caspar the actual name of the nineteenth-century German master—"a genius in a morning coat" and "a gifted petit bourgeois" with casserole reek. It's not that there are no politics in Schwitters; viewed holistically, his is as political a project as can be imagined. But believing as he did—in accordance with the principles of Merz—that "Everything is true. And also its opposite" of course got him *nul points* for political consciousness. That particular "club" was bound to blackball him. Basically, Schwitters's starting position is as a double reject; a *refusé* by the *salon des refusés* that was Dada; an individualist who persisted in making and espousing—and living and breathing—art once it was well out of fashion in those progressive circles. A Quixote.

Because, make no bones about it, Schwitters failed. How could he do anything else? It's indicative that in two pages of testimonial quotes assembled at the end of a monograph on him, there are none at all from 1921 to 1957—practically from his first eruption on the scene to ten years after his death! The man had no prime, no maturity, no obituaries, or nothing worth noting! That's not how success looks. He had no movement, no followers, no patrons with deep pockets, no tame critics, and Hanover as a base. All that he did relied much too much on his own energy and charisma to launch it and guide it. It needed the breath from his lungs, his wit and contrariness, his dexterity, his advocacy, his combativeness. Originality gave it its moment. Personality held it together. But he couldn't always be there to paste something blue into a corner, or to raise his force-ten voice and ululate. His projects, like a numerous and unruly family, tugged at his sleeves, clamoring for attention. His work fell into physical disrepair as its range and ambition became implausible.

In the end, nothing more honorious than guinea pigs made free with his Merz installations. (But, Schwitters might have countered, what better? One of his projects was to turn an island off the coast of Norway into a museum, to be visited only by animals.)

His work, inevitably, was divided up and became the province of teams of separate specialists: the graphic designers, the installation artists, the sound (or "vocovisual") poets, the admen and Märchen men, the abstracters and collagistes and Weimaraners and Dadanauts, each made uncomfortable by the others, and sometimes all of them dismayed by something else, like the persistence in Schwitters of conventional landscape painting (in Norway, and then in the Lake District) and portraiture, which seems to scare everyone. Included in a compendious and generously all-pardoning catalog of Schwitters activities, the Dada historian Hans Richter has "painting really terrible portraits, which he loved, and which he then cut up and used piecemeal in abstract collages," as if he were talking about some retrograde but footling vice like taking snuff. Richter, with his happy abstract ending, is a victim of his own sentimental progressivism. He disregards the crucial second sentence in the Schwitters left-right combination, the "And its opposite." In point of fact, these good doctors and dentists—their likenesses left and delivered whole—were not painted simply in return for treatment or money; are not an unconsolably ironic cri de coeur at the awful humiliations of exile (England, of course, as one would expect, slightly worse than Norway); and are not some even deeper, more obscure form of mockery either, some triple persiflage. They are a perfectly ordinary and, as we would say, "owned" part of Schwitters's oeuvre. There is always something more simple-hearted—at times, almost simple-minded—in Schwitters than his radical admirers seem to want to think. He really isn't as "withering" or as "hilarious" as they say. Either it was his training or his background, but he had an eye for quality, workmanship, value for money, given as much as received. He wanted his bourgeois contented as much as épater'd. I wonder if Schwitters ever had the sort of nutritious pride, aggression, and contemptum mundi required for the avant-garde. Even in the heady days of 1920, in a piece called "Merz," he writes rather modestly and demurely: "I play off sense against nonsense. I prefer nonsense, but that is a purely personal matter. I pity nonsense, because until now it has been so neglected in the making of art, and that's why I love it," but in 1940, or 1947, when push came to shove, nonsense, though still dearly loved, must have seemed more like an occasional luxury. Even his wildly overrated hit poem of 1919, "An Anna Blume" is sustained more by naïve feeling and folksy Berlinisms than by anything stranger or more corrosive. It's not quite "Tea for Two" but it's not all that different either:

> Oh You, beloved of my 27 senses, to you I love!
> You, yours, you to you, I to you, you to me,——we?
> That (incidentally) is beside the point!

(It suffers dreadfully in translation, but the translation at least is Schwitters's own.)

So what's left? Only the windmills, the tenderest, most perishable, most idiosyncratic elements of Schwitters's production, a butterfly diaspora scattered over the world's great modern collections, one here, one there, some of them no bigger than the palm of your hand (and smaller than most reproductions), others the size of a sheet of newspaper and about as robust, rarely looked for in advance by the visitor but instantly and unmistakably recognizable even across a room, an autobiographical fleck, an abstract stain, a validation as pure and concentrated and resolutely singing on a wall as a stamp on the corner of a postcard: the collages. Nothing else gets the sweetness, the melancholy, the joie de vivre, the wit, and the upsettingness of the man as they do. How mechanical and relentless the verbal collage work is by comparison, the blunt intrusions stuffed inside parentheses, no luminosity, no preciosity (not even in the word "bunion"), no gravity, no edge, no swing, how it smugly strains after oddness: "Translation of the artist's worldview. (Bunion treatments in a society at peace, war merchandise.) Total experience greens the brain, but what matters is the shaping." Whatever you want to call it—the depth, the care, the touch, the talent, the interest, the control, the form—the writing is mostly defective in it. The collages encompass the "everything and its opposite" of Schwitters's aspirations like nothing else, like a dream: they are physical and metaphysical (because of course a cutoff word like "Versaille-" or "Zeitu-" [from *Zeitung*, a newspaper] is nothing if not metaphysical); they are personal communications and exercises in abstract rhythm and construction; they are material and immaterial, scooping up ingredients from maize cigarette papers and feathers and gauze to wood and lumps of old iron and artificial bones; topical and effortlessly timeless ("Immortality isn't everyone's cup of tea," Schwitters observed); not long ago they were offered for sale for a few marks or given away to friends, now they are beyond price; their component parts—dance cards, cigarette packets, bar bills, all the fragrant and blatant detritus and *déchets* of commerce—are subsumed but never extinguished in the design of the whole; they can be read as color, as line, as words and letters, as forensic evidence, as coded message; they are, according to the critic John Elderfield, tiny epistles in diary form, made of the materials of the day, which gives them a sort of double reality and double expressiveness. When the painter Edvard Munch—who liked to hang on to things, and look after them badly or not at all—said of his pictures that they would be improved once they had got a few holes in them, he should have been thinking of Schwitters, who seems to use only old and worn ingredients in his collages, things that have *already lived*. (It's one of the attributes that make them so moving, just as badly heard or badly reproduced music is more moving than expensive acoustic perfection can ever be: Keep it with Mono, said the 1970s British label, Stiff Records, at least on one side.) The colors come with provenances: one can imagine a favorite lost toy, a beloved shirt, the color of the rubber jujube inside a glass marble as unique as an iris, theater tickets and billets-doux furnishing them forth. Schwitters's colors are the souls of colors, because they are taken from the afterlife. They are ennobled by successive layers of use and disuse: those ochers and bisters, the tart cerise, the bluey-greeny-gray-ey contamination of mold or tarnish or verdigris. Some are dry as straw (like *Miss Blanche*, of 1923), others look lushly underwater (like *Merz Picture Thirty-one*). It would take a color awareness as acute and unconventional as Rilke's, schooled on Cézanne—that "old-fashioned blue letter-paper" in the poem "Blue Hydrangeas" with its hints of "yellow, and violet, and gray"—to match the subtlety and exquisiteness of Schwitters's palette. The lost keeps the found in equipoise, because these collages do not approach you with the triumph and self-congratulation of redemption. They never say: This is what you were looking for, I have it right here. What is in them is still lost, as rambling and fortuitous as the contents of a long-unconsulted desk drawer or pocket. Their mystery is absolutely intact. It has merely found its own provisional arrangement: swirls of squares, the heart and then another heart in *Rossfett* of 1920, determined clockwork cogs in an airy new machine. Luck, glamour, adventure, travel are regular elements, as witness playing cards, skittles, numbers, date-stamped tickets, advertisements for beauty products, flowers, and fabrics. These by-products from a man who tried his hand at much else, and gained relatively little attention for any of it, who lived with his parents and then in the house he inherited from them in a no-account place in Germany, and then in exile, are among the few wonderful and imperishable things of the twentieth century.

ARTHUR SCHNITZLER

None of the Moderns saw very much of the nineteenth century. (The word "modern" itself only started to come into general use in the 1880s and 1890s.) There is an odd twilit group of writers who straddle the centuries but who carry any amount of nineteenth-century baggage intact. Among them I would count the Austrian—nay, the Viennese—playwright and story writer Arthur Schnitzler (1862–1931). When Peter Gay wrote his magisterial study of the nineteenth-century bourgeoisie, he called it *Schnitzler's Century*. Other "pre-Moderns" for me would include poets like Yeats (born in 1865), Cavafy (1863), and Rilke (1875), and prose writers like Chekhov (1860), Hamsun (1859), and Svevo (1861). They are on the cusp. They are still sequential, social writers. They come before abstraction, atonality, anomie, and the cult of difficulty. The novel is not yet part poem, part essay. The poem not yet a heap of beautiful syllables in foreign alphabets. Things may be out of kilter—Chekhov and Yeats are largely about that—but they still believe in kilter. At the very least, they remember it.

Schnitzler's reputation may have dipped somewhat, but that's still only relative: in his lifetime he was a hugely popular and scandalously controversial writer. His plays were given big productions one after another, and when they weren't—his *Reigen* (or *La Ronde*) had to be pulled in 1921 in Vienna and Berlin after anti-Semitic and neo-puritanical sentiments were unleashed in tandem at this "most vulgar bordello piece" written to incite "the prurience of Asiatic intruders" (i.e., Viennese Jews)—why, then, it was even bigger news. Collections of his stories and novellas—even the list of titles fills two pages in the S. Fischer Verlag catalog—went through forty, sixty, even a hundred printings. Not now, sure, and not in English. But there are still many people who have seen Kubrick's *Eyes Wide Shut* or David Hare's *The Blue Room*, or who remember Max Ophüls's 1950s film of *La Ronde*, and wondered about the author and the texts they were adapted from.

There are two new translations of Schnitzler's fiction, by Margret Schaefer: a collection called *Night Games*, containing the novella of that name, and "Dream Story" (the original of Frederic Raphael's screenplay for the Kubrick film), and seven shorter stories; and *Desire and Delusion* (the title is the publisher's, or the translator's), comprising three novellas: *Flight into Darkness*, *Dying*, and *Fräulein Else*. The situations are tense with promise, the stories are shapely and, as we would say, "deliver," and if your tastes run to some of these "pre-Modern" authors, or Maupassant, or the shorter Dostoevsky, then these are probably for you.

The shorter stories have more in the way of obvious action: they turn on such things as duels and gaming debts, seduction, dishonor, betrayal, and sudden death. None of it is particularly serious; it's as though even in his prose, Schnitzler is still the playwright, putting on a spectacle, amusing his audience. He gives you protagonists but not characters. With very few exceptions, the young men and officers and professional types and married women and harlots in his stories seem to cry out for actors and actresses to give them a little reality. Schnitzler himself noted that he was more interested in "cases" than in individuals. This can be attributed to his analytical, if not cynical, cast of mind, and his medical objectivity—his father was a doctor, and he himself practiced, briefly—but I feel it more as a literary shortcoming in him. (Certainly, it's not something one can say about Chekhov, who was also a doctor.) There is not the increment in inwardness or intensity one might expect from the private form; but as I observed earlier, this is still social writing. One reads with suspense, pleasure, sometimes amusement during the more extravagantly cynical stories ("Baron von Leisenbohg's Destiny") but without any profounder attachment or vulnerability.

As a writer, it seems to me Schnitzler has two somewhat contradictory principal gifts: he is methodical, and he loves to surprise. In the novellas in *Desire and Delusion*, written somewhat later, the emphasis is on the former, perhaps as a deeper, more reputable quality in literature. The first two pieces observe a long process to its culmination. In *Flight into Darkness*, it's the morbidly suspicious nature of Robert, the central figure, finally erupting in a murderous attack; in *Dying*, which is a much better story, it's the progression of Felix's fatal illness and its effect on himself and his sweetheart, Marie. The illness, or the prognosis, destabilizes their relationship; it's almost like a ménage à trois. Here, Schnitzler is absolutely intent and believable; if there's a shock, it's the shock of truth, not a coup de théâtre. The fluent array of feelings he shows in his couple is kaleidoscopic: "Marie did not stir from the sickbed. What an endless afternoon it was! Through the window, which was left open upon explicit orders from the doctor, came the gentle odors of the garden. And it was so quiet! Marie mechanically followed the dance of the sunbeams on the floor. Felix held her hand almost without interruption. His own was cool and moist and gave Marie an unpleasant sensation." All life and all pleasure are away from him. It's a wonderfully—savagely—surprising end to quite an idyllic little passage.

The third novella, *Fräulein Else*, is some sort of masterpiece. It makes it into the literary histories as the earliest sustained example of stream-of-consciousness writing in German—or even outside French! (Dujardin's *Les Lauriers sont coupés* from 1888 was the first; Schnitzler's earlier story from 1900, "Lieutenant Gustl," had been a lesser assay.) Description can't really do justice to this piece. One would like it to go on forever. The feeling is like being behind someone else's frontal bone. Else is a pretty seventeen-year-old, on holiday in the Tirol with wealthier cousins. When the story begins, she's abandoning a tennis match to go back to the hotel; a telegram has advised her to expect an express letter from her mother. The news turns out to be dire: her father is in sudden urgent need of a large sum of money; the parents have tried all the avenues open to them in Vienna, without any success; then it occurs to her mother that one Herr von Dorsday, a wealthy art dealer staying at the same hotel, who might even be thought to owe them a favor, could be approached by Else. It's a typical Schnitzler setup (the one in *Night Games* is similar), but because it's told in the first person, and in real time, the accusations of melodramatic contrivance and shallow characterization fall away. Nor can Schnitzler do without his usual surprise— another telegram arrives halfway through to say the required sum is not thirty thousand but fifty thousand gulden—but that little ratcheting doesn't really matter.

One can quote from almost anywhere in the story to catch the speed and brightness of the girl's mind and her desire to have some sort of effect on life now both perverted and made more urgent by the sudden exigency: "The Alpine glow has faded. The evening is no longer gorgeous. The whole place seems dreary. No, it's not the place. It's life itself. And I'm sitting here calmly on the windowsill. Papa is to be locked up. No. Never, never. He mustn't be. I'll save him. Yes, Papa, I'll save you. It's very easy, after all. Just a few nonchalant words—I'm good at that."

I notice that both the passages I've quoted are couched in terse, powerful sentences. That isn't typical; generally, Schnitzler's prose is a bit long-winded. It can be read with pleasure and ease, but rarely with delight. He hasn't been helped by his translator, whose work I found stodgy, without the suavity that makes the long-windedness bearable, and with diction that's both dull and uncertain. I don't know that you can "contemplate phrases" as you're preparing to speak; to be concerned with one's "postmortem reputation" doesn't sound right to me, nor does "the multifaceted sound of people talking." "She couldn't banish the feeling of well-being that had begun to pervade her whole being" is pretty calamitous, especially when the next sentence is, "She just felt good." A character "gave the room a cursory inspection," only, again in the next sentence, to find "It was roomy . . ." The dictionary will offer "compulsion" and "attitude"— probably two of the most skewed words in English right now—for "*Zwang*" and "*Haltung*"—so in the context of a passage in praise of dueling they're unusable. These are all tiny things, not ruinous by any means, but still they add up over the course of a book or two books. It comes down to tact, or feel. Here are two excerpts from "Dream Story," the first is Margret Schaefer's translation, the second is by J.M.Q. Davies:

"'It's nine o'clock,' the father said. 'Time for bed.' And as Albertine had also bent down to her, the parent's [sic] hands now met on the beloved forehead, and their glances met with a tender smile no longer meant only for the child."

"'Nine o'clock,' said her father, 'time for bed.' And as Albertine too had now bent over the child, the parents' hands touched as they fondly stroked her brow, and, with a tender smile that was no longer intended solely for the child, their eyes met."

Which is the better one? Well, I would suggest it's the one that doesn't use "met" twice, that doesn't contain "the beloved forehead," that permits touching, and that doesn't end with the child. (What happens next isn't going to involve it.) It's no great mystery, and nothing much to do with German. Both "translate" the German, but I'm afraid only one of them writes English.

THOMAS BERNHARD

The Austrian novelist and playwright Thomas Bernhard (1931–1989) once said: "You have to understand that in my writing the musical component comes first, and the subject matter is secondary." It's a strange thing for the professional controversialist and Austropathic ranter to say—somebody who bombards us with content, and bombards content, and bombards *us*—that we should attend to the form, balance, and measure in his work, when everything in it would seem to lead to the giggle and gasp of hurt given or received, or the hush and squeal of scandal, but it is sound advice. Before we talk about the quality of the opinions, or the kilotonnage of the diatribes, or the relentlessness of the perspective (is *anything* exempt?), we ought to talk about the patterns of repetition and variation of the unspooling sentences in the unparagraphed prose. If Bernhard is anything, he is a stuck harpsichord record, bleeding and knocking out its trapped and staggered shards of shrilly hammered phrases.

Old Masters (1985) is Bernhard's penultimate novel. It comes before *Extinction* and after *Cutting Timber* (also known as *Woodcutting* and *Woodcutters*), which was seized on publication, because the couple who thought they recognized themselves in it, the Lampersbergs, old friends of Bernhard, had an injunction taken out against it. (Publicity not being an advantage to them in their circumstances, they eventually relented.) *Old Masters* is typical of Bernhard in that it is both a parodically eccentric version—it's not sure, or one isn't sure, as often in Bernhard, if it's a skit or a pured, laboratory version—of life, but it is at the same time reassuringly solidly mounted. A Bernhard novel is a bizarrely skewed but immediately familiar planet, whose rules and concerns we grasp as readily as those of *Le Petit Prince*. *Old Masters* takes place in a single location, more or less in real time, and yet is able to take in its purview most things under the sun. Come to think of it, including even the sun: "He avoids the sun, there is nothing he shuns more than the sun," it says in Ewald Osers's calm and thoughtful translation. Nothing happens, and little is revealed; it is mostly talk and remembered talk, and thought and remembered thought.

Reger, music philosopher and for the past thirty-four years Vienna music critic for the *Times* of London, for which he knocks out (as he complacently puts it) "those brief works of art which are never longer than two pages" (could there ever be such a figure!?), recently widowed, has summoned his friend Atzbacher to meet him at half past eleven in the Bordone Room in the Kunsthistorisches Museum in Vienna, where, for many years, he has been in the habit of holding court every other day—a court of one, or one and a half—and where, mostly coincidentally, Tintoretto's painting *White-Bearded Man* hangs: Atzbacher, the younger man, working on some chronic and unpublished work of philosophy, and very much in thrall to the domineering Reger ("my imaginary father"), comes to the museum an hour early, so that he can stand next door in the Sebastiano Room and, as it were, warm up by observing Reger without himself being seen; watch his interactions with the museum attendant Irrsigler ("Jenö!") whom Reger has, over the years, converted into a sort of auxiliary personal retainer as he has made the settee in the Bordone Room into a sort of exclusive public headquarters and thinking place for himself; and replay their old conversations to himself, and Reger's trenchant views on this and that. At the set time, Atzbacher appears—he knows the value Reger places upon punctuality—and the conversation—no longer remembered or reconstructed, but "live" or "actual"—is intensified, until the book ends with a cautious stab at a little more of the world: Reger has—ill-advisedly in view of much that has gone before—purchased a couple of theater tickets and invites Atzbacher to take in a show with him. It is Kleist's comedy *The Broken Pitcher* at the Burgtheater. "The performance was terrible," notes Atzbacher in the book's last put-down. It is a real ending, slight but real, no mean feat.

It's a personal thing, but also an Austrian thing. In *The Man Without Qualities*, Musil says, "The man of genius is duty-bound to attack." Perhaps it's the sweetness and pleasingness of the rest of the culture that means that anything honest or anything good will always be critical. Anyway, Bernhard has always had his superior ranters spitting pessimism and disaffection, leaving, as Germans say, "not a good hair" on anything or anyone. They are said to be based, in life, on Bernhard's grandfather, the totally obscure Austrian writer Johannes Freumbichler who, as the English say, "took him in hand," and to whose memory and example he remained devoted. The role of the baobab in St.-Exupéry is played by the grandfather in Bernhard. *Gathering Evidence*, Bernhard's five-part autobiographical memoir, begins with the eight-year-old Bernhard borrowing his "guardian's" (a nervous word for the man who later became his stepfather) bicycle, which is several sizes too big for him, and making a doomed attempt to ride it up hill and down dale to his grandfather's house in another town. It seems probable to me that the re-valuation of all values (Nietzsche) required to make one a writer took place very early in Bernhard's life, when he decided that Freumbichler was not a talentless wastrel who made life miserable for everyone around him (which seems on the face of it a view with much to commend it) but a misunderstood genius whose every word was worth recording; and by the same token that the world was not mostly a dim and well-meaning sort of place, higgledy-piggledy and inefficient but broadly correct and, in any case, hopelessly set in its ways, but a sinister and perverted conspiracy that produced only deformed individuals and institutions and that should be opposed and exposed every step of the way, ideally by a grand, insouciant, terrifying, and old soliloquist (and the greatest of these, somehow, is old: master is good, but old is better, in age only is our salvation, and Bernhard, alas for himself, did not live to be old). If the whole world, all received opinion, all authority, all ease and rewards are in one pannier, one's duty is to jump into the other without even looking, Jeanne Moreau–style. The unwritten motto of Bernhard, in life and work, is *contra mundum*. In other books, this Freumbichler figure takes on the world or its Austrian microcosm by himself in arias of virtuosic hatred, here it is more the braiding of Reger's dominant voice with the alert, repertorial voice of Atzbacher, and the copying voice of Irrsigler, who has, "over the years, appropriated verbatim many, if not all, of Reger's sentences," in a sort of lopsided barbershop trio. One that sings, as it were, only the black notes.

A normal novel is at pains to differentiate among its characters, by making them talk, about themselves and about each other, in distinct, individuated ways. He does the police in different voices, and so on. In Bernhard, though, there is a convergence of voices: everyone speaks the same way and says the same sorts of things. It's one reason why we take these things, these views so seriously and attribute them so readily to the author: they are not relativized, there is no argument, no opposition. In a sense, the views are all we have. They are novels of impassioned generalization. Not only are Reger and his opinions everyone's special subject, including, of course, Reger's own; not only does Reger sound just like Atzbacher's recollection of him and Irrsigler's appropriations of him, but such minor characters as there are resemble him too! A well-accessorized "Englishman from Wales" who one day sits down on Reger's settee in the Bordone Room, wearing "high-quality Scottish clothes" and—as we are given to understand—Reger's make of aftershave, soliloquizes and exaggerates just like Reger, who is further put to the trouble of explaining to him: "Thousands of old masters are stolen in England every day, the Englishman said. Reger said, there are hundreds of organized gangs in England who specialize in the theft of old masters, especially of Italians, who are particularly popular in England." Looks like Reger, smells like Reger, talks like Reger, impresses and dresses like Reger ("everything I wear comes from the Hebrides")—it must be a duck. Reger, incidentally, "had repeatedly made Irrsigler presents of clothes he no longer wears, truly top-quality treasures from the most superb tweed material"; but then you could say he kits out everyone in the book with his style and opinions anyway. Everyone wears, so to speak, the Reger tartan. Even the woman Reger rather bizarrely came to marry—Irrsigler steered her to that same Bordone Room settee—is valued by him principally on the basis of the time and indoctrination he has put into her: a sort of advanced Eliza Doolittle.

All this goes to show just how different Thomas Bernhard's novels are from the usual run of novels. They are sculptures of opinion rather than contraptions assembled from character interactions. Each book is a curved, seamless rant. (I like to think they could be made more negotiable for the reader by the inclusion, not of paragraphs, which is a barbarous idea, but, as in a nonfiction book, of running subject headings, which would include things like: children's education, the Catholic church, the Austrian state, Heidegger, Mahler, the sentimental regard for the working classes, and so on and so forth.) There are in fact no moving parts. The figures pool their wisdom—or their fury—rather than take issue with one another. And by the same token, speech and thought are heavily mannered or stylized, by imputation authorial, almost abstract in their rhythms. Take the diatribe from Reger:

> The art historians are the real wreckers of art, Reger said. The art historians twaddle so long about art until they have killed it with their twaddle. Art is killed by the twaddle of the art historians. My God, I often think, sitting here on the settee while the art historians are driving their helpless flocks past me, what a pity about all these people who have all art driven out of them, driven out of them for good, by these very art historians. The art historians' trade is the vilest trade there is, and a twaddling art historian, but then there are only twaddling art historians, deserves to be chased out with a whip, chased out of the world of art, Reger said, all art historians deserve to be chased out of the world of art, because art historians are the real wreckers of art, and we should not allow art to be wrecked by the art historians who are really art wreckers.

The passage loops like a villanelle, from "the art historians are the real wreckers of art" to "the art historians who are really art wreckers." In between, there are various other technical-seeming shifts: "twaddle" as verb, then noun, "art" as object, then as subject, "art historians" in a general proposition, and then as individually experienced, "driven out" to "chased out." Absolute terms abound: "the real," "killed," "all art," "for good," "the vilest," "only." Figures are strictly obvious: driving flocks, trade, with a whip. And the one hated term comes up eleven times: art historians. The passage displays energy, persistence, modest variety: it's like someone blowing up a rubber balloon with a pump, and, when he does it properly, bursting it. Bernhard continues:

> Listening to an art historian we feel sick, he said, by listening to an art historian we see the art he is twaddling about being ruined, with the twaddle of the art historian art shrivels and is ruined. Thousands, indeed tens of thousands of art historians wreck art by their twaddle and ruin it, he said. The art historians are the real killers of art, if we listen to an art historian we participate in the wrecking of art, wherever an art historian appears art is wrecked, that is the truth.

The first ending was a trick ending, the passage doesn't really end— the balloon doesn't really die—until "that is the truth" (which is a recurring phrase in the book). Bernhard has added another loop: this attack happens to be a figure eight. The dread term "art historian" comes up another seven times, and a different set of shifts are negotiated, or played out; here it's from "listen" to "see, and it's about organizing a contamination of the singular from the plural (those "thousands, indeed tens of thousands"), so that the argument goes from "one" to "many" to "each." It's as though—and this seems quite a tenable point of view to me—Bernhard's real loathing and real fear is of anything in the plural. "People are not interested in art, at any rate ninety-nine per cent of humanity has no interest whatever in art, as Irrsigler says, quoting Reger word for word": numbers and statistics are never good news in Bernhard. I agree the style and the approach seem to be somewhere at the comic end of things, but I'm not sure it's comedy. Certainly, one thing it isn't is British character comedy, as in comic turns or Perrier Awards. Bernhard hasn't dished up these people for us to laugh at them and find them foolish; they're not silly-billies, and it's not Rowan Atkinson. It may happen to work—in England—as comedy, or to suggest comedy—to us—because it's broad or pitiless or unsubtle, but what if it was just broad and pitiless and unsubtle? Something is being clobbered so hard that we—quite possibly mistakenly, and out of the goodness of our hearts—laugh. We're nervous, we don't think anyone could say it and mean it. He means it, all right. Still, there is something relished and performed in this writing. Listen to how many different ways I can come up with to say this, it seems to be saying. See how many times I perpetrate the discourtesy—the maniacal drivenness—of refusing to find alternative forms (as for "art historian" here, or "twaddle") until the words are left jangling and droning in your head; see, conversely, how many fierce synonyms I can string together—"wreck," "ruin", "kill", "shrivel"—and always mean the same vague thing.

The "art historian" passage happened to be figure eight, but there are all sorts of other forms. Here is a statement closely backed up by three substatements in verbal and rhetorical parallel:

> The Austrians are positively congenital *coverers-up* of crimes, Reger said, the Austrians will cover up any crime, even the vilest, because they are, as I have said, congenital opportunist cringers. For decades our ministers have committed ghastly crimes, yet these opportunist cringers cover up for them. For decades these ministers have committed *murderous* frauds, yet these cringers cover up for them. For decades these unscrupulous Austrian ministers have lied to the Austrians and cheated them and yet these cringers cover up for them.

This swelling repetition, Wodehouse's Hollywood mogul backed up by his three yessers and three nodders—"our ministers"—"these ministers"—"these unscrupulous Austrian ministers"—"yet"—"yet"—"and yet"—still manages to accommodate the thrillingly excessive "*murderous* frauds." Then there is the connecting, the braiding of ideas or phenomena, which enables both to be sent to their deaths together:

> Nature is now enjoying a boom, Reger said yesterday, that is why Stifter is now enjoying a boom. Anything to do with nature is now

very much in vogue, Reger said yesterday, that is why Stifter is now greatly, or more than greatly, in vogue. The forest is now greatly in vogue, mountain streams are now greatly in vogue. Stifter bores everybody to death yet in some fatal manner is now greatly in vogue, Reger said.

A lot of Bernhard must be logistical, how to pace, how to rank, how to hide. When to deepen the attack, when and how to move on. When to use a concrete detail—often malign in its pathos (a green coat, a Glasgow aunt)—and when like Marvell to roll all his sourness into one ball and come up with something like: "all these writers write totally brainless and sham-philosophical and sham-homeland epigone rubbish" or "the whole Prater reeks of beer and crime and we encounter in it nothing but the brutality and the brazen feeble-mindedness of vulgar snotty Viennesedom"—instances of what I would call Bernhard's more rubbery sentences, full of spluttering and vocabulary and rather unstructured aggression.

Bernhard may not be funny, but he is—what I've quoted hasn't been misleading—clean. That's another way he differs from comedy. There are no four-letter words. Even when the subject is lavatories, he's not lavatorical: "The Viennese, and the Austrians generally, have no lavatory culture, nowhere in the world would you find such filthy and smelly lavatories, Reger said." Bernhard accepts the difficulty and the diligence of continuing to come up with terms—generalizing terms like "lavatory culture" or particular terms like "Mozart's music is also full of petticoat and frilly undies kitsch." He makes moral-aesthetic judgments: "abysmally hideous," "charlatanist nonsense," "utterly rotten and *demoniacal* state," "Heidegger had a common face," "anything else by Mahler I reject." He goes on judging. If he were to relent and say, "bunch of fucking crap," that would be an abdication. That would be letting us off the hook. That, for the life-long invalid, would be dying.

GÜNTER GRASS

Bertolt Brecht has a famous poem from 1933, "O Germany, Pale Mother!" (Helma Sanders-Brahms later used the words as the title for a film.) The poem has an epigraph: "Let others talk about their shame, I will talk about mine." Grass has done the opposite: he has carefully incubated his particular shame for sixty years, all the while encouraging others to talk about theirs. Now, possibly threatened by its imminent disclosure—the relevant documents surfaced in Grass's Stasi file—or in a bid to keep some sort of "authorial" control over it, he has published it, and impertinently required readers to pay for it, the only significant revelation in a long and miserably bad book. This lifelong silence, and, more yet, the manner of his breaking it, have hurt Grass's reputation in ways from which it will never recover, and which, depressingly, he seems not even to have understood.

It transpires that the seventeen-year-old Grass—who had never previously admitted to being anything worse than a "*Flakhelfer*," a conscripted civilian ack-ack gunner—volunteered and briefly served with the elite unit called the Waffen-SS. When this was made public, the whole of Germany ground to a halt. Grass tried to limit the damage with a long exclusive interview (and homemade *al fresco* lunch thrown in) with representatives of the leading conservative newspaper, the *Frankfurter Allgemeine Zeitung*, and in a series of public events, and has generally gone on as though nothing has happened; but this is something that will not get better or go away. The postwar "conscience of Germany" now has to suffer his name to appear disfigured with the double lightnings of the SS.

Peeling the Onion covers the years from 1939 to 1959, when *The Tin Drum* was published; it is an autobiography of Grass's youth. I didn't read it during the kerfuffle of 2006, but coming to it now, in both the inadequate original and in Michael Henry Heim's always spirited English translation, things seem, if anything, even worse. There is a kind of plainspoken and rueful candor that is apparently entirely outside Grass's gift; perhaps it can only be done by Anglo-Saxon writers. One thinks of the noble line of Edmund Gosse, J. R. Ackerley, or Laurie Lee, or more recent accounts of such "difficult" lives as Janet Hobhouse's *The Furies* or Tobias Wolff's *This Boy's Life*. This is what Grass, by equipment either a rococo fabulist or else a polemicist, cannot do: stand at the end of a life and—however crooked—tell it straight. There are important categories, such as "the poetry of fact," but also even "the truth of fact," that are inimical to him (they are no good to a polemicist or a fabulist). The oddest, most dismaying thing about *Peeling the Onion* is that Grass should ever have attempted anything of the sort, so unwinning, unresonant, unstylish, and unconvincing is the result. (And that too makes one think this was not a voluntary exercise.)

The revelation of the SS membership comes too late in the book (not unnaturally, one turns the pages, impatient for it to come—pp. 109 to 111), and then, when it is gone, one feels too winded—literally, too punched—to carry on through the rest of it. (I actually put it down for two weeks, unwilling to continue.) It is both too heavily trailed and too much put off, too perfunctory and too dilatory, too defensive and too aggressive. They are two pages of failed writing that should be put in a textbook and quarried for their multiple instances of bad faith.

The whole episode is announced by a break in style, an end to Grassian gabbiness and a new, manly brusqueness: "Nothing about the journey there." Then the Waffen-SS makes its first appearance, not as a principal, in the nominative, but in the genitive, "a drill ground of the Waffen-SS," just as "I" appears not as "I" but as "the recruit with my name" (a habitual and awful periphrastic tic throughout the book). There is callous hard-bitten military jargon ("a pocket like Demyansk forced open") followed by a dismaying, and dismayingly rare, statement of fact: "I did not find the double rune on the uniform collar repellent." There is a disquisition on the historical von Frundsberg, a sixteenth-century mercenary, who gave Grass's unit its name: "Someone who stood for freedom, liberation." There is a bizarre note on the international composition of the Waffen-SS (to the boy who knew, apparently, next to nothing of what he was letting himself in for?) that makes it sound like the League of Nations: "It included separate volunteer divisions of French and Walloon, Dutch and Flemish, and many Norwegian and Danish soldiers." And then the *Fazit*, sounding rather more self-justificatory than it needed to: "So there were plenty of excuses." And the last, pat sentence: "I will have to live with it for the rest of my life"—though one should note, that, here, of all places, the German uses an impersonal construction!

As a plea, an account, a confession, this is so bad as to be easily counterproductive. Still, aside from the gravity of its content, it is really no worse than what comes before and after: the endless invocations of the onion, memory (though also of the amber, memory); the strings of rhetorical questions, sometimes as much as half a page of them, one after another; the tedious speculative reading lists of books read (or not read) at a certain time; the intercalation of irrelevant and largely flippant episodes; the cross-references to Grass's work in fiction; the places and persons revisited, years later, in greater comfort, by Grass and his wife; the indifferent use of consequence and inconsequence to match the "now I remember, now I forget" *tenue* of the book; the underlying but sharply unmistakable whiff of self-congratulation attending the whole thing.

"Even in formation I was a loner, though I took care not to stand out," Grass writes: "I was a schemer whose mind was forever elsewhere." Bland and pat and dreamy enough, you might think, but in German it is, again, a little worse. Grass's terms are not the near synonyms "loner" and "schemer," but the near opposites *"Einzelgän-ger"* and *"Mitläufer,"* the one who walks alone and the one who runs with others. The horrible suspicion arises that Grass's deepest project here is the destruction of meaning. Not so much "peeling the onion" as "applying the whitewash."

STEFAN ZWEIG

Romain Rolland, one of Stefan Zweig's many illustrious friends (he seems not to have had any others), expressed surprise that he could be a writer and not like cats: "*Un poète qui n'aime pas les chats!*" It's only one of an unending series of things—as if the man didn't have a shadow—that strike one as being "not quite right" about this popular-again popularizer, like the *Kitschmeister* Gustav Klimt glitteringly and preposterously back in fashion, and neither of them any better than they were the first time round.

Polygrapher Zweig ("twig"), dubbed "Erwerbszweig" (something like branch of the economy or branch of industry) in catty, envious Vienna: this anxious success and oh-so-modest failure; best-selling and most-translated German-language author before World War II, and now again book of the week here, rediscovery of the century there, and indulgently reviewed more or less everywhere; this uniquely dreary and clothy sprog of the electric 1880s; un-Austrian Austrian and un-Jewish Jew (where Joseph Roth—who has certainly spoiled me for Zweig—was both, to the max); neither pacifist much less activist but passivist; professional adorer, schmoozer, inheritor and collector, owner of Beethoven's desk and Goethe's pen and Leonardo and Mozart manuscripts and busy Balzac proofs and contemporaries out the wazoo, plus four thousand *manuscript collection catalogs*; who logged his phone calls and logged his letters and logged his books, and, who knows, probably logged his logs; this cosmopolitan loner and blue-riband refugee, so "hysterically discreet" he got married by proxy and to a man; who, in the words of the writer Robert Neumann, "spent his life on the run. From the Great War to Switzerland. From the symbolic firing-squad across the Channel. From Blitzed London to the safety of provincial Bath. From Hitler's threatened invasion of England to the USA. From Roosevelt's impending entry into the war to Brazil. He even fled Rio for a Brazilian mountain resort. From there there was no more running"; who left a suicide note that, like most of what he wrote, is so smooth and mannerly and somehow machined—actually more like an Oscar acceptance speech than a suicide note—one feels the irritable rise of boredom halfway through it, and the sense that *he doesn't mean it*, his heart isn't in it (not even in his suicide); someone whose books I briefly thought I wouldn't mind reading, before, while setting down the umpteenth of them amid groans (it was the novella *Confusion*)—adding the stipulation to myself: yes, but only if they'd been written by someone else.

Stefan Zweig just tastes fake. He's the Pepsi of Austrian writing. He is the one whose books made films—eighteen of them, and that's the books, not the films (which come in at a stupefying thirty-eight). It makes sense: these hypothetical and bloodless and stiltedly extreme monuments and monodramas for "teenagers of all ages," as someone said, books composed for the bourgeoisie to give itself culture or a fright, needed Hollywood or UFA to make them real, to give them expressions, faces, bodies, rooms, and dialogue; and to drain some of the schematic *guignol* out of them. Of course he failed the Karl Kraus test—who didn't? Kraus quotes some driveling yeasayer to the effect that Zweig with his novellas had conquered all the languages of the world, and adds two words of his own: "except one." The story went the rounds—it was far from being just a piece of Nazi propaganda—that Zweig had his manuscripts checked for grammatical errors by a German professor, which gets most things about

Zweig: the ineptitude, the eagerness to please, the respect for authority, and the use of others.

It's not easy to think of a writer so poorly thought of by his maybe peers, and it can't all be attributed to envy or resentment of his great inherited wealth, easy success, unproblematic seductions, and vast readerships. Even among writers, there may be odd moments of honesty. Hugo von Hofmannsthal, who for the best part of thirty years shared a publisher with Zweig—Anton Kippenberg, founder of the Insel Verlag—wrote literally to dispraise him; when Kippenberg, foolishly trying to change Hofmannsthal's ideas, informed him, publisher-paternalistically, that Zweig had won a poetry prize, Hofmannsthal wrote back in a (for him) strange blaze of candor, that the prize wasn't a prize at all, but a bursary, and that Zweig had had to share it with "eight other sixth-rate talents." When Hofmannsthal and Max Reinhardt started the Salzburg Festival in 1919, it was one of their stipulations that Zweig—who had recently moved to Salzburg—be rigorously excluded. (Zweig took to absenting himself from Salzburg every summer, while the festival was on, mostly, one imagines, to spare his own feelings.) Hofmannsthal's friend Leopold von Andrian put himself through a Zweig novella—that same *Confusion* I mentioned earlier—"reluctantly, a spoonful a day, like a nasty-tasting medicine," and, in the course of a comprehensive, paragraph-long taking-apart, wrote: "each sentence incredibly pretentious, false and empty—the whole thing a complete void." In his memoirs, Elias Canetti recalls a meeting with Zweig, who had come back to Vienna for two reasons: to get his teeth seen to, and to set up a new house that would publish his books. The next sentence is: "I think almost all his teeth were pulled." The malicious and inescapable and (in a master like Canetti) perfectly deliberate undercurrent is that of course Zweig's books are not worth talking about. The teeth are more important, and even their *exeunt omnes* is a better outcome than anything to do with the publication—or extraction?—of the books.

Even Joseph Roth, a complicated friend of Zweig's who more or less lived off him for the last ten years of his life, picked holes in the style of each successive book he was sent, partly as a way of discharging his debt, and partly to preserve his independence. Then the veteran Germanist Hans Mayer remembers a visit to Musil in Switzerland in 1940. Musil couldn't get into the United States, and Mayer was suggesting the relative obtainability of Colombian visas as a *pis aller*. "He looked at me askance and said: Stefan Zweig's in South America. It wasn't a bon mot. The great ironist wasn't a witty conversationalist. He meant it. [. . .] If Zweig was living in South America somewhere, that took care of the continent for Musil."

Nor was it just the Austrians, to whom such *Schmäh* was in their mothers' milk. Hermann Hesse thought neither Zweig's poetry nor "his many other books" deserved to outlast the day. When Kippenberg heard that his author had a part interest in a factory, the publisher is said to have quipped back: "What—another one?" When Zweig moved to England in 1934 (and was naturalized in 1938), that was taken semijocularly in many literary quarters—again, not Nazi—to be a major item in that ongoing "punishment of England" ("*Gott strafe England*") that had been on the German agenda since 1914. The composer Hanns Eisler records a meeting between Brecht and Zweig in London. Brecht, "of course never read a line of Zweig" (one admires the economy of effort), sees him only as a possible source of funds for his theater; Zweig, one guesses, in adding the notch of another great man to his metaphorical bedpost. Brecht asks Eisler for a tune. Unfortunately, the tune he asks for is "Song of the Vivifying Effect of Money," and it's not lost on Zweig. Later—in spite of everything, one would think—the two writers go for lunch together, and when Brecht comes back, Eisler—again, really lovely, the stringent cut-to-the-chase of these Marxist types!—asks him how much Zweig shelled out for lunch. "Two and six," replies Brecht, a Lyons Corner House or something, the multimillionaire Zweig at the time was residing in Portland Place, and then it's straight back to the revolution. Farther west, in Princeton, or much farther, in Pacific Palisades, Thomas Mann and his family spent diverting evenings— this in 1939—debating which of Zweig, Ludwig, Feuchtwanger, and Remarque was the worst writer. Emil Ludwig himself, in an obituary, wrote that none of Zweig's writings had had an effect on him that could compare with his death. It's a well-meaning but damning and finally ineluctable summation. I have seen the Brazilian press photograph of Zweig and Lotte, his second wife, lying dead of their overdoses of veronal on two pushed-together single iron bedsteads, he on his back, mouth a little agape, in a sweat-stained shirt and knitted tie, she on his shoulder in a floral wrap and clean hair, and you can practically hear the ceiling fan going round. It makes Weegee look tame.

Of course the forty-third president of the United States knew whereof he spake, and there is such a thing as misunderestimation. As well as knowing him best, a man's contemporaries have every reason for getting him wrong, but the fact remains that there is an unusual consensus here—Mann, Musil, Brecht, Hesse, Canetti, Hofmannsthal, Kraus—to the effect that Stefan Zweig was a purveyor of *Trivialliteratur* and, save in commercial terms, an utterly negligible figure; when from the distance of Britain or America one erroneously supposes something more like the opposite to be the case: that here is someone who is among the best his country and language and period have to offer, and who comes with the good opinion and endorsement of his peers. Partly it's the distinction—far more rigidly observed in Germany than in the English-speaking world—between serious and popular (*e* and *u* in German parlance, *Ernst* and *Unterhaltung*), but there's more to it than that. There is something touchingly wrong about Zweig. He had a trammeled life and preached freedom; he gave himself to public causes and had little to say; "the least personal biography he ever wrote," thus John Fowles, "was his own"; he was obtuse and hypersensitive and worshipped at the altar of friendship. He is like someone walking up a down escalator, his eyes anxiously fixed on Parnassus—all those people and friends whose manuscripts he collected—toiling away and not coming close. He, by the way, knew it—he deprecates himself and means it; he lists authors who are more important than he is, and means it; Friderike, his first wife, wrote to him, "Your written works are only a third of yourself," with little fear of contradiction from him; he is the modest man in the story with plenty to be modest about—it's his apologists who need telling. In 1981, the last time a Zweig revival was plotted—that one failed; this time, with Pushkin Press's nice paper and pretty formats and with new translations by the excellent Anthea Bell, it seems to be succeeding—John Fowles (a thoroughly representative Anglo-Saxon *e* and *u* crossbreed) wrote: "Stefan

Zweig has suffered, since his death in 1942, a darker eclipse than any other famous writer of this century. Even 'famous writer' understates the prodigious reputation he enjoyed in the last decade or so of his life, when he was arguably the most widely-read and translated serious author in the world . . ." Fifty languages and millions of copies in circulation, but "serious author"? Ain't no way. I have seen Zweig referred to in German as "an exemplary subrealist" and "the notorious writer of bestsellers," which is more like it. The Viennese critic Hilde Spiel deemed his fiction—which has taken the lead in the present reinflation of his reputation—as "closest in spirit to Schnitzler's—and not a patch on it." That seems fair to me.

In Thomas Mann's great story "Tristan," the bourgeois Klöter-jahn has trouble even reading the handwriting of the writer Spinell; Mann's admirably ironic conclusion is that writers are typically people who write rarely and with great difficulty. Zweig is one writer I can think of who enjoyed writing, and to whom it came easily, all of it: from his teenage poems, straightaway put out by the august publishers of Dehmel and Liliencron (in 1901, when he was barely twenty), to his first shot at a feuilleton, accepted by the paper his parents subscribed to, the *Neue Wiener Presse*, while Zweig briefly cooled his heels in the editor's office, to his translations of the Belgian poet Emile Verhaeren (in 1905 and 1910) and others; to the essays and popular biographies, on Verlaine, Dostoevsky, Balzac, Dickens, and dozens and dozens of others, which Paul Bailey, an admirer of at least some of Zweig's fiction, describes as "slightly embarrassing"; the lectures and statements and appeals; the intermittent plays and libretti (for Richard Strauss, once Hofmannsthal's opposition and tenure had lapsed with his death in 1929); the stories and novellas, mainly framed narratives, encounters with strangers and madmen—unfortunates with stories, one thinks of them as being—mediated always by the same sane, starchy voice. Zweig himself speaks a little smugly in *The World of Yesterday* of "this preference of mine for intense, intemperate characters in my novels and novellas." "The typical Zweig story," notes the critic William Deresiewicz cooling to his subject in an afterword, "is a tale of monomaniacal passion set loose amid the veiled, upholstered civility of the Austrian bourgeoisie, the class into which Zweig was born." The only form to resist his suit at all was the novel; he managed in fact only one, *Beware of Pity*, published in 1939 (*The Post Office Girl* was a posthumously published two-part wreck and an excellent argument against any novels by Stefan Zweig: it encouraged his prolixity, and he had no idea how most people walked and talked and lived in the world—as an original conflation of John Fowles with Uri Geller put it, "The silver spoon that met him when he entered the world was later to become something of a crucifix"). He loved and approved all aspects of writing and publishing, from the fetishistic *cura* of the works of genius in his collection to his own bibliophile editions with Insel Verlag, which he praises for appearing without a single misprint that he was aware of (and he would have been aware). He wrote some twenty or thirty thousand letters. He loved his days researching Magellan, say, or Mary Queen of Scots, at the British Library. When he went to India, it's unthinkable that he would have come back without his poem on the Taj Mahal. If Hofmannsthal had his "Chandos" crisis of language and expression, Zweig bespeaks something very like the opposite: an abundant, facile, and unhindered lifelong logorrhea.

At some time, curiously, Zweig's actual methods swung from one pole to the other. I find both descriptions—and conditions—alarming. In 1899, as a very young man, he wrote to an editor:

> I realize . . . that this Novelle, as with most of my pieces, is slapdash and over-hasty, but . . . I find that when the last word is written I can make no more corrections, in fact I do not even check through for spelling and punctuation. This is a silly and obstinate way to go about things, and it is completely clear to me that it will prevent me from ever achieving anything great. I do not know the art of being conscientious and diligent . . . I have burned hundreds of my manuscripts—but I have never altered or rewritten a single line. It is a misfortune not easily to be altered, since it is not a purely external thing but probably lies deep in my character.

It is a strange performance, the clash of callow self-certainty with a certain innate modesty, resolved in a (typically Zweigian) stance of passivity and helplessness and evasion ("probably"). Compare this to the insight into his processes provided in Zweig's last work, the post-humously published *The World of Yesterday*:

> So if my books are sometimes praised for sweeping readers along at a swift pace, it does not come from any natural heated or agitated approach to the work of writing, but is entirely the result of my system of always cutting unnecessarily slack passages—anything at all that, like radio interference, might distract the reader's attention. If I have mastered any kind of art, it is the art of leaving things out. I do not mind throwing eight hundred of a thousand written pages into the waste-paper basket, leaving me with only two hundred to convey what I have sifted out as the essence of the work.

Here, the modesty is paired with a methodical application of that "conscientiousness" and "diligence" he earlier castigated himself for—or boasted of?—lacking. Even then, it is oddly unconvincing, part of a spiritedly oxymoronic two-page attack on "anything tediously long-winded," that is itself chock-full of redundancies and questions begged. What are phrases like "tediously long-winded" or "unnecessarily slack" but examples of what's wrong? (And what happens, one wonders, to those passages that are "necessarily slack"? Presumably they are nodded through.) What is the dreary and inept simile "like radio interference" but an awful instance of something that needlessly "distract[s] the reader's attention"? (Roth in his letters is forever taking Zweig to task for his hammy way with comparisons.) What does the last clause of the quotation, the nineteen words from "leaving" to "work," really add to the sentence? The German expression "[only] to cook with water," [*auch nur*] *mit Wasser kochen* (sort of the opposite of "cooking with gas") describes the unexceptional, the uninspired, the sublunary, the mortal. Zweig, in strangely praising—like a jam manufacturer—the role of water in his processes ("my system"), apparently fails to realize that every page of his is sodden, formulaic, thin, swollen, platitudinous.

Take some instances. Here is the English widow, Mrs. C., in *Twenty-Four Hours in the Life of a Woman*: "In essence, I regarded my life from that moment on as entirely pointless and useless. The man with whom I had shared every hour and thought for twenty-three years was dead, my children did not need me, I was afraid of casting a cloud over their youth with my sadness and melancholy—but I wished and desired nothing more for myself." It's not so much riveting as riveted. Here is a description of the servant-woman Crescenz in the story "Leporella" (Zweig seems to be especially bad at those sudden changes to which, as a writer, he is so dependably drawn): "The sluggish heaviness suddenly left her rigid, frozen limbs; it was as if since she had heard that electrifying news her joints were suddenly supple, and she adopted a quick, nimble gait." Here is another old woman, the mother in *The Post Office Girl*: "But then a confused torrent of broken, half-intelligible sentences burst from her toothless, working mouth, interspersed with floods of wild triumphant laughter. Tears roll down her cheeks and into her sagging mouth as she stammers and waves her hands, hurling the jumble of excited words at her bewildered daughter." Here—lest it be supposed that it's only older female characters who somehow escape Zweig's otherwise "meticulous but at the same time condensed style" (Anthea Bell in an afterword)—is Zweig's narrator in the novella *Amok*: "I had seen a new world, I had taken in turbulent, confused images that raced wildly through my mind. Now I wanted leisure to think, to analyse and organise them, make sense of all that had impressed itself on my eyes, but there wasn't a moment of rest and peace to be had here on the crowded deck." One appreciates the ease, the fluency, perhaps most of all the fearlessness of the writing, but I fail to see the least dash or economy or precision (let alone beauty) in this clubbing and relentless and unaware deployment of parts of speech that stands in for a style, and is everywhere the same. Zweig is at one and the same time an absolutely natural and absolutely dreadful writer; the one quality of course does not preclude the other.

Zweig finished *The World of Yesterday* in 1941, shortly before his death in February 1942, but neither the new form nor the old subject, neither being in the New World nor the probable end of the rest of it, neither his turning sixty (as he, something of a Peter Pan, wished never to do) nor whatever thanatophile twinkle he had in his eye enabled him to transcend his ordinary possibilities. It is indeed his "least personal biography." Hermann Kesten, Joseph Roth's sometime friend and fellow exile, and later his editor, mused expertly:

A reader of Zweig's autobiography could be pardoned for thinking this Zweig must have been a colourless individual. In fact he was a strange and complicated person; fussy and interesting, bizarre and cunning; brooding, calculating and sentimental; helpful and distant; amusing and full of contradictions; comfortable in his manner, sometimes anything but in the things he said; actor-ish and hard-working; always intellectually stimulating; banal and devious; easily excited and quickly tired . . .

The World of Yesterday is orderly, often bland, sometimes honest, sometimes disingenuous, occasionally unintentionally funny, from time to time downright stupid. Fowles is cross with a biographer ("one of his less gifted biographers") for remarking "with an infelicity bordering on the sublime, that 'no one has ever accused Zweig of a sense of humour,'" but I really don't know why; it's so obviously true. Then, all his life, Zweig prided himself on his lack of any political nous. He is in Belgium in August 1914, and so sure is he that the Germans won't invade that he offers to hang himself from a lamppost if they do. A few hours later, they do, and he doesn't. A book that says—of Maxim Gorky!—"there was nothing striking about his features" (just as it does, incidentally, and with more justice, about Rainer Maria Rilke: "features, not in themselves striking") isn't going to raise the bar for perspicacity or boldness. Accordingly, the human portraits are not among the best things here: the pages on Vienna, Berlin especially, and Paris are much to be preferred to the sanctimonious, almost slobbering passages on Hofmannsthal, Verhaeren, Rilke, Rathenau, Rolland, and Strauss, full of the sort of adulatory humbug that was Zweig's real element. However, saying that his choice of publisher—the later Nazi Kippenberg, who put him through a long and painful and expensive separation that hurt his reputation and earned him years of scolding letters from the fiery Roth—"could not have turned out better" is in a different class of untruth: a sort of sentimental and half-deluded, half-diplomatic twaddle.

Zweig's worst whitewashing is reserved for his sentiments at the outbreak of World War I. In his guileful paraphrase (and in a chapter titled none too bashfully "The Fight for International Fraternity"), he describes an essay he published in September 1914 in a Berlin newspaper ("After all, I was a writer, I had words at my disposal, and I therefore had a duty to express my convictions in so far as I could at the time of censorship"), titled *To Friends Abroad*: "I addressed all my friends in other countries, saying that I would be loyal to them even if closer links were impossible at the moment, so that at the first opportunity I could go on working with them to encourage the construction of a common European culture." Then this and that, mostly to underline Zweig's bravery and isolation, and then over the page, "fourteen days later, when I had almost forgotten the article"—so much for his convictions, one thinks—he gets a letter from his pacifist friend Romain Rolland: "He must have read the article, for he wrote: 'I for one will never forsake my friends.'" As told, the story makes no sense. Here's Zweig, sticking his neck out, courting danger and even a run-in with the censor, and here's the protestation of loyalty from his friend. Why? Why is it so clear that Rolland has read the article? Why the strange, rebuking sound in Rolland's sentence? Isn't everybody being brave together? Well, no, not when you read the words Zweig actually addressed to his foreign friends, quoted in Donald Prater's 1972 biography: "This hatred for you—although I do not feel it myself—I will not try to moderate, for it brings forth victories and heroic strength . . . Do not expect me to be your advocate, however much I may feel this my duty! Respect my silence, as I respect yours!" Inasmuch as this ghastly jelly-wobble of a passage says anything, it prorogues Zweig's foreign friendships for the duration: no wonder the German censor found little to take exception to! German poet sends French poet to Coventry—it's exactly right, it's *magnifique* and *comme il faut*! Imagine Zweig's humiliation, then, when he got Rolland's letter! That ringing sentence, slicing through Zweig's vermicular dither and duplicity, "I for one will never forsake my friends!" You have to hand it to the French! And then imagine living with that for twenty-five years, and then writing it in your autobiography, not what happened, nor what you wish had happened, but the whole thing just so obfuscated that it makes no sense, and the relief you feel when you've done that! And you call it "The Fight for International Fraternity." You talk about your "immunity to this sudden patriotic intoxication" and you wonder, a little repetitiously, but then you're like that, about being "perhaps the only person to be shockingly sober amidst their intoxication," and you swear "an oath that I kept after 1940 as well—never to write a word approving of the war or denigrating any other nation," which perhaps wasn't such a great idea in 1940 as it might have been in 1914, but let that go, when on the next page of Prater's biography there is a letter from Zweig to Kippenberg: "My great ambition, however, is to be an officer over with you in *that* army, to conquer in France—in France particularly, the France that one must chastise because one loves her," and then you might have understood that Hesse is wrong to say that he dislikes your books but admires your convictions, *Gesinnung*, he says, using that rather unpleasant word, because separations of that sort don't really work, and the rottenness of your writing isn't just confined to your style, because rottenness isn't like that, and perhaps more to the point, style isn't like that either—remember, Buffon said *le style, c'est l'homme même*—and you admit, not before time, that you are just putrid through and through.

ROBERT WALSER

So irregular, so appealing, and—if one may say—so pitiable a figure is the Swiss writer Robert Walser (1878–1956) that he comfortably resists summary description. Even his biographer, Robert Mächler, begins by warning himself, via a feisty sentence of his subject's: "No one is entitled to behave towards me as if they knew me."

It's not that writing about Walser can't be done, it can be done endlessly and beautifully, but it seems unlikely to accomplish anything much. He offers so much scope for true statement, insight, and original expression. You write your piece, make your comparisons, press your claims, and at the end of it all you look up and see Walser, looking not much like your likeness of him, only slightly battered for having been the object of your attentions. It's like nailing the proverbial jelly to the wall. Susan Sontag talks about him slipping through the net of comparisons. It's perhaps not beside the point to recall that when a very young man, Walser wanted to be an actor, and while that ambition may have been squelched in the course of a typically humiliating encounter with an established actor who merely motioned toward the door, there remains something protean about him, even as a writer.

Walser inspires critics and admirers—and really he no longer has any of the former, only the latter—to feats of brilliant emulation, so that they outdo themselves, each other, and their subject. As a result, he can strike one not as a writer for readers, or even for other writers, so much as one for the commentators. Thus, to Susan Sontag (than whom one cannot easily imagine a more contrary personality or temperament), he is "a Paul Klee in prose—as delicate, as sly, as haunted. A cross between Stevie Smith and Beckett: a good-humored, sweet Beckett." Christopher Middleton writes: "Well before the 1920s, the text for Walser is a non-thing, as much so as a Cubist guitar or Magritte's apple ('*Ceci n'est pas une pomme*')." Other comparisons on offer include the composer Satie, the painter Rousseau, the inevitable Kafka, and a further trinity of mad writers, Hölderlin, Nerval, and Christopher Smart. The more genial and indeed congenial William Gass describes Walser more modestly: "He was a kind of columnist before the time of columns." And a further, more modest name is offered: "The signature Harmless Crank could be appended to quite a few without discordance or much malice." So we have Walser variously as yea- or nay-saying (does a "sweet Beckett" say yes or no?!), as priestly whiff of incense and as humdrum green ink, as artsy and crafty, as writer and eraser, eccentric and universal, recessive and bold. None of these is discounted by me; all, I think, are true. Just as true is another pair of opposed statements, Middleton again: "As author and individual, Walser articulates a large and general cast of mind, such as strictly 'personal' writings seldom do." And Gass again: "If Walser is a descriptive writer, and he is surely that, what he is describing, always, is a state of mind . . . and mostly the same mind, it would seem." And to sum up the admirable summaries? That honor should go to Christopher Middleton, Walser's first translator—rare that that accolade should belong to someone working in the English language!—and his champion for nigh on fifty years, for whom his author remains "a wild particle," whom one reads "for his blithe difference from colleagues in any age or condition—for his perfect and serene oddity."

Start over. This is the essayist Franz Blei's recollection of his first meeting with Walser, in 1898:

> A few days later, he stood in my room and said I am Walser. A tall rather lanky fellow with ruddy, bony features, under a thick blond thatch that fought off the comb, dreamy blue-grey eyes and beautifully formed large hands protruding from the sleeves of a jacket too small for him; they seemed not to know what to do with themselves, and wished they could have crept into the trouser-pockets so as not to be there. This was Walser, half journeyman apprentice, half page boy, all poet. He had brought along what I'd asked to see. And he pulled out a lined school jotter bound in black linen: there were the poems. They were all he had. They were thirty-odd in number. They filled the thin notebook with their beautiful, crisp handwriting, which ran smoothly and evenly, without anything unruly or fancy. It was rare for a single word to be crossed out and replaced in what was nonetheless a first draft. [. . .] This young person gave every impression of having heard there was such a thing as poetry from hearsay or report, that he had invented the music and the instrument on which it was played at the same time, so wholly unformed by reading or literary taste were these poems.

Walser was twenty. The passage takes its place next to other celebrated early sightings, say, of Malcolm Lowry by Conrad Aiken, of Hugo von Hofmannsthal by Stefan George, of Rimbaud by Verlaine, of Whitman by Whitman. Blei captures what later observers would see too—what good readers of Walser could even intuit for themselves, I think—the strange mixture of ungainliness and delicacy, the rough, oxygenated outdoorsiness and the sheepish punctilio, the strong growth and the dreaminess, the evidence of health and the suspicion of pain, the high color and its confining translation into symbols on paper, the spiritual agency (speaking in the hands and the eyes) in an improbable and uncouth physical setting that is not, however, despised (any more than it is in Whitman). It shows Walser's self-aware, occasionally prickly poverty, his rough desire to please in the context of his independence, his extreme civilization—bashfulness, poems, beautiful hands that fear being seen—paired with his extreme wildness. All his life, it seems, he had a relish for the human animal, writing with notable, undissembled pleasure of walking, swimming, eating, but also a difficult flair for courtesies. Manners as difficulty, as confusion, as bristling or bridling defense, by the way, never as pleasantry or lubricant. (Walser wrote his own account of the meeting in a defiantly cringing, tormentedly grateful piece with the speaking title, "*Doktor Franz Blei*." The squid in its cloud of ink encounters Cousteau.) It might be a scene reasonably early on in Caspar Hauser. The "page boy" is also no figure of speech or mistranslation; it is a recurring figure both in Walser's life and in his writing, the desire to be in service. At a later meeting in Munich, with a group of writers and publishers—notionally his equals and coevals in a joint venture, called *Die Insel*, the island—Walser promptly offered his services, Friday-like, to one young man, as it were, Blei's successor. There is a scene in service in Walser's first novel, *Geschwister Tanner*, where Simon goes to work for a woman who practically indentures him on the street, while the whole of his third, *Jakob von Gunten*, is set in an academy for—observe the self-contradiction—aspiring servants, like the one Walser himself attended in 1905. It is an expression of a whimsical but agonizing social and erotic desire, a relieving if also embarrassing admission of (then easily ironized) inferiority in a black-and-white world without gradations but offering instead a "place." (See the stories "Tobold" or "Simon: A Love Story" in *Masquerade*.) The man who feels such a thing is clearly all at sea, with an endless craving for protection, disguise, or alibi, a uniform. (He enjoyed his time in the Swiss military.) He would like to give himself away but doesn't know how. It hardly needed Blei to note later, "but it turned out he could neither polish silver, nor iron a top hat."

Twenty years later, 1919, another meeting, this time on Walser's own terrain, the Blue Cross Hotel in (Walser's birthplace) Biel, Switzerland, where he lodged for the best part of seven years in a garret. The man meeting him on this occasion, Emil Schibli, a Swiss writer, had come to express his admiration. Initial difficulty in establishing Walser's identity. He is somewhere among a group of workingmen taking their evening meal of coffee and potatoes (I think of the daunting ugliness captured in Van Gogh's early picture *The Potato*

Eaters)—only which one is he? All look much of a muchness. Schibli makes inquiries of the waitress, duly intercepts Walser on his way out, explains his errand, would he care to walk with him awhile? Walser, not overjoyed, a little suspicious, agrees. They walk beside the lake in gathering darkness. Walser, thawing a little, begins to talk. Schibli realizes his last train home has left: what would Walser say to walking back with him in the night, it's two hours on foot. Walser promptly agrees:

> The writer then stayed as our guest for a couple of days. Should I say something of his appearance? Well, he doesn't look the way a reader of his books would imagine him, or a painter paint him. All his books have something light, delicate, burbling, cheerful, elaborate, perhaps on occasion over-elaborate. The writer by contrast is heavy, taciturn, roughly built, a labourer, mechanic or engineer, it seems to me. At any rate he strikes me as being a thoroughly healthy man. His books are curious, eccentric, original, really bizarrely personal; the author is unremarkable, stolid, wholly unexceptional. Only his eyes are striking.

The page boy and the poet are effaced, but the longed-for anonymity is perfected. Only the eyes are left as a suggestion of an inner incongruity, a deep failure to match up or shape up. The behavior, already stiff in the early encounter with Blei, where one has a sense of someone negotiating a new presence and unfamiliar situation largely by sense of *smell*, is now even stranger: the traumatized hurtle of sympathy and trust from someone now and already almost beyond human contacts, frozen into habitual silence and self-communion, in which the burly frame and its delicate productions stare at one another aghast, in mutual suspicion and irony. Imagine Kafka as fat! Two rival identities, counteridentities, pretenders or pretendants. The difficulty of housing within oneself something so alien, or, conversely, of finding the human envelope so malapropos. Imagine Mishima in spreading middle age, or consider Franz Werfel's poem "Fat Man in the Mirror" in the translation by Robert Lowell: "O, it is not I." But Walser's situation is worse: it is not one part of himself betraying or disappointing another, they are each at it. The centaur is neither a good human nor a good horse. Almost the most heartbreaking details in the accounts of him are the regular comments on his rude good health and his ultimately cordial if obstructed nature.

A third meeting, ten years on, in 1928, in the wake of a failed attempt to arrange a reading for Walser in the Swiss town of Thun. The recording visitor on this occasion is one Adolf Schaer-Ris, the setting the last of Walser's numerous short-term lodgings in Bern:

> The badly dressed, gaunt figure that timidly appeared at the crack in the door, looking as if inclined to shut and bolt it immediately, has never left me in its moving helplessness. Nothing at all, nothing but the staring, soul-filled gleaming eyes betrayed the presence of this uncommon man. But for those eyes, one might have taken him for a common labourer. The voice sounded shaky, though perfectly friendly, warm and well-disposed. It proved impossible to get a proper conversation started. I had the feeling I was assisting at a human tragedy, and the name Hölderlin sounded in my head.

Hölderlin, who spent thirty-seven of his seventy-four years, half a lifetime in the words of his most celebrated short poem, in a state of what in German is called *Umnachtung*, benightedness—in the sense of having the balance of his mind impaired. In the following year, hearing voices, Walser is hospitalized and diagnosed with schizophrenia. He is—and later becomes—institutionalized. Opinions differ as to the reality and gravity of his condition. He continues to write and publish for a time, but later ceases—it appears almost consciously in order to conform to the expectations and conditions of madness. He dies on Christmas Day of 1956, from a heart attack while out walking.

The prevalent movement in Walser's writing—whether in sentence, paragraph, story, or entire career—is toward defeat. I don't quite like either of Susan Sontag's terms, "musicality" and "free fall"—musicality because it's a vague and rather tyrannical way of saying "I like this, even if you don't get it," and free fall because it's untrue, in Walser you get fall of a most encumbered and musing and incident-filled kind—but they suggest the general area. The notion of defeat of course says nothing about the gallantry, the frolicsomeness, the imaginativeness, or the sheer assiduousness of Walser's writing, which remains the reader's overriding impression, but I don't think one can escape it. It remains a losing battle, and Walser's great qualities are displayed in an ironic, a rearguard or, most precisely, a Pyrrhic way, not least because he mistrusts an aesthetic of victory. Defeat, I think, is everywhere in him. Whether it's in possibly his single most famous sentence, his resignation from the Swiss writers' union of 1924, "Esteemed sir. After calmly considering the matter, I hereby announce my resignation from your union, signed Most Respectfully Robert Walser," to almost arbitrarily selected beginnings and titles of pieces: "During this performance several people walked out" ("An Essay on Lion Taming"); "His birth was brilliant. If I'm not mistaken he was the outcome of an illicit relationship" ("Hercules"); *"And now he was playing, alas, the piano . . ."* (these instances all from his volume of short pieces, *Speaking to the Rose*), there is a Buster Keaton–like indomitably sad cheerfulness.

Puncturedness and swollenness appear indivisible, indistinguishable, it's impossible to say which condition brings on the other. The author is blowing into a wounded balloon. It's really no different in the early stories, in the other English collections: "The Boat" begins with a sinking feeling, "I think I've written this scene before, but I'll write it once again." "Poets" begins: "To the question: how do authors of sketches, stories, and novels get along in life, the following answer can or must be given: they are stragglers and they are down at heel," and ends on the same note of ghastly jollity: "Every true poet likes dust, for it is in the dust, and in the most enchanting oblivion, that, as we all know, precisely the greatest poets like to lie, the classics, that is, whose fate is like that of old bottles of wine, which, to be sure, are drawn, only on particularly suitable occasions, out from under the dust and so exalted to a place of honor." Here, incidentally, in that overqualified and hedged-about last sentence, put together from provocative falsehoods ("enchanting oblivion," "like to lie") and patnesses ("like . . . old bottles of wine," "exalted to a place of honor"), is an instance of that blending of motivelessness and utter deliberateness, of control and abdication, that Walter Benjamin appreciated in Walser; he seems, by turns and putting it very bluntly, too stupid to be cynical and too cynical to be stupid. A sort of repro aesthetic ("Walser paints a postcard world," says Gass) seems equally likely to serve a straightforwardly lyrical end as parody or persiflage: "Rarely have my eyes, ever eager to soak up beauty, seen a more delightfully and daintily situated little town than the one in which a quiet dreamer once requested, in an open, sun-splashed square, that a young intellectual with designs on becoming an authoress be so good as to inform him whether he might entertain hopes with regard to her excellent person" ("A Small Town"). One doesn't know whether to prescribe Don Quixote as an ideal reader for this sort of sweet Dulcinea tosh, or declare the adjective off-limits to the author. Certainly, he doesn't scruple to use them, either in a Roget-rrhoeal stream ("now there passed over the lake an exceptionally windy wind. It was a regular whirlwind racing over the clear, blue, beautiful, jubilant, bouncing, amiable, good water") or with a bizarre, almost surreal pointedness.

In structural terms, the effects are similar. The story "Kleist in Thun," a manifest remake of Georg Büchner's grievous masterpiece "Lenz," has a most peculiar coda. First Kleist, his work, his depression, the beauty of the Swiss landscape, and then he leaves the story in a stagecoach when his sister comes to rescue him. The story, though, continues for another half a page. "Last of all," says Walser—though it's far from being the last thing—"one can permit oneself the observation that on the front of the villa where Kleist lived there hangs a marble plaque to indicate who lived and worked there." There already is the mustache on the *Mona Lisa*, but Walser isn't finished: "Thun stands at the entrance to the Bernese Oberland and is visited every year by thousands of foreigners. I know the region a little perhaps, because I worked as a clerk in a brewery there. The region is considerably more beautiful than I have been able to describe here, the lake is twice as blue, the sky three times as beautiful." And then, with crowning, with quite superb bathos: "Thun had a trade fair, I cannot say exactly but I think four years ago." This strange blandness, these final chords on tissue paper and comb, is absolutely characteristic of Walser. He refuses to take himself seriously, he insists, if you like, on disappointing and, in the course of the disappointment (a plaque on the wall, a clerk in a brewery, a trade fair), slipping himself into his story. Increasingly—though it is hard with a huge production like Walser's, of many hundreds of pieces, of which I've read perhaps a quarter, to identify a trend—parody, upset, call it what you will, works back to the beginning and the whole conception of a story. Walser read and recycled romantic pulp, with a mixture, one may imagine, of wickedness and actual yearning. Dismayed perhaps by the difficulty of his life, and the persistent objections not of editors, who tended to be more enlightened and to appreciate him more, but of actual readers, who would write in to the editors to protest, he seems to reply, "You like popular, you want popular, all right, I'll give you popular," the results being of course among his most hilariously disturbing. The following comes from a one-page story from 1925 called "Je t'adore":

> Chocolata sat, swathed in the smartest brown, which itself spoke the most distinguished of tongues, in the automobile; Fragmentino, a gallant just like in books but otherwise imbued with quite practical views on life, stood, with his hat respectfully removed, beside the vehicle which was all set to set off and proudly glittered and glanced in all directions. The chauffeur awaited Chocolata's slight signal, but she seemed in no hurry to give it. Fragmentino's way of standing there had something shopclerkish about it. His suit was treacherously redolent of the speed of its purchase in the ready-to-wear shop. What an unrelenting style I'm writing here!

There is something twice-processed about this writing; it is a *petit four*, a romantic biscuit. The writer praises himself for his mastery of a "low" idiom, for his "unrelenting style." "Just like in books" is high, ironic praise. As often with Walser, one thinks of Sterne or Quixote.

It is said that the short piece remained Walser's basic unit of production, the disquisition, the article, the scene, even in his novels: what the metal merchants and engineers of contemporary fiction call "riffs." In themselves, therefore, the novels are also Pyrrhic. They crumble. Even where they exist, they are disrupted, and where they cease or alter they are so again. Characters make long speeches in which they say what they think of each other or themselves, or they write long and improbable letters, or (in *Jakob von Gunten*) compose a curriculum vitae. *Geschwister Tanner* is even supposed to consist of twenty chapters, each of ten pages: the novel is, as it were, an assemblage of Procrustean miniatures! And then there is the question of the content of these books, which again may strike one as Pyrrhic. *Jakob von Gunten*, the first of the early novels to have been translated, is the diary of a young man (or an old boy—Walser claimed sometime in the 1920s that "youth was among his gifts") at a small, rather rackety school for servants. It ends with the death of the headmaster's sister, and the quasi seduction of the headmaster who sets off an around-the-world tour with the hero. *Geschwister Tanner* (the Tanner Siblings, the Tanners, or—my suggestion—Meet the Tanners) is a story of the comings and goings of the various Tanners, closely corresponding to the comings and goings of the various Walsers, over a period of a year or two. It begins with a hilarious presentation of Simon Tanner at a bookseller's (like Walser as a young man, Simon had employment and plenty of it, but never for very long) and ends with him retelling the whole story of himself and his brothers and sisters to a sympathetic female ear. *Der Gehülfe* (The Assistant), for my money Walser's best book, is about a few months when he found himself as secretary to an inventor. Here, somehow everything comes together: rapturous descriptions of seasons, landscape, and weather, delighted consumption of food and coffee and wine, the deep enjoyment of a temporary parasitic status—the inventor is going to the dogs, and sooner or later everyone knows it—and sharp insights into family, society, and even capitalism. Both *Der Gehülfe* and *Geschwister Tanner* have recently appeared in English, published by New Directions, and translated by the gifted Susan Bernofsky, who has taken on this eccentric author from Christopher Middleton.

These three novels came out in 1907, 1908, and 1909 from the respected firm of Bruno Cassirer (who later took on Wolfgang Koeppen). They represent Walser probably at the zenith of what it seems a mistake to call a career in anything but the most literal (and punning) sense. Walser was living in Berlin, sometimes in the house of his brother Karl, a famous and successful illustrator (he did an exquisite cover for *Der Gehülfe*), and making his way. But probably even then: a dearth of friendship, love, and money. Employers and relatives did duty for friends, and chance optical infatuations with waitresses or well-dressed ladies for lovers. Walser was never other than independent, and that only with some difficulty. He was short-tempered and high-maintenance, suspicious, quarrelsome, and demanding. Most of his life—like Rilke, of whom his writing persistently reminds me—he conducted by correspondence, but even being within epistolary reach was probably too near for many of his associates and employers. After his three novels, it must have seemed to his publisher that he could not sell this author, and to the author that he could not live from such books. Subsequent novels were lost, destroyed, rejected, or left incomplete. Walser retreated to the production of short prose pieces, and he retreated also to Switzerland, first to his sister, then to the hotel garret in Biel. Included in *Masquerade* is something from 1919 called "The Last Prose Piece"; it wasn't, but it shows enough bitter necessity to have nonetheless informed such a thing: "This is likely to be my last prose piece. All sorts of considerations make me believe it's high time this shepherd boy stopped writing and sending off prose pieces and retired from a pursuit apparently beyond his abilities. I'll gladly look about for another line of work that will let me break my bread in peace." Walser found further retreats and retirements. He went into employment again; he discovered the joys of apartment hopping ("I confine my nomadism to the city, a type of peregrination that seems very agreeable to me, because I am able to say I appear to be reasonably healthy, which is to say, I look to myself to be blooming" in a piece called *Wohnungswechsel*, "Changing abode"); he fell out, as already mentioned, with the Swiss writers' union.

One might think things could go no further, but then Walser fell out with his pen: from 1924 he wrote in pencil, and in "microscript." So tiny were the letters—two millimeters, a quarter of an eyelash or so—that for decades it was assumed—I don't know why, belt and braces presumably—that this was a private code. It wasn't, it was regular German, or Walser's version of it, but it was very small and very perishable. Five hundred sheets of this, often eccentrically but speakingly found on already literarily marked pages—rejection slips, postcards to himself, and so forth—were read, employing an optical device used for the counting of threads in weaving, transcribed, and spread into normal type to make up a further two thousand pages, six further volumes in addition to the twenty of Walser's writings.

This was the *Bleistiftgebiet*, the pencil area or pencil terrain. (It includes one entire novel, *Der Räuber*, a jaunty, glancing, elliptical book, translated already by Bernofsky as *The Robber*.) Some other pages from there are included in the latest short selection from Walser by Christopher Middleton, *Speaking to the Rose*. There, in Walser's typically ornate but spoken style, we come across passages like this, from "I would like to be standing" of 1927: "Moreover I make with pleasure the confession—which perhaps characterizes me—that while writing I might have been silent about rather much, quite unintentionally, too, for as a writer I preferred to speak not of what could be irksome, or difficult to express, but of lightness, whereas into what has occupied me here I did open out, with all the heaviness in me, though fugitively, of course, as seems to be my wont." In Zurich, I saw a street named after him, where he couldn't possibly have afforded to live, and in a station somewhere a train, which he—who once walked to Stuttgart—couldn't possibly have afforded to take. John Berryman wrote, "The Bach-Gesellschaft girdles the world." So it goes.

ACKNOWLEDGMENTS

Acknowledgments are due to the editors of the following, where many of these pieces first appeared: *Australian Book Review*, *The Guardian*, *London Review of Books*, *Modern Painters*, *The New York Review of Books*, *The New York Times Book Review*, *Poetry*, and *Poetry Ireland Review*.

Most of "Robert Lowell" was given as a talk at the Aldeburgh Poetry Festival (and appears at the kind suggestion of C. K. Williams), and "*The Passenger*" was written for a collection of essays on film scenes projected by Robert Ray.

"Robert Frost and Edward Thomas" was originally commissioned as an introduction to *Elected Friends*, edited by Matthew Spencer and published by Other Press in 2004; "John Berryman" was an introduction to the reprint of *The Dream Songs* on the occasion of the centenary of his birth; "'Remembering Teheran'" was a contribution to Nick Gammage's book of tributes to Ted Hughes on the occasion of his seventieth birthday, *The Epic Poise* (Faber and Faber, 1999); the essay on Gottfried Benn led off my 2013 selection, *Impromptus: Selected Poems and Some Prose* (FSG, 2013).

"Ted Hughes" (as "Stare at the Monster") was awarded the 2005 Editors' Prize for best review-essay in *Poetry*.

Mary-Kay Wilmers and Chris Wiman were a joy to work for, Chris Richards was both warmhearted advocate and cool adviser, and Mareike Grover read the manuscript with wonderful and alarming acuity. Thanks are due to all, but especially to one: Jonathan Galassi.

A Note About the Author

Michael Hofmann is an acclaimed poet, translator, and critic. He has published six books of poetry and has translated more than sixty books from the German, including Gottfried Benn's *Impromptus: Selected Poems and Some Prose*, as well as works by Ernst Jünger, Franz Kafka, and Joseph Roth. His criticism appears regularly in the *London Review of Books*, *The New York Review of Books*, and *Poetry*. He currently teaches poetry and translation at the University of Florida.